Helping people

THE TASK-CENTERED APPROACH

Helping people

THE TASK-CENTERED APPROACH

LAURA EPSTEIN

Professor, School of Social Service Administration,
The University of Chicago, Chicago, Illinois

Illustrated

The C. V. Mosby Company

ST. LOUIS • TORONTO • LONDON   1980

The C. V. Mosby Company
11830 Westline Industrial Drive, St. Louis, Missouri 63141

Library of Congress Cataloging in Publication Data

Epstein, Laura.
    Helping people.

    Bibliography: p.
    Includes indexes.
    1. Social case work. 2. Social work
administration—United States. 3. Task
performance and analysis. I. Title.
HV43.E67   361.3   79-21084
ISBN 0-8016-1509-7

GW/VH/VH 9 8 7 6 5 4 3 2 1   05/B/604

Preface

This is a book about how to help people. Step-by-step guidelines to alleviate common problems in living will be explained. These guidelines are based on the task-centered model of social intervention developed at the School of Social Service Administration, The University of Chicago.

Practitioners and students in human service occupations have two basic problems. First, plans of action are usually not specific enough to guide regular and ordinary work assignments. Second, the social welfare system in the United States is so complex that the provision of services is often overwhelmed by the workings of the structure and style of agency programs. Especially, new practitioners lack disentangled road maps of the terrain of social welfare. Direct service professionals need to know what features of an agency program and what features of their clients' lives constitute barriers to carrying out helping actions. Unsatisfactory results are by no means necessarily attributable to the practitioner, although that is where the onus is often placed. The guidelines that staff members follow with great effort are often defective. Agency programs exist in a charged political atmosphere. They are frequently as good as they can be in the circumstances, but programs can and do inhibit good practice.

In this book practice guides, client problems, and agency organizational context will be depicted. The aim is to arm practitioners with useful ways to have impact on their clients' problems and to protect practitioners as much as possible from being lost in a morass. Logic would demand laying out first what the big map contains before moving into the small components. Logic, however, is going to be compromised here. The most urgent question practitioners ask is, *What do I do?* Knowing what to do is necessary but not enough to get through one case, one day. Techniques, or technologies, are always affected by the characteristics of an agency's programs, the pattern of beliefs that a profession and its practitioners espouse, social sanctions and expectations, changing knowledge, and subjective reactions. With this warning, the questions about what to do will be dealt with first—but in general. Readers can use this book for the technical guidelines alone. These are summarized in the first chapter and are given in detail in all of Section two. In between will be found information concerning what social welfare services are and are not, what they can and cannot accomplish, why there is so much conflict and misunderstanding about the effectiveness of services, how to conduct one's practice despite organizational problems and the diversity among clients, and how to make the task-centered approach work on behalf of clients.

The size of the literature about social welfare is enormous. New work appears constantly and older works sink into obsolescence. People in the field can never know enough, but they can learn a basic problem-solving framework that is sufficiently flexible to accommodate most circumstances and bend with change. If this book raises enough important and right questions, as well as gives some answers, it will have done its job, or I could say its "task."

This book is the result of eight years of work developing the task-centered model of practice. The work began and continued through my collaboration with my colleague and friend, William J. Reid, School of Social Service Administration, The University of Chicago. Support was received from Dean Harold A. Richman and Associate Dean John R. Schuerman. Over the years about 125 graduate students participated in the project. It was these students who suffered through all the trials of the model, testing and refining the work. A number of doctoral students were exceptionally helpful in conducting studies, supervising students, and developing the task-centered model in many new, ingenious ways. Thirteen social agencies in Chicago collaborated by affording fieldwork placements for the students.

The mission of the task-centered project for the field of practice was to develop technologies that could be learned efficiently and could increase the effectiveness of direct services offered in social welfare. It was believed that utilizing the results of practice research, testing and changing these findings in the world of real practice, and changing practice in accordance with research indications were justifiable in and of themselves. More significant, one of the important avenues for increasing the impact of practice was to clear out debris accumulated over years—to begin a process of revision and renewal so that effectiveness in practice could be developed.

The first three years of the project, roughly from 1970 to 1973, were devoted to designing the basic task-centered model. Its processes and effects were studied in that part of agency practice carried out by the students in their fieldwork. With the publication of *Task-Centered Casework* (Reid and Epstein) in 1972, the model attracted interest in agencies throughout the country and abroad. Practitioners and researchers from many settings took the initiative to test and develop the model. As a result of a grant from the Social and Rehabilitation Service of the United States Department of Health, Education, and Welfare (SRS Grant no. 18-P-57774/5-03), the project was able to conduct more sophisticated research. The tests of the task-centered model included approximately 1300 cases handled by students in the Chicago agencies between 1970 and 1977. Of this entire group, a smaller number became the sample for the research on processes and outcome.

The case examples used in this book have come from actual cases handled in the project. A few are from a public welfare agency outside Chicago, made available through a staff training project. Two case examples are taken from my own practice. All cases have been disguised, and the names of the agencies are withheld in order to prevent improper disclosures.

The technical guidelines described in this book are my attempt to distill and arrange the product of the past eight years of model building. Whenever possible, the guidelines are derived from practice research conducted in the project and from currently available practice research conducted elsewhere. Errors of interpretation are mine. Hopefully, they are few. The guidelines are written for practitioners to apply directly and immediately. Therefore detailed documentation to justify the guidelines is not provided in the body of the descriptions. The criterion of inclusion of research in this book is my judgment about usefulness to practitioners. The attempt is to translate a complex body of research into sets of quick and ready guidelines for action in the field. This attempt is justified, even though the product is imperfect, because practitioners need all the guidance they can get about what *probably* works best. I have tried to keep in mind the real world of agencies and the real hazards of work in the field of social welfare.

Although many questions about the operation of the task-centered model remain, the product of these years of research-based practice and evaluation supports the conclusion that task-centered practice is effective to a reasonable degree in reducing many of the problems encountered in a wide range of agencies. In fact, many of the central ideas of the task-centered model have spread and become attached to ideas of practice that have other origins. The task-centered model itself hardly sprung de novo from this project at The University of Chicago. Its own origins are varied and represent selections and revisions from a host of ideas and practices that preceded it.

The many clients, students, and agencies who cooperated by giving their effort and resources to this endeavor have been indispensable in making the work possible. Helen Mansfield, the Department of Health, Education, and Welfare, was of enormous aid. I could never properly acknowledge or repay particular colleagues: William J. Reid, George Herbert Jones Professor, The University of Chicago; Lester Brown, Instructor, University of Wisconsin at Milwaukee; Ronald Rooney, Assistant Professor, University of Wisconsin at Madison; and Eleanor Tolson, Assistant Professor, The University of Chicago. The unique skills and unbelievable patience of Gwendolyn Graham put all of what follows into readable shape.

Laura Epstein

Contents

10 Third step: task achievement, problem reduction, problem solving, 213

11 Fourth step: termination, extension, monitoring, 257

Helping people

THE TASK-CENTERED APPROACH

Section one

THE MAKEUP OF HELPING SERVICES

CHAPTER 1

Task-centered model: what it is; how applied

TASK-CENTERED PRACTICE IS A SET OF PROCEDURES

Task-centered practice is a technology for alleviating explicit problems. These are *target problems* perceived by clients, meaning the particular problems the client knows of, understands and acknowledges, and wants to attend to. Important other people who care about the clients or who put pressure on them influence and shape the target problem. Authorities sometimes require work on some problems; in other words, *some problems are mandated.*

Task-centered practice has a particular way of unfolding. It consists of a Start-up and four steps. Steps are carried out in a certain sequence, although they overlap (Fig. 1). The regularity of the steps is important just as the steps of an escalator have to be separate and follow one another. But the escalator of the task-centered (TC) model is not made of steel. It is more like hard cardboard. Under the pressure of problem solving it can soften and twist, but it can usually be righted with repair work. A cardboard escalator is better than one made of Jell-O.

The regularity of the task-centered steps provides a basic structure for problem solving. Regularity refers to being methodical according to a preferred logic. Regularity means being systematic. To the extent that practice is systematized, it tends to be as thorough as circumstances permit. Being systematic can protect clients and practitioners from extremes of bewilderment, frustration, and irrelevancy. Systematic practice helps to minimize waste of time, effort, and money and to encourage effective practice. The influence of structured practice on good outcomes has been demonstrated in studies that cut across various fields of practice and various helping occupations (Reid and Epstein, 1972; Reid, 1975; Epstein, 1977; Reid and Epstein, 1977; Reid, 1978).

3

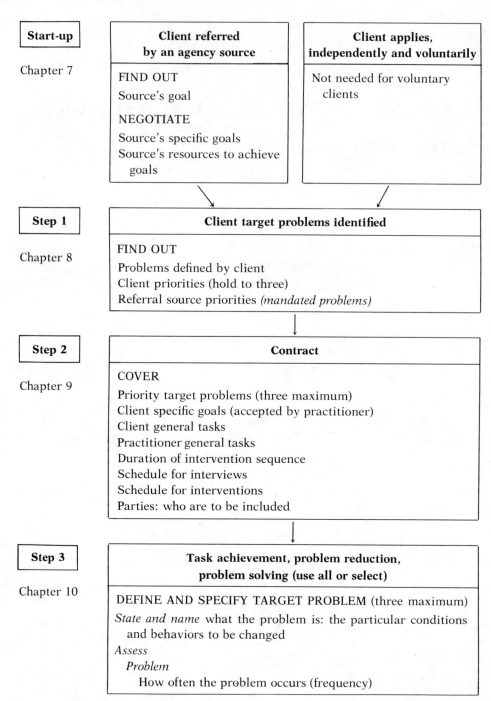

Start-up	**Client referred by an agency source**	**Client applies, independently and voluntarily**

Chapter 7	FIND OUT
	Source's goal
	
	NEGOTIATE
	Source's specific goals
	Source's resources to achieve
	  goals
		Not needed for voluntary
		  clients

Step 1	**Client target problems identified**
Chapter 8	FIND OUT Problems defined by client Client priorities (hold to three) Referral source priorities *(mandated problems)*

Step 2	**Contract**
Chapter 9	COVER Priority target problems (three maximum) Client specific goals (accepted by practitioner) Client general tasks Practitioner general tasks Duration of intervention sequence Schedule for interviews Schedule for interventions Parties: who are to be included

Step 3	**Task achievement, problem reduction, problem solving (use all or select)**

Chapter 10	DEFINE AND SPECIFY TARGET PROBLEM (three maximum)
	State and name what the problem is: the particular conditions
	  and behaviors to be changed
	Assess
	  Problem
	    How often the problem occurs (frequency)

Fig. 1. Detailed map of the task-centered model.

| Step 3 | **Task achievement, problem reduction,
problem solving (use all or select)—cont'd** |

Where it occurs (site)
With whom (participants)
What immediate antecedents
What consequences
What meaning
Social context: What social conditions precipitate and maintain
   the problem
   Work-school circumstances
   Health care circumstances
   Economic status
   Personality-intelligence traits
   Family organization
   Peer group organization
   Housing state
   Cultural background
   Other

GENERATE ALTERNATIVES
Find out and identify a feasible range of possible problem-solving
   actions
Negotiate supportive and collaborative actions of other persons
   and agencies

DECISION MAKING
Design intervention strategy
   The basic interventions
   Timing and sequence
   Participants
Get client agreement and understanding
Get agreement and understanding of necessary others

IMPLEMENT (carry out strategy)
Develop tasks
   Get client understanding and agreement to tasks
   Get client understanding of rationale and incentives for tasks
   Devise plans for client task performance
   Summarize tasks
   Summarize plans for task performance
   Review task performance   *Continued.*

Fig. 1, cont'd. Detailed map of the task-centered model.

Step 3	Task achievement, problem reduction, problem solving (use all of select)—cont'd
Chapter 10, cont'd	*Support task performance* 　Review number of sessions outstanding 　Obtain and use resources 　Find out obstacles to resource provision 　Show client how to perform tasks 　　Give instruction 　　Give guidance 　　Do simulations 　　Accompany client for modeling and advocacy 　　Discuss cognitive barriers 　　　Fears 　　　Suspicions 　　　Lack of knowledge 　　　Lack of cooperation from others 　　　Lack of resources 　Find out obstacles to task performance 　Plan and state practitioner tasks 　　Inform client of practitioner tasks 　　Review implementation of practitioner tasks 　Review problem state VERIFY (check, test, confirm, substantiate probable effects of intervention) Monitor and record problem status regularly Revise contract, or some parts of it, if 　Progress unsatisfactory 　Progress exceeds expectations 　New problems emerge 　Problem takes on different characteristics Revise tasks not performed or poorly performed Revise supports and resources if ineffective Revise practitioner tasks if not feasible or ineffective

Step 4	Termination
Chapter 11	End *Extend:* Only on evidence of client commitment *Monitor:* Only when mandated by law, court order, or formal agency requirements

Fig. 1, cont'd. Detailed map of the task-centered model.

Task-centered practice will take a lot of weight and still produce reasonable results. Take a look at this case, which is a routine example of task-centered practice (Nieminen, 1978).

Example: Lester

Lester is 30. Family, friends, residential care personnel, and social workers say: "He looks mentally retarded." Pushed to explain what such a look is, they say he is thin and has buckteeth. He looks like Andy Gump, a figure in old comic books—a skinny dumb "nebbish." Most of us tend to rely on such stereotypes to form our commonsense appraisal of others, but it is deplorable if such stereotypes are exalted as "diagnosis."

Lester comes from an average family, which means they have a complicated life. His father is a truck driver. His mother died when he was 15. The father was left with Lester, his twin brother, and a small child of 4 years who was a cerebral palsy victim. As children, both twins seemed "dumb." Shortly after their father became a widower, he married an attractive woman. She was divorced and had custody of her two young children.

The stepmother could not undertake the care of the big teenage twin boys, as well as the handicapped son and her own children. Looking for a way to take care of the twins, the parents had them evaluated at the local psychiatric clinic. Tests showed that both had IQs in the fifties. They were committed to a state residential facility for the mentally retarded. They were sequestered in a place where they could be educated and cared for.

As such places go, the institution was good. The twins attended school. They were supposed to be prepared for "independent living"—meaning self-support. They received vocational training in ceramics, sawmill work, and dairy farming. The locale of this history is a western state with lots of tourist trade (who might buy ceramics), lots of trees (which can be sawed in mills), and lots of cows (for milking). The cost of this care and training for fifteen years was estimated at roughly $50,000. What did Lester and his brother get out of it? A 20-point jump in IQ. The twins learned a lot of the things tested on IQ examinations, and that is obviously all to the good. With IQs in the 70's, they were no longer so "dumb."

The twins were a product of the way programs were organized in the early 1960s, when they entered the institution. The *deinstitutionalization* movement was starting then. Several national trends were converging to create a climate favoring care of the mentally retarded in the community rather than in institutions. That movement was worldwide and is continuing. Over time there began an exodus of residents of state custodial institutions. Funds to carry out deinstitutionalization were provided under the Mental Retardation Facilities and Community Mental Health Centers Construction Act (1963) and subsequent amendments.

Lester's brother was released first. He fared satisfactorily. Lester stayed inside for another two years. Fifteen years after his admission, Lester was sent to his father, and this started a huge contretemps. The other twin was living in a rooming house where the father visited him occasionally. But Lester was home, just sitting around, a strange, helpless 30-year-old man—in the way, scarey, disrupting the home. His father and stepmother were furious, overwhelmed, in a panic. They demanded that the local welfare office take Lester off their hands—at once.

But should it be done and how to do it? Parents are supposed to like and want their children and to offer them care and protection. When the parents came to the office to be interviewed, they defined two and only two target problems: (1) they did not want Lester at home and (2) they could not afford to pay his rent, feed, and clothe him elsewhere. The welfare office should take Lester off their hands!

No. The regulations of that state governing income maintenance (providing cash) prohibited such benefits (Lester was "ineligible") to able-bodied, single men, and Lester's IQ was now too high to qualify him for disability benefits, a special category of income-maintenance programs.

Could Lester's parents take a course of counseling to think about how to adjust their style and habits with Lester at home? To think about how they could make him self-supporting?

No. The father's income was too high. He would have to pay a fee for counseling and could not get it free. The father was of no mind to be counseled, let alone pay for it.

What did Lester think was his problem? (1) He had no job and (2) he did not know his way around the city to look for one.

What was the practitioner's judgment? There are all kinds of possibilities. It could be stated that the father was a narrow-minded bully or a selfish, opinionated, passive-aggressive personality, that the stepmother was a rigid, obsessive personality, and so forth. Taking such positions would box the practitioner into a corner. As soon as these labels are attached to persons and problems, current logic is that counseling is "needed" to alter the personalities involved, which in this case meant the people would need to change so that they could adapt to the new person in the home; after all, he was a son. This particular practitioner steered clear of psychological myths. He suggested that work be done to decrease the problems targeted by the parents and son, using about eight interviews with the son. Lester was eligible for free counseling because he had no income, and the agency was responsible by administrative regulations for counseling those recently deinstitutionalized. The father would be consulted by telephone (to get around the fee charge). Lester's father said this sounded good: "We'll do what you want; you're the boss."

At the end of that first and only interview with the parents, the father added another target problem: Lester was lethargic and unhelpful around the house. He had been home one month, had not gone out, and had not lifted a finger *(target problem specification).* Operating on the general assumption that people do what they know how to do and avoid what they do not know how to do (i.e., they have or lack social skills), the practitioner gave immediate advice. He advised the parents to teach Lester how to do things in the home, as long as he was there, hopefully temporarily, and to treat him as if he had a reasonable amount of brains.

Lester was advised to come for a series of eight interviews, once weekly.

Meanwhile the practitioner took on his own tasks. He phoned a halfway house to find out if they could give Lester job-finding services. They were willing but, as it turned out, not able to find him a job. The practitioner phoned the vocational rehabilitation office. They were willing to accept Lester for job training but could not accomplish anything because he was erratic about workshop attendance. The practitioner consulted a public psychological testing service for a retest for Lester. If his IQ was lower on a retest, he might be eligible for financial support. This was dropped. In truth, Lester was not a case of low intelligence any more. His problem was lack of knowledge about the city map, streets, and how to talk to ordinary people about the ordinary things people talk about daily.

No one rescued the practitioner. Other agencies were reasonable but ineffective. Each of the other agencies had a particular work focus and style. They all did what they thought they were supposed to do and what they could. The practitioner should have understood this but did not. Feeling stymied, he did himself what needed to be done, but he felt "let down" by the other agencies.

In interviews with Lester, the practitioner worked out tasks designed to get him a job and a room in a boarding house. The start-up tasks were (1) to make a list of possible places to go to ask for work and (2) to make a list of possible rooming houses where he might live.

These are ordinary and unexciting things, yet for Lester they just made the difference between knowing and not knowing, doing and sitting around, having tolerable circumstances and intolerable circumstances. Self-actualization, fulfillment of one's potentialities, comes down to tolerable versus intolerable circumstances. When solving problems, no neon signs light up; no cymbals clash. Problems get solved and life looks better after a hundred details are taken care of.

To get Lester's tasks done, the practitioner sat down with him and looked over the want ads and notices from the public employment service about vacancies, as well as the for rent ads and lists from real estate firms. He taught Lester first how to make the lists, then how to approach a businessman and a landlord: what to say, what to expect, what to do, think, feel. Interview after interview Lester tried, and his results were nil at first. The worker and Lester drudged on. The road to Rome is paved with tiny concrete blocks.

Meanwhile at home the parents were teaching Lester to use the dishwasher and vacuum, to make his bed, and so forth. They made the effort to talk straight to him and have reasonable expectations. From time to time they felt defeated (depressed), afraid and enraged. They called up the practitioner and complained and hollered. He suggested things they could do and described how they could do them.

The Lester case illustrates an application of the task-centered model to a type of problem situation that is frequent in social welfare. It is not the hardest or easiest, but somewhere in between.

SCOPE OF THE TASK-CENTERED MODEL

The task-centered model can be used with hard cases, easy cases, and those in between. There is a peculiar perception in social agencies that all cases are extraordinary. People who work in social agencies appear anxiety ridden. They speak about how unusual, surprising, exhausting, devilish, or overwhelming their cases are. The issue seems to be "seriousness," in the sense of gravity or the highest possible degree of importance and risk. This kind of interpretation is hard to live with and is false. The great majority of cases are ordinary. All the work of social agencies is other people's troubles. Virtually all problems in living are ubiquitous. Everybody has them, in greater or lesser quantity, throughout life. That makes them ordinary and not exceptional. *Most troubles have two components: (1) the person lacks resources for alleviating a problem and (2) the person lacks skills for alleviating a problem.*

Seriousness, or exceptional problems, are those which jeopardize life—our client's life or that of someone else. Direct service professionals usually do not have to be responsible for handling threats to a client's own life. Exceptions include working in a medical facility with critically ill people and in a psychiatric facility where one necessarily intervenes in the lives of people judged to be suicidal. Another type of seriousness is the possibility that the client is endangering the lives of others, which is occasionally encountered. However, resources are usually available for arranging to protect people from this high degree of danger.

Protection in case of danger is always a shared undertaking. Courts, hospitals, jails, and the police are the basic resources for protection when it is essential. Families and friends provide the protective social network. The real reason for high anxiety about seriousness lies in lack of knowledge. In the social sciences these is little exactness or certainty about how to control human actions. The tense attitudes among the public and professionals exist because of unrealistic expectations, ambiguous goals, and fear. It is possible to cope with these work anxieties by adopting reasonable and feasible expectations and by clarifying and specifying goals.

In the ordinary instance, there is a client *target problem*. There is a state of being agitated, a distress, an uneasiness or upset, a turbulence, malfunction, handicap, perplexity, a threat to goals and expectations. Particularly, there is a focus that the client has. Clients have opinions, beliefs, judgments, knowledge. They know or believe that a particular event or occurrence is the center of the trouble. The target problem is what a client thinks is the problem: what should be alleviated, what should be worked on to get a problem cut down. In task-centered practice, everything begins and usually ends with the client's target problem. People are generally able to make a coherent statement in words defining their target problem. When they cannot do so, practitioners can help clients in various ways to develop a target problem statement. Practitioners can also collect the opinions of important other people to identify these problems with and for the client.

Side by side with the target problem of the client are opinions about him or her. Often there are demands by influential other people as well as by social institutions, for example, courts, parents, spouses, children, peers, professionals, physicians, or teachers. The collection of opinion about the client is one section of the *target problem context*. These opinions have to be identified, sifted, and evaluated. The client has to be relieved of unnecessary stress caused by these opinions and demands. The climate of opinion has to be reorganized so that it helps rather than hinders the client. In the Lester case, persuading the parents to treat the young man respectfully and to teach him skills illustrates such a reorganization of opinions.

THE TASK-CENTERED MODEL: IN BRIEF AND IN GENERAL

Task-centered intervention is a set of procedures for alleviating the explicit target problems perceived by clients. When people are referred or obliged to use a service, that is, when they are *involuntary clients*, there is a start-up sequence. These preliminaries draw out the clients' problems in their own words and draw out the problems identified by the referral agencies. To alleviate target problems, one depends on *problem-solving processes.* *Goals* are specific and tangible. The existing particular interests and concerns of the clients are the basic power source. Stretching out a client's motivation is normally not necessary. What is necessary is that the client obtain the *resources* and *skills* for *problem-solving work.* Clients are nearly always motivated for something that makes sense. None of the traditional goal-stretching practices is effective.

Basic steps

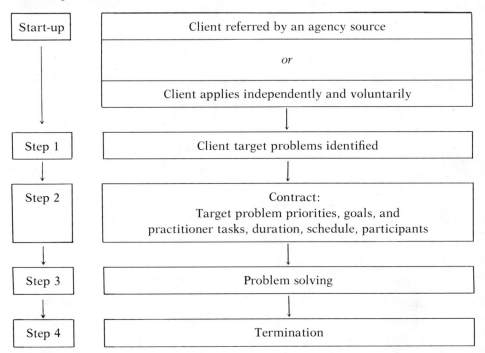

Start-up	Client referred by an agency source
	or
	Client applies independently and voluntarily
Step 1	Client target problems identified
Step 2	Contract: Target problem priorities, goals, and practitioner tasks, duration, schedule, participants
Step 3	Problem solving
Step 4	Termination

Case planning

The *general strategy* for a case plan consists of (1) *assessment* and (2) a *problem-reduction program* of action. The focus is on *client target problems.* The assessment is small in scope. It is elaborate about the particular details of the problem occurrences in the present.

The program of action is constructed by making judgments about what changes can be expected to reduce the problem. This judgment is arrived at by considering the following:

1. The substance and direction of action the client is willing to undertake

2. The resources and rules of the particular agency responsible for the case
3. Available information of a formal type estimating best actions to have impact on the problem

Implementation

A *contract* is made to organize the problem-solving work. *Tasks* state exactly what the client and practitioner are to do. To overcome *obstacles* to the client's task performance, the practitioner concentrates on providing clients with the resources for getting tasks done. The client is instructed in the skills needed for accomplishing the stipulated tasks. Goals, problems, and tasks are set firmly, but with reserve flexibility. The practitioner's responsibility is to create a favorable climate for task performance. The practitioner *procures resources; instructs the client* in relevant social skills; *negotiates* resources and favorable attitudes in other agencies and with the family, peers, and important others; *reviews the client's task performance,* adjusting tasks for the best fit; *reviews progress on problem alleviation;* and arranges to *terminate, extend,* or *follow up (monitor)* the original contract.

Tasks

Tasks are framed to state what the client is to do. A task may state a general direction for the client's action. These general tasks are broken down into more tangible task specifications. Tasks change form and content as intervention occurs. Some tasks drop out; others are added. Target problems change sometimes. *Practitioner tasks* are commitments to clients for actions to be taken on their behalf by a representative of the agency.

Assessment

Assessment of the case is concentrated in the initial phase, the first two sessions. Assessment consists of *finding out* the problems (exploration), together with *classification* and *specification* of the problems. The influential conditions in the environment, *the problem context,* should be identified. The person's special traits, talents, abilities, and problem behaviors are noted. Assessment is confined to the logical boundaries of the target problems. A target problem is classified according to its best fit into a typology that limits the scope of assessment (Chapter 8). Assessment would not extend beyond problems that could be subsumed under the target problem classification.

Reassessment occurs if and when the target problem has to be changed. Some recycling of the treatment design is then made.

Psychiatric classifications. Labeling the person according to speculation or confirmation of a mental disease has limited use in task-centered assessment. Psychiatric classifications are helpful when one apparent cause of the problem is physical or neurological, when drugs or other biological interventions are being administered, or when delusions or hallucinations are present. Social workers seldom use information about origin and history of the problems; therefore history they obtain may be sketchy. Information about the problem's duration and some of its changes or stability over time is sometimes helpful. Attention is given to what the problem means to the client *in the present.* Long duration of a problem may or may not color its meaning in the present.

Personality or behavior theory. It may help to obtain an explanation of the person, at least to some extent. Some clients acquire a stronger grasp of their actions if they have a credible explanation of themselves. Any theory or combination of theories than can help to understand and explain a situation is acceptable. Personality theory can have a high degree of eclecticism (Chapter 4). There is no general acceptance of any one personality theory in social science or psychology. No single existing theory can adequately explain the range of problems dealt with in practice. When there are obscurities or impasses to treatment, personality theory may be helpful in charting a direction. Reexamination of the problem is more valuable. Most valuable, when it can be obtained, is social science knowledge about the nature of particular problems. Information from the technical literature on types and effectiveness of strategies for the reduction of a class of problems can be profitable, if available.

The task-centered practitioner must be appropriately responsive to the client. What is done, said, and communicated is crucial. It is rarely necessary to portray any particular image. A courteous, respectful posture during a work relationship develops naturally. In most instances no special nurturing is required.

ADMINISTRATIVE SUPPORTS

To carry out this model, certain basic administrative and supervisory supports should exist. Normally such supports are attainable. The task-centered approach, properly carried out, is capable of reducing many client problems and organizing work. Both these objectives are priorities of agency administrations. There are, however, problems in the administration, super-vision, and program designs of agencies. Implementing the task-centered model requires administrative supports. There should be an opportunity to practice the model enough to be familiar with its details. Access to consulta-tion and information is also necessary. There should be a reward system for clients and practitioners that makes efforts along these lines worthwhile.

About dirt, neglect, and learning disabilities; an illustration of task-centered practice: Joseph and Rita

Joseph is 11; his sister Rita is 8. They are black children living in a deteriorated neighborhood. Before 1968 this neighborhood was crowded. Two main business streets were heavily trafficked and noisy. There were lots of shops. The merchan-dise was overpriced. Bright, ugly signs grabbed you. The"El" train ran on top of one of the main streets. Every block had taverns, gyp joints, greasy spoons, wel-fare offices, banks, and gambling and drug joints. Gangs fought. This was before Joseph and Rita were born. For ten years the neighborhood burned. Today, empty lots are cluttered with bricks. Buildings are shells. Here and there a block or a building stands in the rubble. It is dangerous to ride the El. The two main streets are deserted. Urban renewal high rises and town houses show up strange-ly. The real estate speculators are there. The urban renewal experts are there. The school attended by Joseph and Rita used to be a loud, teeming place. Now it has empty rooms and lots of special education classes.

Joseph and Rita live in an apartment with their 31-year-old mother and two younger sisters. Their mother is on welfare. She came to this northern city from the South twelve years ago. She has never had any paid employment. She has been on welfare during most of her years in the city.

Joseph and Rita were referred to the school social worker because of being dirty. This is a mandated problem but of relatively low power; that is, no one is likely to be deprived of liberty or subjected to police action for poor body hygiene. But there are potential powers: the mother might be labeled "neglectful" and be-come subject to child welfare investigatory procedures; the children and mother might be pressured by school officials, reported to the welfare department, and so forth. Cleanliness is a high priority in our society. It is sometimes believed that a parent who fails to keep children clean may be doing worse things, may be guilty of neglect. It is also often believed (probably falsely) that intervening to see to it that children are clean provides entry into a home so that one might find out (explore) if worse things are going on and if worse things can be prevented. Exactly how the "engagement" of clients and the prevention are to be done is a mystery. Such investigations are time consuming if done and, more often than not, are fruitless. The usual result is a collection of disconnected pieces of information, a large percent of it speculative; and an information overload that is difficult to sort out, interpret, and use for case planning.

The teacher who referred Joseph and Rita for a dirtiness problem had both the children in her room. She had an ungraded learning disability (LD) class. The two children were interviewed by a social worker. Joseph was a spontaneous, lively, talkative child. Rita was his follower—quiet, shy, hanging onto big brother to talk for her and fight for her. When Rita wanted to add something or change something that Joseph was telling the social worker, the girl would gesture to Joseph and speak to him softly, rather than speak up herself.

The social worker told the children the reason for the referral. They denied the accusation. They are only dirty from being on the playground. They had different woes (target problems): (1) the teacher is unfair to them, singling them out for criticism when they act no differently from the other children; (2) they do not know why they were put in LD; and (3) they do not know what to do to get out of LD.

The kids agreed that the social worker should visit their mother. She found the apartment appropriately clean, the laundry facilities adequate, the quantity of clothing adequate. The mother showed the social worker her things to defend herself against the false accusation of uncleanliness. The mother's target problems were that (1) she was never informed her children were to be placed in LD, a violation of law in that state, if true, and (2) the white teacher is prejudiced against black kids.

The practitioner's judgment was that Joseph and Rita were average, in her experience, in cleanliness and in their mother's attention to cleanliness. What came through was the family's distress and indignation at the children's being labeled LD—dumb. The blame was put on the school officials. The cause was thought to be race prejudice and general unfairness of the teacher.

Discussion of the case of Joseph and Rita

Start-up, Steps 1 and 2 combined. The information just summarized came out in the first two interviews, one with the children in school and the other with the mother at her home. No case is perfect. This one is no exception. Along with good points, there were errors. The good points are that the mother was immediately contacted and her opinions obtained; the home was observed to get a direct impression of it; and the practitioner paid acute attention to concentrating on the problem as viewed by the clients.

   The error is that the practitioner did not confer and negotiate with the referral source (teacher) to find out how often, when, and to what degree the children were dirty; why they were in LD; what their learning disability consisted of; what they could be expected to learn, how fast, with which educational program; what the teacher wanted to change and why; and what the teacher could do to help change along. In other words, the start-up step was bypassed. Steps 1 and 2 were done together, and Step 3 was begun, which is often the case in actual practice. In that way the model is adapted to fit the real circumstances. However, in making these combinations, the necessary parts of the steps should not be overlooked.

   The content from Steps 1 through 3, which occurred in the first two interviews, was that target problems were identified and that goals and/or general tasks were stated as follows:

1. Joseph and Rita were to obtain an understanding of why they are in LD.
2. Joseph and Rita were to get along better with the teacher.
3. Duration was to be six weeks, the children to be seen twice per week for 30-minute sessions, together or separately.
4. Their mother was to be seen as needed, alone or with the children.

Step 2: contract. This contract is on the right track but lacks enough specifics to move things along. The errors follow:

1. The target problems have been given a practitioner twist, altering the way the children and mother want to go. The clients want information and redress of grievances. They could be expected to have high motivation to get action on those problems. However, when the practitioner influences the children to think about ways to cut down on conflict with the teacher, the children's motivation will not be high.

2. Work with the mother, who has certainly been interested, exists somewhere out on the sidelines. The contract is really only with the children. The practitioner should have been pinned down how often the mother would be seen and for what and whether the children would be seen separately or together. The most efficient way to get action here may well have been to see all three together.

3. There should also have been practitioner tasks to find out from the school officials why the children were in LD; whether their rights had been violated; what the teacher recommended regarding uncleanliness and school program; what the teacher could do to get the desired changes; and if the charges of unfairness and prejudice had any observable basis.

Step 3: problem solving. Interviews 3 through 12 took place over five weeks. These interviews were with the children together and with their mother by phone. There was virtually no assessment. The practitioner developed one client task only and with the children only: the children were to ask their teacher why they were in LD. This task was steady and unchanged in interviews 3 through 8, six 30-minute sessions. The children did not do the task.

The immediate obstacle was that they did not know what to say to the teacher. This obstacle was worked at by discussion, instruction, simulation, and role playing. They did not do it anyway. The children said that on some days they had no opportunity because the teacher was absent due to illness. On other days she was in a bad mood.

The children acted as if they liked the sessions. They recited for the practitioner what the task was and rehearsed repeatedly, but they never did it in real life. The practitioner urged them on, mentioning that the sessions had a time limit. Also, during the sessions the children became lively when talking spontaneously about their "Dad", but information they provided about their father or about problems related to him was not recorded, if it was obtained—not even who he was. In addition, the *problem context* was fuzzy. At the end of the eighth session, the practitioner decided to take on the tasks of conferring with school officials and involving the mother with school officials to work on the target problem.

Why were the errors made? It seems that the practitioner made a judgment: to give the children maximum independence in solving their own problems. This judgment has a certain moral attractiveness but is unrealistic for an 11- and 8-year-old in these circumstances. These children and their mother do not have enough clout and self-assertiveness to take on successfully a formal bureaucracy such as a school system. They need a mediator. That should have been what the practitioner did at once.

By interviews 9 and 10 the children were telling the practitioner that they felt smarter than kids in the regular classrooms, that they did their work conscientiously, and that *no one has explained to them or their mother why they are in LD*. The target problem again. The practitioner-imposed task is not even being attempted by the children. Belatedly, the practitioner hears. She contracts herself for these tasks: to arrange with the teacher for an appointment for Joseph and Rita; to accompany the children to that appointment; to request a staff meeting with appropriate school officials to explain to the children and their mother what the LD placement is all about; and to obtain copies of the laws and regulations dealing with LD placement pro-cedures and rights of the parties. The children and the mother were pleased.

In interview 11 Joseph and Rita seemed foggy about the purpose of the intervention sequence. The social worker prepared them for the staffing scheduled for the following week. The children were given an explanation of where the meeting would be held, who would be there, what they should say.

Meanwhile the practitioner had learned that the school officials insisted they had fully followed regulations governing special education placements. The teacher was enthusiastic about the forthcoming meeting. She sponta-neously asserted that with some "home intervention," Joseph and Rita could be ready for regular class placement the next school year. By home interven-tion the teacher meant help from the mother with homework. The teacher stated that uncleanliness was no longer a problem.

The staffing took place. Present with the family and practitioner were the teacher, the adjustment teacher, and the principal. The school people brought forth a signed form showing that a parent gave permission for LD education placement. At first the mother did not recognize the signature. It then came out that the children had been taken for psychological tests by the mother's boyfriend and that he had signed the paper. The civil rights mystery was solved. The staff recommended that Joseph practice at home on a typewriter (he had no typewriter) to improve fine motor skills, that he keep a notebook to identify words he did not know, and that he be relieved of a baby-sitting job (it was just discovered he had one) which kept him up every night until midnight. Rita (the follower) was not mentioned in the staffing. That was an oversight.

Step 4: terminating. By session 13 the target problem disappeared. All now knew why the children were in LD. The children and their mother were satisfied. Joseph and Rita agreed the teacher was not so bad. Joseph was going to move soon to a regular classroom. Rita would be left behind. The mother was to pay special attention to Rita.

Conclusion. What happened in sessions 9 through 13 could have been done in sessions 1 through 4. A plan for Rita should not have been overlooked. Such a plan could have been worked into the intervention if so much time had not elapsed before the practitioner corrected the strategy. The focus would have been more correct if the problem context had been assessed and if the logic of the clients' target problem had been followed.

CASE EXAMPLES ARE REAL LIFE

Throughout this book other real cases will be presented. They will illustrate different types of problems and the work of a number of practitioners in various settings. Case vignettes often read as dry as dust. Reading the narratives about Lester and about Joseph and Rita, one can ask: Where is the drama? Where is the sense of mission and the caring? The big bang of helping, rescuing, and making an important impact? Is task-centered work only about looking at want ads, drilling a client in making lists, reading a city map, having a meeting with school authorities?

Lester's life was a shambles—a bewildered, terrifying disorder. Imagine the father, an exhausted and tense truck driver, coming to his "dream home" to find a slobbering son, a crippled son, an enraged and unfriendly wife. Imagine Joseph and Rita's despair about being publicly proclaimed dumb and the hidden anxiety about revealing the presence of a man in the house— "Dad"—who perhaps did not know and never told what he had done when he signed a paper putting his girlfriend's kids in a class for "dummies."

In the course of this book other cases will be narrated dealing with the despair of people. The point of these illustrations is to confront this despair with analysis and to organize the human situation clearly enough so that systematic intervention becomes at least possible. It may appear that the problem situations are simplified. They may seem drained of most of their color, even though they deal with death, separation, abuse, failure to learn, terror in the face of life's demands.

Novelists, poets, playwrights do a better job of communicating the essences of cases that wind up in agencies. All the people in cases are hurting, despite the neatness of case examples in a textbook. We must let these words into our minds:

> . . . those who can never put themselves together out of their component bits and pieces . . . , the neglected who have never been given anything for nothing, the underprivileged whose wildest dream is to be next to the last, those who live with their backs to the wall, always looking for a place to hide, cringing before they are threatened, . . . those who never get picked for either team in the school playground, whose hats always get sat on, those who walk straight into every flying gob of spit, apple core, or burning cigarette butt, those who get the leftover pudding or wife, . . . who are always being asked how they are by people who are already walking away . . . let all those come who want to; one of us will talk, the other will listen; at least we shall be together.*

*From Konrad, George, 1974. *The caseworker.* New York: Harcourt Brace Jovanovich, Inc.

REFERENCES

Epstein, Laura, 1977. *How to provide social services with task-centered methods: report of the task-centered service project* (Vol. 1). Chicago: School of Social Service Administration, The University of Chicago.

Nieminan, Edward A., 1978. Personal communication.

Reid, William J., 1975. A test of a task-centered approach, *Social Work 20*, 3-9.

Reid, William J., 1978. *The task-centered system*. New York: Columbia University Press.

Reid, William J., & Epstein, Laura, 1972. *Task-centered casework*. New York: Columbia University Press.

Reid, William & Epstein, Laura (Eds.), 1977. *Task-centered practice*. New York: Columbia University Press.

CHAPTER 2

Practice: what is done and who does it

Human service professions tangle with some of the oldest and most profound dilemmas in the world. How should people live? How should some of us—professional practitioners—influence failing members of society? What happens to us when we get involved with clients? Are we rescuers, Robin Hoods, hypocrites? Does anything we do matter or work? Are we responsible for our clients? For our own actions?

We confront the pain and sorrow of the human condition. "To live authentically . . . is to live in anguish" (Plant, 1970). Consider Dysart, the psychiatrist in the play *Equus:*

> I'll heal the rash on his body. I'll erase the welt cuts into his mind. . . . I'll take away his field of Ha Ha, and give him normal places for his ecstasy—multilane highways driven through the guts of cities, extinguishing Place altogether. . . . With any luck his private parts will come to feel as plastic to him as the products of the factory to which he will almost certainly be sent. . . .
>
> And now for me it never stops: that voice of Equus out of the cave—Why me? . . . Why me? . . . Account for me . . . ? In an ultimate sense I cannot know what I do in this place—yet I do ultimate things. Essentially I cannot know what I do—yet I do essential things. Irreversible, terminal things. I stand in the dark with a pick in my hands, striking at heads! . . . I need . . . a way of seeing in the dark. What way is this? . . . *What dark is this?* . . . There is now, in my mouth, this sharp chain. And it never comes out.*

THE ESSENCE OF PRACTICE

Given the range of activities in practice, what is the essence of the work? Regardless of professional affiliation, practitioners do two basic things: (1) they provide tangible resources and (2) they educate, reeducate, or train per-

---

*From Shaffer, Peter, 1975. Equus. New York: Atheneum Publishers.

sons in social skills. Direct service workers provide resources and train people in social skills on a *case* basis; that is, they concentrate on a single unit such as an individual, family, or group. Indirect service workers (community organizers, planners, managers) concentrate their attention on a condition, a state of affairs. These conditions are usually composed of *deficits* in resource programs or *excesses* of hazards to life, health, and well-being. The overall objective of practice is the reduction of social problems.

REDUCING SOCIAL PROBLEMS

Social welfare services deal with social problems (Chapter 3). These are barriers stopping people from achieving basic desirable and legitimate goals. Such barriers are personal in the sense that they are directly felt to be risky and oppressive by individuals, families, and small groups—in technical words, *microsystems* problems. This is not the whole story. Personal problems never—*at no time under any circumstances*—exist in a vacuum. Nevertheless, private problems cause pain to be felt and misfortune to occur. The direct service practitioner works toward the reduction of personal problems, engineering or constructing some change. The change may be in the physical environment, the interpersonal environment, or the afflicted person's feelings, attitudes, beliefs, and actions. For example, in the Lester case (Chapter 1) the strategy was to reduce the young man's helplessness. In the case of Joseph and Rita (Chapter 1) the strategy was to reduce the children's apparent victimization by the school system. There is immense variability and diversity among the problems dealt with in practice: from a child's being neglected by parents to a child's being misunderstood by foster parents; from a wife's being beaten up by her husband to a wife's making her husband feel like a worm; from a child having temper tantrums to a child being mute; from stealing a car to practicing prostitution; from staying out all night to sleeping all day; and a myriad others.

No case is the first one of its kind in the world. The various social sciences and professions develop typologies, or ways to classify problems. There is no one correct way to classify personal, or *microsystems*, problems. All the various schemes, both past and present, are guesses. They have more or less practical use. My preference for how to classify personal problems ordinarily encountered in practice is two dimensional: (1) a lack of resources to diminish the problems (lack of money, friends, food, shelter, medical care, or their substitutes) and (2) a lack of social skills (problem-solving skill, interpersonal relationship skills, self-esteem, self-confidence, education, information). Most human problems come down to deficits in material resources and know-how. From this viewpoint, work to reduce personal problems is repairing these deficits to the extent possible.

Personal problems may be classified according to a medical metaphor. It can be said, and often is, that they are caused by persistent unsuccessful adaptations to stress (Frank, 1973). The resulting problems thus become an emotional disorder or mental illness. From this viewpoint some people are more prone to develop a maladaptive solution than others because of adverse early life experiences. Another prominent view is that behavior, including problem behavior, is a learned response to individual interpersonal and social circumstances (Bandura, 1977). From the application of medical thinking to social problems arises the idea that work to reduce an emotional disorder or mental illness is "therapy." From the learning perspective, reducing social problems means reeducation, which may be compared to therapy.

Social problems have a dimension in addition to the immediate pains of daily life, influencing daily life and opportunities immensely. These are the *macrosystems* social problems, resulting from the way large-scale institutions of society function: government, welfare, health, education, housing, security, industry, and their subparts. Macrosystems social problems occur in relation to particular historical, economic, and cultural trends and conflicts. They become issues in the play of power among contending centers of influence current in a society. The practitioner's role with macrosystem problems is *social planning* and *community organization*. Examples of these activities are making choices among alternative policies available to an organization; planning and organizing the provision of social services; organizing consumers; lobbying politically; aiding community groups to achieve particular objectives such as reducing community conflict, coordinating services, applying group pressures; and managing, evaluating and changing an organization (Gilbert and Specht, 1977).

PROVIDING SERVICES

Practitioners are service providers. Services are resources created by the large-scale social institutions. They are of two types: *hard (concrete)* and *soft (intangible, psychological).*

Hard, or concrete, resources

Hard services are goods: cash, food, clothing, housing, medical care. Hard services are organized and paid for by the government and to a small extent by private philanthropy. It is always intended that these resources should be distributed to people needing them and unable to purchase them outright or through credit. However, gatekeepers prevent "runs" on the resource banks and try to make the distribution fair. Human service professionals, among their other duties, are the gatekeepers. They make a judgment, based on an agency's general policies and rules. They decide whether a particular person is eligible to receive public assistance, food stamps, supplemental social security benefits, payment of medical bills, payment of child care bills, and similar resources. Human service professonals exercise judgment about *eligibility*. They form an opinion of the clients and their circumstances. Judgment is based on professional knowledge. It is influenced by pressure of duties and beliefs about what is or is not acceptable practice in an agency, community, or profession.

Soft, or psychological, services

Soft services are mental: knowledge and skill. Direct service profesionals impart knowledge and skill to clients. The problem may be gaps in the client's ability to perform in necessary, suitable, and desirable ways. These gaps are sometimes labeled "deficits in coping skills." The practice of enhancing clients' knowledge and skills is referred to as *counseling*, or it may be called *therapy* or *casework*, depending on the language habits and preferences of a particular branch of the delivery system. Recipients or beneficiaries of services are called "patients" when receiving a service under medical auspices and "clients" of nonmedical agencies and practitioners. In housing agencies, recipients are called "tenants"; in prisons, "offenders"; in employment service, "applicants"; and in schools, "pupils." All these words convey approximately the same thing. They label the status of the recipient according to the prevailing style of the organization.

Mixed services

Many services mix together the hard and soft, the concrete and mental (psychological) resources. In our individualistic, therapy-oriented society, psychological services dominate direct service delivery. Organizing program and administrative structure dominates the macrosystems, that is, the rules and regulations of social institutions. An example of mixed services is foster care: the provision of several concrete and psychological resources. Foster care provides housing (a proper place for a child to live), food (necessary and healthful), clothing, medical care, and education. Foster care is primarily under the auspices of the social work profession. As a result of historical developments in social work, it became common to assume that children in foster care, whether in large or small institutions or in foster family homes, always or nearly always needed therapy for psychological ills. These ills were thought to be induced by deficits in the children's preplacement lives, particularly and especially deficits in the behavior of mothers. Although such "pathology" does occur, the majority of children in foster care are not mentally sick. They lack concrete resources. They lack social skills for managing fear, suspicion, low self-esteem, envy, bewilderment. Their parents lack adequate income and housing and skills of home and child management.

In the majority of instances, concrete resources are what people need first. These are the necessities of life. The necessities should not be contingent on the clients' adopting a particular life-style, a particular attitude toward professional helpers, an agreeable relationship toward and acceptance of the beliefs of professional helpers. Concrete resources should be provided (1) in a decent atomosphere, in a place that is clean, neat, and close to where the person lives and (2) by courteous, well-intentioned practitioners who respect the client's life-style, preferences, and capacity. Only after the necessary concrete resources are provided, or started on the way, is it proper to look into needs for counseling or therapy or what manner of counseling is desirable and available.

TYPES OF WORKERS

Who are the people who work at problem reduction and resource provision? They are a diverse lot. They arrive at their work by numerous routes. Their educational credentials vary from high school graduation to doctors of philosophy and doctors of medicine. Despite this variety of personnel, something is happening to spur the emergence of a common core in these occupations. Pulling together such a core is confusing, as well as full of conflict and uncertainty within and between the disciplines. Core knowledge and skills will certainly not jell quickly into anything exceptionally firm, nor will it stay for long in one place. The transitional character of human services and the range of personnel are its outstanding features. New cognitive maps are needed at this particular end-of-century: maps taking into consideration the changes in these fields during the last approximately thirty years.

Since 1950 the people-serving sector of the American work force has grown immensely. Between 1940 and 1968 the number of persons employed

Table 1. Distribution of human service workers, by sex and ethnicity (in thousands), 1970*

Occupation	Total	Total		Black	
		Men	Women	Men	Women
Teachers (kindergarten, elementary, secondary)	2845	1024	1821	52	170
Health technicians	264	80	184	8	16
Nurses	819	NA	819	NA	60
Social and recreational workers	274	113	161	16	27
Physicians	256	256	NA†	5	NA
Social scientists	110	89	21	2	1
TOTAL	4568	1562	3006	83	274

*From U.S. Bureau of the Census, 1976, *Statistical Abstract of the United States:* (97th edition), Table no. 602, Washington, D.C.: U.S. Government Printing Office.
†NA, information not available.

in providing human services doubled. The number in the private sector decreased, while that in the government sector increased vastly (Gartner, 1976). The way the labor force is counted makes it difficult to extract a particular figure to represent the numbers of people at work in the social welfare sector. A reasonable estimate is shown in Table 1.

On the basis of these figures, the various human service occupations add up to about 4½ million people. About 66% are women. Men dominate the most prestigious occupations. Among the persons the census counts as "social and recreational workers," the numbers of men and women are more equal. Overall, the labor force is the human service professions is slanted toward women working for agencies in the public sector of the social welfare system. The numbers of men employed are nevertheless high. The private sector is not insignificant. Black human service workers are a distinct minority. Among the black workers the numbers of women are far greater than the numbers of men. The heavy representation of women creates a climate of work that must affect how work is done in these fields. However, we know of no scholarly analysis of the meaning and character of this influence.

STRATEGIES FOR REDUCING PROBLEMS

The business of direct service practitioners is a particular kind of problem-solving work. Clients are helped according to both the established and the developing problem-solving frameworks in the social welfare system. These frameworks are based on generalized *strategies of problem reduction.* They may be classified as follows:

1. The social welfare system is a provider of *supports for people and remedies for problems.*
2. The *direct service,* or *clinical approach* is one major way of bringing the supports and remedies to the population.
3. *Provision of resources* to people is one of the main activities of the social welfare system.
4. *Teaching people social skills* through education and reeducation, or counseling, is another major activity of social welfare.
5. *Counseling* is done in three modes: individual, family, and group.
6. *Community development* is the strategy for problem solving that involves neighborhoods, communities, and special interest groups.

Each of these strategies will now be examined. What workers do is to implement one or several of these strategies.

Supports for people and remedies for problems

Direct service workers operate in the social welfare system. It is difficult to make sense of this system's often impaired or abnormal operations. It is difficult to make sense of the impairments and injuries clients sustain in their lives and their seeming reluctance to respond to professional interventions.

Poverty, inequality of opportunities, sickness, and mental anguish are the prevailing problems. The most devastating problems in America, possibly in the world, are related to poverty—one way or another. The existence of poverty and the fear of poverty blanket our lives. At the same time, all the social problems of America cannot be explained by poverty alone. For instance, poverty is not the sole explanation of inadequate economic participation of women, blacks, Hispanics, and American Indians. Poverty is an insufficient explanation of urban decay, alienation, corruption, and the thousand ills that people are heir to as they are born, start school, start work, get married or divorced, get fired, get sick, pay taxes, get old, die. Poverty, however, is involved in, and theories of poverty partially explain, virtually all social problems.

Ambiguity stalks the working lives of helping professionals. This is due partly to obscuring the difference between two dissimilar sets of beliefs about the solution of social problems. To cut down this ambiguity, it is necessary for practitioners to identify the two basic strategies for understanding and intervening in each case. The *clinical strategy* calls for applying psychological interpersonal influence to support people in the effort to remedy problems. The *strucutral strategy* calls for increasing opportunities through reorganizing social institutions to equalize access to the goods produced and distributed (Pearl, 1977). The clinical strategy is an atttempt to act on a theory that poverty and personal misfortune are caused by individual character defects and *family pathology* (Handler, 1973). The structural strategy is an attempt to act on a theory that attributes the cause of poverty and misfortune to faults in the structure of the social order, especially lack of opportunity in education and work, lack of equality in the administration of legal justice, excessively low wages.

It is not possible for a modern practitioner to take case actions exclusively according to only the theory of individual causation or only the theory of social structure causation. Both are inextricably bonded together in our social institutions, in laws, in administrative policy and regulations, and in each of our heads. But when it comes to techniques of intervention, the clinical strategy dominates because all the intervention technologies for reducing personal problems that presently exist in social work, psychotherapy, and counseling have their theoretical and research base in abnormal psychology. This one-sided emphasis on abnormal psychology creates most of the frustration of daily case practice. It is perilous to forget that every personal problem has a social context. Every social context produces some type of stress, mismatch, and unfairness. Except in special instances, nearly all social intervention practice occurs in the space between the microsystems and macrosystems. For instance, Lester's problems can be traced directly to gaps in services, resulting in excessive stress put on him, his parents, and the agency worker. Joseph and Rita's problems occurred in a context of a nonconventional marital relationship, an incomplete appraisal by the staff, and a harried educational system.

The characteristics of social welfare services have changed in the last decade. People want a share of what's going on. Today the notion that consumers are entitled to a role in offering, providing, and structuring services is prominent. This participatory thrust is particularly strong among clients who are minority group members—blacks, Hispanics, American Indians, gays, women—especially if they are poor, very young, or very old. Along with recognizing consumer rights, there is strong pressure in social welfare for "accountability." This means more responsive services; more effective, more visible, and measurable practices; and more capability for services to be managed, controlled, economical.

Direct service, or clinical, approach to supports and remedies

The direct service, or clinical, system in the human services is: (1) providing resources to supply necessities and (2) instructing clients in one way or another in the social skills needed for managing hostile and depriving environments, whether these be physical, personal, or interpersonal.

The traditional differentiation between social work and other human service occupations such as nursing, pastoral counseling, psychiatry, medicine, and psychology is this: social work is specifically set up to organize, locate, package, and connect concrete resources. Nursing, psychiatry, and medicine emphasize services organized to alleviate social problems viewed as mental disease or its derivative, emotional or personality "disorder." Clinical psychology emphasizes correction of maladaptive behaviors and thoughts, partly based on the medical metaphor and partly based on the study of mental and behavior processes. Social work practice has the objective of combining and selecting practices from its own history and studies of social problems, as well as from the work of related disciplines. This combination is intended to enable its practitioners to deal with a problem in configuration, a psychosocial or a "social situation," as it is usually called. Nurses, the clergy, psychologists, and psychiatrists understand the powerful influence of the environment, that is, the effects of work, family, school, neighborhood, friends, culture, socioeconomic status. A merging and blending of the helping occupations has arisen. There is developing scholarship in fields named social psychiatry, social psychology, psychiatric nursing, and so forth. Social work has developed two relatively distinct concentrations: *social treatment* (the psychotherapy emphasis, which usually includes resource provision also) and *social development* (the emphasis on large social institutions). Sociology, law, and business administration studies are brought to bear to illuminate the field of social development.

For historical reasons, most social work practice has evolved a distinct clinical (or psychotherapy) cast. Some social workers operate with minimal attention to environmental aspects of a problem, as do some clinicians of the other professions. Social workers actually provide almost all the psychological clinical services furnished in America through large service organizations. Psychiatrists and psychologists provide most of the private practice services, although the private practice of clinical social work is on the increase. There is dispute about the definition of *clinical social work*. It sometimes seems that everyone would like to have that title. The term has supplanted the older term *psychiatric social work*, which also was hard to define and fell into disuse. Some social workers like the newer term because they believe it emphasizes the importance of direct interventions with individuals, families, and groups, as opposed to concerns about community, program, and social policy development.

The term *clinical practice* in the human services is of recent origin. Its spreading use has been attributed to the movement to write laws to license human service practitioners. Licensing laws are the prerogative of states. Their extent and provisions vary to a high degree. In social work there is a vague "specialization" often named *clinical social work*, but this term is impossible to define and no one knows exactly what it means. In psychology, social work, and nursing, some practitioners attach the work *clinical* to their titles, presumably for status reasons. The status of practitioners is important because high status usually brings rewards in salary, working conditions, and perquisites or "perks." It is preferable to use the simple term *direct service practitioner*, meaning a human service worker who obtains and dispenses concrete resources (money and goods) and who instructs clients (teaching, advising, guiding, counseling, treating) is ways to upgrade social skills.

Ambiguity about the term "clinical" will probably continue. The current controversy about the term is best explained as an economic and political matter. At present private practitioners of social work or social agencies can rarely receive reimbursements from insurance companies for services falling in the domain of psychotherapy. This is a source of serious economic strain. The policital factors are related to the array of human service occupations, some of recent origin, whose members come from a heterogeneous collection of educational backgrounds and are in the midst of their own struggles to achieve professional recognition. Social work competes with older, prestigious occupations—psychiatry and psychology—which sometimes have more power to obtain resources and prestige, even though their work in many respects is indistinguishable from social work (Henry et al., 1971).

It is probably best at this point to use the broadest and most nonspecific definition of clinical work in the human service occupations. The clinical workers are the direct service providers, the dispensers of the resources funded and organized for distribution by the public and private social welfare institutions: tangible resources and instruction in social skills. "Clinical" is probably the worst possible word because it blatantly assumes that providing services is caused by a medical or quasimedical problem, that the clients are "sick." The term is occasionally used here only because it has become so common.

Providing resources to reduce social problems

When providing a tangible resource, we are implementing an income transfer welfare program. These programs transfer income because funds collected from higher income persons through taxes are diverted, that is, "transferred," to poor people as "grants." Grants may be cash payments, as in a welfare check. Grants may be "in kind," as in medical care and foster homes for children. Direct service providers are the agents of the social welfare system in reducing the inequalities of income that are arbitrary, capricious, or serve no social purpose (Schulz, 1977). These are inequalities arising from structural faults in the society. Discrimination—principally due to race, sex, and age—is perhaps the most prominent fault. Examples of income transfer follow: in a public assistance agency a service worker is assessing eligibility for aid, figuring budgets, ordering payments; in an unemployment insurance office or a social security office, a worker is verifying eligiblity and ordering payments; in a medical facility a worker is preparing Medicare and Medicaid documents stating costs for health care; or in a child welfare agency or state psychiatric hospital the practitioner is computing ability to pay for service. In all these and in other instances the worker is administering a government program to transfer income, reduce inequality, make services available to people who cannot afford to pay for them on the open market.

The *paperwork* required to provide grants is cumbersome and excessive. Improvements in computer technology may in time control the paper somewhat—if they do not increase it! Paperwork is a process in which a direct service worker gets needed information from a client, makes certain interpretations and judgments, routes this information and these judgments on paper to accountants, and secures the resource for the client. The crucial actions of the resource-providing, direct service worker are getting the relevant information from the clients, *interviewing;* making a fair and proper interpretation about what the client is entitled to, the *eligibility decision;* and getting the information to the authorities, *unlocking the vault* (resource bank, funding allocation)—all this is the paperwork.

Many human service workers are under stress to use time to fill out forms for management information systems. These duties are indeed exceedingly time consuming. They seem to have little to do with the pressing problems of helping clients. These computerized systems are new and have many problems, some of which will be solved in time. Their objective, however, is desirable. They are an attempt to collect from the far-flung social welfare system key facts that could be used for improving planning, making fund allocations, and designing services.

Some resource provisions directly transfer cash. Examples are social security benefits and public aid grants. Others deal with reducing inequality of opportunity. Working in Head Start or other early education programs, we dispense a tangible service—preschool education—to supplement the regular educational system. In a manpower and training program we dispense special education intended to match the supply of employees with the labor market demand. In a child welfare agency the organizational structure is established to feed, clothe, and educate children; in a mental health agency, to dispense drugs, give counseling and provide sequestration.

Teaching people social skills

When providing the intangible resources of counseling or therapy, human service workers are all educators. Reeducators is possibly more descriptive. There are many different "curriculums" for counseling. They can be basically boiled down to two: (1) education in how to obtain basic tangible resources and (2) education in how to behave, that is, how to act to get the social supports needed to sustain life and improve its quality. This is what service workers offer when they "do" counseling or psychotherapy.

When practitioners teach clients how to obtain resources, they explore, explain, discuss, and mediate or advocate (Weissman, 1976).

1. *Exploring* means finding out what resources the clients say they want, what for, when, what they think the resource will do for them. If the clients do not know what resources they want, their uncertainty may be due to fear of making straightforward statements or perhaps to being confused or overwhelmed. Under these circumstances the practitioner can find out what problem each client wants to solve and what resources are available to match this problem.

2. *Explaining* is informing and interpreting. Workers inform the client specifically what resources exist. They explain who controls the resources, what are the rules, how the provision will be monitored, what the clients

have to do to obtain and keep the resources, under what conditions they may be terminated, what rights the clients have and do not have, and what is the authority for these rights.

3. When *discussing* resources, workers elicit the client's views, then sift and examine the fears, anticipations, biases, lack of understanding, personal beliefs, and attitudes about the terms and conditions of resource provision.

4. When *mediating* and *advocating*, workers make the necessary contacts —in person, by phone, by letter—with agencies or departments to expedite matching the client and the resource. Mediation means reconciling differences. Advocacy means using strong influence to procure resources.

Counseling

When human service workers do counseling, all four practices just described are part of the counseling activities. Strictly speaking, counseling or psychotherapy refers to using personal influence to increase another's sense of well-being. There is an assumption underlying all forms of psychotherapy that well-being is both a good in itself and a necessary, if not sufficient, basis from which well-doing grows. These assumptions originated in the liberal beliefs developed in the eighteenth century in Europe and elaborated thereafter in Western culture (Arendt, 1958). We do not, however, have any solid agreement about what well-being consists of and how it is obtained. Nor do we know with any certainty that well-being leads to well-doing and how this connection is made. The paths to well-being and from there to well-doing are obscure and tangled. A multitude of personality and behavior theories have been produced, some more interesting than others, some more informative than others. None of them fully explains the idea of well-being and well-doing (Chapter 4).

From a practical standpoint, it makes the best common sense to think of the direct service worker as one who is a good influence, helps a client get straightened out, feel less depressed and anxious, learn, experience some joy in living, think clearly, decide, and plan.

When counseling clients, four areas of information are sampled and combined to organize an intervention framework, or *intervention strategy:*

1. *Client information:* What the client says
2. *Practice wisdom:* What the practitioner's common sense and practice experience indicate
3. *Expert information:* What the experts suggest
4. *Common sense:* What is feasible

As the helping occupations have developed professionalization and links to the disciplines of medicine, psychology, and sociology, the complexities of helping theory have become immense. Probably the most complex and influential practice theory of many workers in the human services is psychoanalysis. Psychoanalysis is fascinating, attractive, prestigious. It addresses a part of life that is deeply felt and sometimes mysterious. In vulgarized form many of its prominent ideas have saturated American life.

However, on the contemporary scene, psychoanalysis has lost its formerly ascendant position. It cannot be subjected to rigorous scientific study. It is inordinately expensive, it is locked into an elitist and exclusive training system that is highly conservative, and its superiority of outcomes is doubtful. The substance of psychoanalysis is foreign to many capable people. Its popularity is primarily an American phenomenon.

In social work *psychodynamic* (meaning psychoanalytic with an environmentalist tail) casework occupies a position somewhat similar to that of psychoanalysis in psychiatry. Psychodynamic casework's basic practices of interpersonal helping to reduce social problems involve forming a working relationship, making an assessment and case plan, clarifying clients' problems and feelings, giving guidance toward change, procuring concrete resources. Lately, however, under the pressure of new and revised knowledge, "casework" has tended to become renamed "social treatment" and to be broken up into a variety of seemingly different approaches and models. The ideological position of casework is that it focuses on the interface between person and society. In other words, its mission is to influence persons to improve their well-being within themselves (internally) and at the same time to improve their relations with other people and their physical environment (externally).

However, neither casework, psychoanalysis, nor any of their derivatives and adaptations have been able to confront fully the interplay of person and environment. The environmental context is big, hard to identify and conceptualize. For many practitioners the environment is not interesting. We do not ordinarily know how to define, let alone explain, everyday problems of living in terms of history, economics, politics, social structure, nor do we grasp, except perhaps fleetingly, the role each of us plays in making the history of our time (Mills, 1959).

Behaviorists in their modern form are producing information about the mechanisms of "doing therapy." They make the connection between identified unwanted problem behaviors and particular environmental conditions studied with research methods in laboratories and in natural settings. Behaviorists concentrate on controlling environmental conditions, that is, the current antecedent and consequent events believed to affect behavior. One group within the behaviorist field asserts that problem reduction is strengthened by cognitive factors, particularly confidence in one's ability to act in certain ways.

In short, one way or another, on the couch or off, in the office or home or institution, with or without graphs and a stopwatch, with the poor or more affluent, woman or man, child or adult, deviant or conformist, what the counselor does is to influence the client to change. What is to be changed is the client's behavior, the behavior of others, or a social condition. Change is thought to occur by learning skills of acting: getting what is needed, staying out of trouble, becoming safer in a dangerous world, possessing as many resources as can be negotiated, having as good a quality of life as can be garnered.

Three modes of counseling. Direct service intervention can take place in three modes: *individual, family,* or *group.* Cost, convenience, and common sense, as well as habits of work, normally dictate the mode.

Individual mode. The individual mode means that only one person is in the client role; that is, one person only is using a particular service and is the "unit of attention." In professional jargon it is said that the work is "one-to-one," or one client is "working with" a counselor. The two typical examples of the individual mode are (1) the client coming voluntarily or under social pressure for some form of psychotherapy because of feeling depressed, anxious, indecisive, "crazy" and (2) the client coming voluntarily or under social pressure to get a concrete service such as day care, physical health care, foster care.

Family mode. The family mode means that several or all the persons in a nuclear or extended family come on their own or under social pressure to reduce problems that all or most share to a greater or lesser degree. Many methods have been discussed in the professional literature for social treatment of families. The opinions about how to do family treatment are extensive, the language often confusing, the particulars of the recommended actions often nonspecific. There is no strong evidence to support the efficacy of family treatment or any one segment of that field. However, there are indications in the literature to lend credence to the basic notion that getting the major actors in a problem together for work on that problem adds power to problem-solving work (Gurman and Kniskern, 1978).

Five perspectives for viewing the family treatment mode (Briar and Miller, 1971) follow:

1. The family is a collection of individuals.
2. The family is a network of interpersonal relations.
3. The family is a small group.
4. The family is a social organization.
5. The family is a social institution.

Probably most of us have all these views in mind. The first two, however, seem to dominate practice theories. By thinking of a family as an assemblage of individuals, we are led to diagnosing or assessing each person separately. The family members present in a session tend to be onlookers at times and to interact at times. This perspective is exceptionally limited for solving problems that are class linked, that is, related to income and social position. Thinking of a family as a network creates a focus on the quality of their sharing, togetherness, respect for one another, and equality among them. Examining how they communicate tends to be the focus. This approach has the limitation of concentrating on family process, rather than on getting the specific problems out of the way. A tendency may also develop to ignore the family's environment.

Thinking of a family as a small group, a social organization, or an institution seems to have merit. Group processes may be an aid to mobilizing mutual understanding and suitable actions. Analyzing how a famliy is organized, as well as its goals and goal attainment practices, should lead to ideas about and possibilities for action. Nevertheless, the technical literature available at present provides few reliable guides for the small group or social organization focus on family treatment.

Viewing the family as a social institution is an approach that has nothing to offer at present in guidelines for practice. This approach, however, decisively affects thinking about family problems because it is *normative*. We have beliefs and make assumptions about what does and does not constitute good (mature, conflict-free, mutual caring, open communications) or bad family life. These assumptions tend to dictate how a family problem will be judged and what interventions will be designed. But for the most part, there is no consensus on what policies should be pursued to govern and support family life, to specify exactly what it ought to be. Surprising as it may seem, there is little hard knowledge about families (Rossi et al., 1978). Differences in normative expectations may be a singularly important source of strain between practitioners and clients.

Group mode. The group mode of intervention means that an unrelated collection of individuals is put together in order to achieve a particular objective (graduate from school, cut down housing violations in the neighborhood, go on recreational trips, elect an alderman, eject a school principal, etc.); to reduce problems of a personal and social type (become more self-assertive, more friendly, etc.); and to enhance personal growth (study art, resolve conflicts about self and others, etc.).

There are numerous perspectives suggested in the literature that can guide practitioners, depending on what approach is familiar to them and is judged relevant to their circumstances. Ordinarily the group practitioner is responsible for the structure and conduct of the group sessions.

The group mode depends on small group processes to influence the group members. Group processes are transactions among the members; between the members and the group's natural and professional leaders; and between the members, leaders, and surrounding environment. Group processes occur and influence group members. Some group processes are consequences of how the group came together, or *group formation.* Once formed or in the process of forming, there are alternative directions to the process of developing and deciding the group's *purposes.* The primary purposes may be *affiliative* (a source for making friends and interacting with people). The group may intend primarily to be *task oriented* (to get certain things done). Some groups' primary purposes are *personal change* (altering feelings and attitudes). Other groups aim for obtaining *socially rewarding experiences* (recreation and education). Most groups reveal all these purposes, but one is usually dominant.

The purposes of a group usually are translated into a *program,* that is, a set of interlocking plans to guide its decisions and activities. In the course of carrying out its program, a group tends to go through stages. Beginning is usually an anxious time because new people and new experiences need to be understood. The middle stage is shaped by the degree and quality of cohesion and conflict among members. Ending brings satisfactions and disappointments. Complex and often covert interactions occur all along, helping or hindering the group, depending on circumstances.

As a collectivity the group has a life of its own, different from the sum of its parts. The group can be at its best a source of power to help the individual members. It may also be a disastrous struggle at times (Roberts and Northen, 1976).

A perspective on choice of mode. Direct service practitioners sometimes know how to manage all three modes—individual, family, group. Most are at home in one or two. It is not difficult to be familiar with all three, but some practitioners have strong personal preferences for a particular mode, feel more secure with one rather than another. Such preferences are legitimate and should be recognized and accepted.

If a particular set of problems is held in common by a whole family or an important family subpart, efficiency dictates bringing together all the influential actors if it can be done. A particular individual who is shy and inhibited confronting a practitioner solo may relax more with the family present or with a group of strangers. Some clients, as well as some practitioners, dislike and become anxious about the confusion and conflict that can exist in a family or group meeting and are more comfortable alone. Other practitioners prefer sitting down with a family or nonrelated group because it is more stimulating, less boring, less intimate. Still other practitioners are shy and do not like the exposure of families and groups. Research is being done to clarify differential effectiveness among these modes, but no general statements can be made with assurance that any one is generally superior to any other.

Community development: social planning and community organization approaches to problem reduction

Community development is planning, organizing, and carrying out actions to change a social institution. These actions may be on a small or large scale, but their basic purposes are the creation of new resources and the revision of existing resources. The objectives are to increase the opportunities available for a particular population and to make resources more accessible.

What is referred to here as "community development" also goes by many other names: community work, community organization, social planning, social development. Advocacy actions to some extent could be considered in this sector, or in the direct service sector, or both. Advocacy means negotiating with or for the client with agencies or dominant persons who control access to resources and who are opinion creators. The negotiators' goal is obtaining particular resources or arranging particular climates of opinion to relieve stress on a client or a group of similar clients. Advocacy normally is getting maximum benefits for the client within the existing rules and regulations, defending and supporting the client powerfully.

Practicing in the community area can be as complicated as, or more complicated than, direct personal service. Community-oriented work cuts across many fields: social work, urban planning, health planning, public administration, management of private enterprises, political action. The community worker is an agent of change in a complex field of social interactions that are difficult to identify, understand, or manipulate. Power and politics are often at the heart of the issues of concern. *Comprehensive planning* refers to developing projects with a multiplicity of goals and interventions that involve numerous groups, and to a greater or lesser extent it is related to the political arena. *Incremental* or *adaptive planning* is on a smaller scale and concerns arrangements to implement as effectively as possible policies and objectives already formulated.

Most practitioners of community work are involved in local social action: "mobilizing people directly affected by adverse conditions and helping them to organize action on their own behalf" (Perlman, 1977). Local social action often results in small-scale, sometimes temporary gains for a particular population. People may learn basic skills in asserting themselves in concert, gaining a better response from agencies and government, creating a climate in which to alter policies and programs over time. There are no big results and no big breakthroughs.

It has been suggested that community organization practice proceeds by way of the following three models (Rothman, 1974):

1. *Locality development:* Organizing a relatively wide spectrum of people to set goals and take action, for example, organizing parents to put pressure on school and legislative bodies to upgrade public education
2. *Social planning:* Making scientific studies of problem areas, for example, juvenile delinquency or bad housing; analyzing and manipulating the roles and performance of managing bureaucracies so as to establish, arrange, and deliver goods and services to people identified as in need, for example, reorganizing management personnel, starting up a community mental health agency
3. *Social action:* Organizing a disadvantaged section of a community to make demands and wrest some redistribution of power and resources, for example, welfare rights organizations, women's liberation

NORMS AND VALUES: RELATION TO PROBLEM REDUCTION

All human service workers carry out their basic jobs in certain climates of mind and attitude, according to norms of good and bad. These norms rarely are firm and finite. They approach firmness when the norms are widely supported by most sectors of society, such as widely approved laws prohibiting murder, assault, home invasions, theft. These norms have power because their violation can cause loss of liberty and onerous deprivations, primarily imprisonment. Most norms lack the power of criminal law. They consist of shifting sets of values, complex and contradictory objectives, uneven and changing knowledge, collections of rules of procedure known as "methods" or "regulations." Norms of low power are capable of affecting clients' lives by saturating them with pervasive attempts to influence them, with or without their consent, and in ways that make it necessary for them to pay attention to the opinions and beliefs of agencies and their staffs. For example, in the case of Lester (Chapter 1) the normative central position was that an adult person should be self-supporting. This position clashed with another norm, that a disabled person should be cared for by the state or by close relatives. The working out of the case illustrates one way in which direct service workers make decisions between conflicting norms. Lester's worker brought resources to bear to enhance self-support opportunities and simultaneously influenced the relatives to take a little more care of him—temporarily.

The norms of practice are related to "professional values." These are sets of ethical standards. In the United States, and to greater or lesser degrees elsewhere in the world, ethical standards are those of the Judeo-Christian religious tradition and of the Enlightenment era. Specifically, these values (*Social Work*, 1958) hold that:

The individual is the most important unit of society.

Individuals and society are interdependent.

Individuals have responsibility for one another.

Individuals have both common and unique needs and characteristics.

Self-actualization and social responsibility are both essential attributes.

Society has responsibility to enhance self-actualization.

It is often believed that the social role of social welfare is to put these values into practice. But the objectives of social welfare programs are really more mundane: to provide survival income to those not working, to limit the amount of income transfer so that work incentives are kept high, to put a ceiling over parents' neglect and abuse of children, to limit the excesses of children and youth in their pursuit of aggressive acts, to minimize aberrant behavior of adults and children, to guarantee literacy, to maintain health. The mundane objectives of policies and programs are expressions of a collective social need and also, in many instances, of the wish to control the acts of people who are regarded as deviant. Policies and programs are necessarily reflections of political, cultural, and moral sanctions. Policies and programs develop and die as shifts occur in politics, culture, morals, and economics.

One of the functions of practice knowledge is to promote informed application of norms and values. Information and its interpretation is produced by three processes: handed down in traditions, deliberately created in knowledge development centers such as universities, and naturalistically created by persons during ordinary social life through everyday observing, testing, hypothesizing, validating, and generalizing from experience. Knowledge about people and social conditions, although extensive, is nevertheless full of gaps, inconsistencies, contradictions. It is cluttered up with all kinds of biases and beliefs masquerading as knowledge. Methods of practice, although sometimes specific, usually are expressions of beliefs containing mixtures of values, objectives, and knowledge.

It is little wonder that human service workers are beset with dilemmas and awash with anxiety when it comes to their daily jobs. It is little wonder that they are also zealous and enthused about helping people, eager to acquire at least the illusion of mastery over such a frightening and important reality.

What the usual direct service worker does—the actions taken—often boils down to the following:

- What the supervisor directs
- What one's individual inclinations suggest
- What a co-worker says was done in a similar instance
- One's own interpretation of agency policy
- What the client directs
- A suggestion from a recent conference with consultants or experts
- What one reads in a book
- An exhortation in a newspaper or on television
- What a present (or former) teacher says or implies should be done

The usual objectives of the direct service worker often are:

- To cut down the noise (demands in letters received, memoranda received, verbal orders received, plaintive requests received), that is, to organize sets of conflicting and high-pressure demands
- To improve the client's well-being
- To do what will be rated acceptable by agency authorities
- To conform to one's professional image

WORK HAZARDS AND SURVIVAL IN THE WORKPLACE

Keeping onerous and sometimes hazardous responsibilities in order requires health, freedom from fatigue, *and above all clarity of intentions.* Without clarity, the work situation becomes a struggle with enemies: the bureaucracy, the clients, the supervisor, co-workers.

Here are the words of a caseworker:

> My caseload was impossible to service [500 cases plus another uncovered load, he said]. It seemed like all I had time to do was change addresses, visit clients requesting furniture, and visit new cases. The rest was totally wild. The personal pressures were enormous, dealing with all those urgent needs. Sometimes when I couldn't find a way to get money from the state, I'd give people money out of my own pocket. And the amount of money the department was spending was just astronomical. . . .
>
> Getting ineligibles off the rolls, that's the way I see my primary function today. . . .
>
> And there is still real human tragedy about this system. . . . Welfare creates a dependency. There are so many people out there who are never ever going to get off aid and help themselves. Some can't because they're handicapped or sick or old, but others just never will. I've had my present caseload for three years and I see it happen. Sometimes I get on them about it. I go out there and I say, "What are you going to do? I've been coming here four years [sic] waking you up or finding you still watching TV. What are you going to do?" I ask them. "When are you going to get a job?" A lot of times they say, "Oh yeah. I think I'll go to school, improve myself, yeah, I think I'll go to school.". . . .
>
> Welfare keeps people from starving to death . . . and that's what it was designed to do. . . . People do get by, though, I admit, I don't know how they do it. . . .
>
> Think about it. If you were married with a kid and paying $135 a month rent and buying clothes and sending your kid to school, could you get by on $216 a month plus food stamps?*

You are at your office. Your office is a huge loft in a converted warehouse, abandoned factory, or supermarket. It's either gray or dirty cream. Big pillars divide it. The state has laid down rows of small desks, in two's, with one phone for every two to five desks. One phone is shared by Brownstein and Kempward. The clients refer to either of them as "Brown-ward." There are five desk drawers full of clutter. On the desk top are two- to four-foot high stacks of "files"—ubiquitous dossiers filled with carbon copies of forms, illegible letters and notes, and typescript—THE RECORD. There is this constant

---

*From Roberts, Margaret, June 21, 1978. Seven years on the case. *Chicago Journal 2*, 3.

but intermittent noise knife—the phones. You stand up with a phone at your ear, balanced on your shoulder so you can write; you flirt, look up at the ceiling, watch the others, worry. Somebody is always signaling that you are late for a meeting. You have to refer to some paper. You start flipping papers on top of the desk, looking for something. Not there. Somebody passes—a messenger—and dumps some more. You pull out a top drawer and let your fingers walk inside. You cut yourself on a paper edge. Not there. You pull out the next one, then sit down so that you can reach the bottom. You stand up and squint. You start on the other side. Pull down. Push down. You yell to someone: "Have you got a 207A?" Notes, papers, heartbreak. The client on the phone is crying. The neat professional voice of a distant social worker is telling you off with contemptuous politeness. A resident in an emergency room is ordering you to do something impossible. Whatever. Chaos—inside your head and outside your head. You think to yourself: What should I do? Somebody! What should I do?

A teacher is screaming. "He did it! He did it again!" The words are coming out fast, falling over each other. I do not know what she is talking about. Who did it! What? He BM'd in the water fountain. You want to laugh—a lot. That's quite a trick.

He is 4 years old. The kids in the day care center were all quiet at a nap time on the little cots. One teacher and two aides are "supervising." The water fountain is ten yards down the hall. The kid's head only reaches halfway to the top; it's an adult-sized water fountain. He had to escape unnoticed from the nap room, walk unheard ten yards, shinny up the water fountain, take off his pants, and BM—a feat. He did it. *What* are you supposed to do?

You have four choices: fight, flee, negotiate, organize. All are legitimate. Fighting usually makes things worse. Fleeing is okay temporarily if you need time to collect yourself. Negotiating and organizing get you further.

•   •   •

The first scenario—the dance of the desk drawers—calls for organizing because what you have on your hands is many parts that lack arrangement or system. The second scenario—the assault on the water fountain—needs negotiating because what you have on your hands is contention, rage, dispute.

The work of human services is to provide resources and to teach social skills. You pick out the priorities that concern deficits in resources and social skills. If you think in terms of these two priorities, you can see what is foreground, what background, and what is not relevant. Irrelevancies can be ignored. If an irrelevancy heats up, gets a lot of pressure on it, you deliberately rearrange the priorities. You may have to do this often or only occasionally, depending on circumstances controlled by others. You will have to attend to powerful controlling others by negotiating with them to get your work back in order—until the next rearrangement comes, and it will.

The task-centered approach is an aid to maintaining order in these pressure cooker settings. It is an aid to sorting out thoughts, impressions, and demands by means of its basic strategy: to give priority to providing resources and teaching social skills.

CRUCIAL QUESTIONS

Following are the crucial questions for the direct service practitioner in the human services:

1. Which problems do I work on?
2. How do I know and understand the people who are my clients?
3. How can I find my way through the social welfare system?
4. What am I to do? How? What is best to do?

The following chapters will try to give basic answers to these questions.

REFERENCES

Arendt, Hannah, 1958. *The human condition.* Chicago: University of Chicago Press.

Bandura, Albert, 1977. *Social learning theory.* Englewood Cliffs, N.J.: Prentice-Hall, Inc.

Briar, Scott, & Miller, Henry, 1971. *Problems and issues in social casework.* New York: Columbia University Press.

Frank, Jerome, 1973. *Persuasion and healing.* New York: Schocken Books, Inc.

Gartner, Alan, 1976. *The preparation of human service professionals.* New York: Human Sciences Press.

Gilbert, Neil and Specht, Harry, 1977. Social planning and community organization: approaches. *Encyclopedia of social work* (17th issue, vol. 2). Washington, D.C.: National Association of Social Workers.

Gurman, Alan S., & Kniskern, David P., 1978. Research on marital and family therapy: progress, perspective and prospect. In S. L. Garfield & A. E. Bergin (Eds.), *Handbook of psychotherapy and behavior change.* New York: John Wiley & Sons, Inc.

Handler, Joel F., 1973. *The coercive social worker.* Chicago: Rand McNally College Publishing Co.

Henry, William E., Sims, John H., & Spray, S. Lee, 1971. *The fifth profession.* San Francisco: Jossey-Bass, Inc., Publishers.

Mills, C. Wright, 1959. *The sociological imagination.* New York: Oxford University Press.

Pearl, Arthur, 1977. Poverty: strategies for reduction. In *Encyclopedia of social work* (17th issue, vol. 2). Washington, D.C.: National Association of Social Workers.

Perlman, Robert, 1977. Social planning and community organization. In *Encyclopedia of social work* (17th issue, vol. 2). Washington, D.C.: National Association of Social Workers.

Plant, Raymond, 1970. *Social and moral theory in casework.* London: Routledge & Kegan Paul, Ltd.

Roberts, Robert W., & Northen, Helen, 1976. *Theories of social work with groups.* New York: Columbia University Press.

Rossi, Alice S., Kagan, Jerome, & Hareven, Tamara K. (Eds.), 1978. *The family.* New York: W. W. Norton & Co., Inc.

Rothman, Jack, 1974. Three models of community organization practice. In F. M. Cox et al. (Eds.). *Strategies of community organization.* Itasca, Ill.: F. E. Peacock Publishers.

Schulz, James H., 1977. Income distribution. In *Encyclopedia of social work*, (17th issue, vol. 1). Washington, D.C.: National Association of Social Workers.

Working definition of social work practice, 1958. *Social Work 3*(2), 6-9.

Weissman, Andrew, 1976. Industrial social services: linkage technology. *Social Casework 57*(1), 50-54.

CHAPTER 3

Problems: where services start

Which problems do I work on? Who decides? How is it decided? What is the rationale for a particular choice? How much problem change is necessary, according to what criteria? How much problem change is sufficient? What are the consequences of failing to have an impact on a problem?

WHAT PROBLEMS TO WORK ON

All practice issues that confront the practitioner eventually come down to the question: What problems do I work on? The task-centered approach advocates a practical answer to this question. The *target problem* is the one, two, or three conditions producing *in the client* the most perturbation, the greatest threat to present life goals. Clients know what their target problems are. They may need help in stating them and understanding them. Some clients may understand them perfectly. Often the client's target problem seems to be at odds with the problem identified by a referral source or with a professional view of what the problem ought to be (the case of Joseph and Rita in Chapter 1). Uncertainty and confusion about the problem are major sources of a practitioner's work-induced anxiety.

One way practitioners try to deal with confusion about problem identification is the *conference system*. Nearly all agencies establish case conferences as a vehicle for technical in-service training, administrative control, and sharing of risky decision making with "the team," which usually includes some high-status, powerful professional experts. One of the usual agenda items in case conferences is problem identification and selection of focus for work.

Not infrequently, decisions about focus are connected to a judgment about *diagnosis*. There is a belief that if you get the diagnosis right, the rest of the intervention process should fall in place. Not so. Two things are needed to get an intervention in place in dealing with particular problems of individuals and families: (1) pinning the problem down specifically and (2) put-

49

ting into effect a systematic problem-reduction strategy for which there is some evidence of effectiveness, if possible, and which is logically related to the target problem. These two basic intervention principles are disarmingly simple. Their virtue is parsimony. The rest of this chapter will look into the issues surrounding problem focus in order to analyze the dilemmas a practitioner faces.

Dilemmas illustrated: the Kent Corey case

Kent Corey was 45, gaunt, nondescript. Laconic and without spontaneity, his most frequent remarks were: "Gee, I don't know." "Gosh, it's all my fault!" "I never did anything right." He also frequently said: "Gosh, I don't know what to do." He could not find a job. Though a highly skilled construction worker, his work was specialized. At the time, the building industry was depressed. Jobs were indeed scarce. Supported by unemployment compensation, Mr. Corey was living in an apartment with his retired father. Kent had no idea what to do with his children, who had been in foster home placements for three years.

Kent Corey was born in 1917, the younger of two brothers. His father—a direct-thinking, direct-talking man—had overpowered Kent as a child. Kent had been close to his mother even though she was a nag and, in her later years, an alcoholic. After they grew up, Kent and his older brother became estranged. The brother became a gas station owner and had five children.

Kent attended a vocational high school. He dropped out at the end of the second year and joined the navy. After his discharge, he ended up in the construction trade. His wages, although high, were erratic so that his yearly income was minimal. He married Jerry, a pretty blonde, demure on the outside and steel on the inside, and they had six children. Jerry gave herself to child-rearing. The children found her endearing, warm, and delightful. Kent found her remote, stern, well organized, determined.

In the seventh year of the marriage, Mrs. Corey became ill. While still being treated for a disease not yet specifically diagnosed, she conceived another child. While she was pregnant, her third oldest, Arnold, died suddenly. After Amy was born, the doctor said Jerry had cancer. She had surgery and radium treatments. Her organized household went to pieces. She was weak and in pain. Often she was away in the hospital or going for radium treatments that left her exhausted. Meanwhile, Kent pretended nothing was amiss. Women relatives and neighbors lent a hand.

The terminal phase of Jerry's illness was gruesome. While Mrs. Corey was dying, she lay for almost a year on the living room couch with the playpen drawn right up to her side. In that playpen were Timmie and Amy. Timmie, at 3 years of age, was a lethargic child with diarrhea and perpetually soiled, wet pants. Amy, the infant, gave no trouble. Kent's mother died shortly after Amy was born, at the time when it was first realized that his wife's illness was terminal.

The Coreys' oldest, Ralph, 7 years old, was a bitter, angry child. Next was Eileen who took after her mother in looks and who was frightened and anxious. After the dead boy was Anne—frightened but resilient. Then came Timmie and the infant Amy.

The agency was phoned by a neighborhood minister. He felt that this beaten family should have someone to look after the sick woman and the children while the father was away at work. The agency placed a homemaker. For eight hours each weekday she kept the house, cooked, and took care of the children and their sick mother. In the evenings and on weekends, Mr. Corey was home with his wife and children. He was mostly depressed, often beside himself and given to rage. With the children he was a top sergeant. He issued orders and ultimatums. The homemaker thought he was cruel. She was antagonistic toward him, but he did not notice. Mr. Corey knew his intentions were good, and he had no idea that his children were miserable. Filled with his own pain, he had nothing left with which to sense how others might feel. Within six months of the agency's placing a homemaker, Mrs. Corey died. She was then 38 years old. Kent Corey was in a daze.

There was in Kent Corey a stolid, persistent, and unremitting push, not only for survival but also to manage his affairs and the world, to understand what the world was about. His personal history demonstrated resolute persistence (some might say he was stubborn) in the face of uncertainty. He was slow and cautious. When he graduated from grammar school he chose to study for a trade. Dissatisfied with vocational high school, he dropped out. He talked to relatives, thought about himself, read the papers to know what was going on. He called this period "drifting." He eventually joined the navy. When he got out of the navy, he talked to friends of his father, did some soul-searching, and apprenticed himself in the construction industry. He found a girl, got married, and had six children. He kept a job, even though he changed often due to the conditions of his trade. He paid rent and later made mortgage payments on a mediocre house, but it was a house and he was buying it. He was a landowner, he had a good job, he had a wife, a family.

After Mrs. Corey's funeral, the agency left a homemaker with the family. At the same time, the agency urged Mr. Corey repeatedly to decide on a permanent way to care for the children. The homemaker's being there was, by policy, a temporary expedient. He placed an ad in a neighborhood newspaper for a live-in housekeeper. His problem was that he had no one to care for the children. He had a plan—to keep his house, keep up the mortgage payments, and to have a live-in housekeeper.

There was only one response to the ad, Mary Helen Thurston. Exactly Kent's age, Mary Helen was an attractive brunette, chic, well spoken. It was quite a surprise for him to find such a woman answering his ad for a housekeeper. He had been expecting to hear from elderly ladies who were homeless and widows. Mary Helen was divorced. Her regular occupation was hotel maid. In spite of her elegant appearance, she was on welfare. She had just been released from the state psychiatric hospital. She had suffered a depression during which she made a suicide attempt. Mary Helen came to see Mr. Corey one evening. She was appalled by the ramshackle, filthy, nine-room house, as well as by the children, the smell of urine, and the boring man of the house. She wanted nothing to do with the job. Mr. Corey asked if he could call her sometime and she said yes. She believed her back was against the wall and that no stone should be left unturned. Mary Helen was not surprised when Kent Corey phoned her at her dingy rooming house and invited her to dinner. Men had always been attracted by her good looks, by her elegance and appearance. A desultory romance began.

Mary Helen was the only person who ever answered Kent Corey's ad, although he ran it for months. No sensible domestic worker in her right mind would have answered that ad. Considering the lower-class neighborhood and the large number of children, a domestic worker would have known that this was a problem job, that the pay would be poor. Mr. Corey's only solution to his family problem, which he perceived as the problem of caring for the children so that he could keep on working, was to put these ads in newspapers. The agency, continuing to keep its homemaker in the Corey home, became impatient.

The agency itself was having a reorganization. A new executive came on board. Staff were getting fired and resigning; new staff were being sought and hired. Change and new programs were the subject of constant meetings. The need to make permanent plans for the Coreys was a top priority in staff meetings. The new approach of the agency called for speed and effectiveness and was critical of the slow pace and loose direction of the agency's past.

Mr. Corey was being given gentle, sympathetic, supportive counseling. He came to believe that he was not a modestly competent man as he had thought. He became aware of his inadequacies. He came to feel helpless because he did not know what to do. Mr. Corey had no strength or inclination to sift out the assorted and twisted miseries of his existence, to confront accurately and firmly what was possible and what was not. He was employed. He was providing the children with food, shelter, and clothing. The agency was reluctantly providing child care—at no fee. Sometimes it crossed Kent's mind that he might make up with his brother, but he did not think it feasible that his sister-in-law could handle her five kids along with his five. So it was not worth the effort to see his brother. The two had never quarreled. They just had nothing in common. Mr. Corey was jealous of his brother's aggressiveness and ambition. It also crossed Kent's mind that his wife's mother and her sister Francesca might help him care for the children. He was frightened of his mother-in-law who was an excitable woman. He thought she probably drank too much. He liked Francesca who visited often, consoled him, and cared about the children. But Francesca had her own troubles with several children and an argumentative husband.

Mr. Corey hinted that there was a woman or two whom he had in mind but who did not have him in mind. The neighborhood minister tried to persuade him to attend church and put himself in the way of meeting someone. Kent looked the other way at the church. Over the years, as he struggled to know what made the world tick—in other words, to acquire a philosophy of life—he became alienated from religion. He could not bring himself to get involved with the minister. He had his own private and secret desires about what kind of a wife he wanted, and they did not coincide with the lonely widows and old maids whom the minister would have pushed onto him.

Dilemmas discussed: the Kent Corey case

The question pressing for decision was *to place or not to place these children in foster care.* That question jumped over the essential first questions: What did Mr. Corey think his problem was? What did the children think their problems were? What could *they* do about those problems which they perceived? What resources could the agency apply to help the family get what they thought was the solution? Then what should the agency do if it were not able to support the family's solution?

Ordinarily there are four alternatives open to a widower with young children. All family plans constructed by individuals or social agencies are one or another variant of these four possibilities. *First,* the father can take the full responsibility on himself, but since he is required to be absent during the workweek, he must be helped by others to fill the gap left by the deceased mother. The gap is filled by some combination, depending on individual family styles, of employed domestic worker and motherly relatives who either move in or come to the family home for specified hours. A *second* alternative is for the father to move in with relatives and give up his own home or to move the children in with relatives while he goes it alone in bachelor quarters. The *third* alternative is to place the children out, either in an independent foster home for which the father pays a fee or in an agency foster home. The latter will be either free of charge to the father or priced at a nominal sum, since it is subsidized by private and public funds. The *fourth* alternative is for the widower to marry—if someone will have him, considering that he often is poor and is offering a prospective bride a lot of work.

In Kent Corey's situation, finding a domestic worker proved impossible. He could not pay enough, and his children were too disorganized for any domestic worker to handle. His mother was dead. His elderly father and brother appeared unlikely prospects. It seemed impractical to attempt a reconciliation with the brother or that the sister-in-law could manage a total of ten children. The maternal grandmother, a widow, was erratic. The maternal aunt Francesca was poor, had her own brood, and a problem husband to boot.

What exactly is the social problem, the urgent troublesome condition, at this particular point, the circumstance that propels the agency to act to make a change? A number of possible problem formulations come to mind:

1. Mr. Corey is doing an unsatisfactory job of rearing his children.
2. Mr. Corey's personality makeup is defective.
3. The children are anxious and insecure; their development will be abnormal.
4. The agency cannot afford the cost of continuing an unsubsidized homemaker indefinitely.
5. The agency cannot invest a homemaker for such a long placement; there is a waiting list of other families.
6. Child care is one of the necessities for social survival; that basic essential is absent.
7. Because of its publicly sanctioned role, the agency is obliged to obtain adequate child care.
8. Mr. Corey is obliged to supply, or allow the agency to supply basic essential child care.

There are four different orders of meaning to these eight problem formulations. The first and second focus on the *particulars of Mr. Corey's deficiencies* as a person. The third focuses on the *negative state of the children.* The fourth and fifth emphasize the *operation of the agency:* its costs and public policy. The sixth, seventh, and eighth identify *a basic obligation* of society. In general, as workers approach a decision on problem focus, they have in mind in most cases *deficiencies in adult behavior, deficiencies in the state of children's lives, agency regulations,* and a *broad social need* as defined by public consensus and law.

HOW SOCIAL PROBLEMS BECOME DEFINED

Social problem is a social construction. The essence of a social problem, whether in its personal or societal form, is opinion (Blumer, 1970). The opinion that certain acts, certain states of mind, certain conditions of life are problems is not whimsical (although in trivial matters this could be the case). Problems are not fixed, explicitly bounded things with firm substance. They ordinarily cannot be clearly recognized in a uniform manner by following particular rules of observation. *Conditions become defined as problems by a complex and fluid process. Problem definers* are those who give voice to an issue. Problem defining takes place in social interactions: in a family; between peers; in a community, labor, or special interest organization; between the readers and writers of newspapers and magazines; between the viewers and producers of television accounts; between teachers and students, workers and supervisors, management and labor; within professional organizations; among scholars and researchers; and among politicians or between politicians and constituents.

Defining problems is a continuous and changing process. Who defines and what is defined reflects how a social order is functioning at a particular time. In present times, social problems are defined and redefined in accordance with the stresses produced by industrialization and urbanization in all parts of our world. The demand for social welfare programs is a response to strains in the social system resulting from the industrial and urban characteristics of modern life (Wilensky and Lebeaux, 1965).

Problem definitions of bygone eras have a way of staying around even when the original condition has changed. Often we have a way of finally arriving at a good solution for a problem that may have ceased or changed. Social welfare is a way of institutionalizing some types of problem defining and problem solving. However, such organized problem definitions are always temporary, hence the frequently shifting styles of defining problems and the altering of consensus about definitions and intervention methods.

For example, at the level of small particulars (microsystems level), in an earlier chapter the problem of uncleanliness of two children, Joseph and Rita, was discussed. The teacher thought the children were dirty. Joseph and Rita thought they were clean and so did their mother. Several weeks later the teacher thought the children were clean. The practitioner never thought they were dirty. Differences in the perception of something labeled a problem in a particular case are universal. Psychiatrists disagree about diagnosis, which is a hypothesis suggesting a class of problems, such as *schizophrenia.*

Disagreements abound about the dimensions and substance of such problems as child neglect, child abuse, drug abuse, homosexuality, even poverty.

Poverty: an example

Poverty is a special case. It illustrates many issues about problem definition. Notions about what might be a tolerable level of poverty vary with the gross national product (Axinn and Levin, 1975). Should we say that poverty is a problem only for the 20% with the lowest income? For all who are malnourished? Only for those without any shelter? For the old or single? For any urban family of four earning less than $5000 per year?

There are two main theories used today to explain poverty: the *structural* theory and the *pathology* theory. Each has variations, depending on particular and special viewpoints. Most of us mix these two theories together, but since they are of quite different orders, mixture invites confusion.

The social structure theory. The theory of poverty that has the most support today in sociology and in the social policy segment of social work is a theory that attributes the cause of poverty (hence many of its attendant ills) to faults in the *structure* of the social order:

1. Lack of adequate opportunity for the poor to participate in the world of work and education
2. Lack of opportunity for the poor to have access to and fair treatment in the legal justice system apparatus
3. Excessively low wages in certain occupations (the *working poor*)

Most contemporary government-supported social welfare programs are set up to correct the structural deficiencies of low opportunity, injustice, inequality, and low wages. The way these structural faults play themselves out in practice can be illustrated by typical case problems, such as the following:

1. An unemployed parent (father or mother) gets job training. After completing training, there are no jobs available for the newly acquired skills at the place where the parent lives. Jobs may be located at a distance from the home, requiring long and arduous daily transportation, with no opportunities for moving to the community where work exists. The person may be discriminated against in the application process for jobs because of race, sex, age.
2. A single-parent family can find no adequate and accessible child care service where the family lives.
3. An employed adult, young or old, cannot break out of menial and de-

meaning, dead-end work because of prejudice, deficient social skills, or depressed labor markets.

4. An adult or juvenile charged with law violation is unable to get competent and invested legal counsel or a fair trial.
5. An adult feels restrained from using appeals procedures to contest actions taking away or limiting benefits. He has no practical way to change an adverse agency decision.
6. A child taken from parents who lack the resources for care is placed in a foster home or custodial institution indefinitely.
7. Children and adults experience demeaning, mass-produced medical and psychiatric care in overcrowded and fast-paced clinics and hospitals. They drop out or get short shrift.

The pathology theory. The competing theory of poverty is that its cause is the special characteristics of poor people themselves, their individual character defects and family pathology. This theory influences agency practice and public responses to programs. The pathology theory of poverty is a modern version of social Darwinism, a view which holds that economic life rewards persons of good character and punishes the "negligent, shiftless, silly, and imprudent"—the undeserving poor (Hofstadter, 1965). Social Darwinism is a moral and normative system of thought. It charges the poor and near poor with immorality. For example, they may be considered to be welfare cheats, sexually promiscuous, neglectful and abusive to children. In an effort to minimize and liberalize the harshness and one-sidedness of social Darwinism, psychological and anthropological theories have arisen. Deficiencies in energetic pursuit of work, for example, can be explained not as immorality but as psychopathology and the effects of a *culture of poverty*. Not being employed, not having a regular income, not having adequate child care, doing poorly at school or at work can be interpreted as defective ego development, impulsivity, immaturity, defective coping mechanisms, inability to form interpersonal relationships, psychosis, and bad culture.

The theory espoused about a problem leads logically to intervention strategy. For example, staying for the moment with the problem of poverty, the strategy of welfare policy has been to prevent the poor from crossing the line between self-support and dependence on public support. The devices for prevention are some combination of financial assistance (coupled with restrictions on the amount and type of aid), provision of mental health education, and *early intervention*.

The philosophy of this view is that a basic financial floor must be provided, but that easy access to public resources drives the poor away from self-dependence. Offering easy access to counseling and reaching out to people to counsel them are thought to be preferable. The intervention policy derived from this set of theories and its philosophy is that the poor should be reformed (Handler, 1973). The understandings and misunderstandings developed in psychology during this century were thought to be of some use in the rehabilitation and treatment of the poor. New social institutions were erected with that objective. The expanding helping professions tried to develop a scientific basis for treating the personal defects of the poor. The programs to restructure some basic economic and social mechanisms of the social order deliver resources through *individual negotiations between the person in need and experts in interpersonal helping techniques or counseling.*

The dualism of the structural and individual theories of the causation of poverty is an old issue. The caseworker's lament quoted in Chapter 2 illustrates the quandry. The fact is that there are many subtheories about the cause of poverty and we do not really know the root cause. We do know many of the attributes of poverty and some ways to mitigate its sting.

CHANGING OPINIONS ABOUT PROBLEMS

The time or era influences opinions about what is a problem. Changing opinions today illustrate the effect of time. Having an abortion once was considered to be a problem. Today, for many it is a solution. Abortion legislation has become a problem for some people—a new problem. Being a homosexual is a condition that has and has not been a problem, depending on the historical era being considered. The urgency of any social problem depends on the power of those who define it. Problem-defining power is the prerogative of an interlocking set of people and institutions: legislators, media people, government and agency officials, fund-allocating bodies, middle-class spokesmen, professional leaders. In times of social turbulence, poor people and oppressed people develop a degree of power through conflicts with the usual power wielders. They can for a time impose their definitions of problems. Strikes, demonstrations, and organized political pressures exemplify how otherwise powerless people achieve a change in social problem definition.

FADS

The passage of time, the diversity of culture and interests, and the shifting bases of power create fads in problem definitions. There is some hard-nosed, empirically based knowledge about social and individual problems, and the quantity of this knowledge increases a bit year by year. But scientific understanding to guide problem definition and to help design solutions is not sufficient by itself to inform practice. Scientific understanding, with its built-in tentativeness and skepticism, drowns in competing ideologies, biases, and myths. Many ideological statements masquerade as science.

Americans are devoted to quick and visible solutions to whatever is defined as a problem. Popular solutions are those which offend the majority least, such as the recent "discovery" of child abuse and the elaboration of psychotherapeutic interventions for it (Steiner, 1976). Unfortunately, faddish approaches to problem diminution fail. Ill-conceived and simplistic, they lead to the well-known reaction, so profound in the human services, of despondency.

CONCEPTUAL PROBLEMS OF DEFINITION

When a society publicly affirms an urgency, it probably is not absolutely essential that a problem be defined in pure and exact terms. When an individual has a problem according to any kind of commonsense perception, it may not be absolutely essential that its definition be exact. The idea of problem suggests that work must be done despite a small or large degree of unclarity and uncertainty. Because of the multiplicity of factors impinging on every client and every practitioner when starting any case, *naming the problem is where every case starts.*

The study of social problems is confusing because the concepts are varied. Experts disagree, and knowledge is not complete. In common usage the term *social problem* has two meanings. One meaning is *particularistic.* A social problem is an attribute of an individual or a small group of related individuals, such as a family, an immediate neighborhood, or a recognizable peer group.

As an example, consider the single *particular case:* a teenage girl and her mother, living in constant turmoil. Both are drained of energy and interest for work, school, friendships. They think that placement out of the home will be a relief but hate the thought of separating. The family is black; the father is gone; the mother works hard at low wages. The intermingling of individual personality, aspirations, and perceptions with economic and social discriminations and deficiencies is apparent.

The other meaning of social problem refers to discrepancies in the distribution of society's resources needed to maintain the quality of life—a *structural* view of social problems.

An example is the supposed erosion of the family as a powerful social institution or, as it is called in newspaper headlines, "family breakdown." Evidence is marshaled to identify the modern family as an "endangered" institution. This evidence is usually summarized by pointing to increasing numbers of families headed by women; increasing numbers of children, especially older children, being placed in foster care; increasing numbers of working mothers; increasing child abuse reports to the authorities; a perceived intensification of parent-child conflicts because of aggressive, acting-out behavior among children; an increasing divorce rate; and so forth. It is assumed that widespread deficiencies of support systems such as day care, counseling, and relief from poverty and inequality comprise the *social structures* responsible for the crises of the family (Keniston, 1977).

These two views of social problems, the particularistic and the structural, are related. However, little is known about exactly how they are related, although there are a multitude of partial theories and many beliefs about the character of this relationship.

To some extent, it is reasonable to aggregate numbers of deviant persons according to some classification such as age, locality, particular acts, then to assume that the aggregation amounts to a structural deficit or excess and is a broad social problem, or a macrosystem. It is, however, entirely irrational to suppose that microinterventions, even if they reached a saturation point, could of themselves prevent, repair, or wipe out problems afflicting a whole social order. Neat, specific interventions tailored to small units can often alleviate particular problems within a modest amount of time.

The individual particularistic problems dealt with in most agencies can be construed as some form of *deviance*. The charge to practitioners is to contain or control this deviance in a particular person or unit of persons. On the other hand, the public seems to expect that particular individualized services to aggregates of persons should diminish a broad social problem. It is doubtful this would happen. The ability of particular individual services to change a whole group of people (e.g., juvenile delinquents) is questionable. Practitioners, however, may believe they are responsible for accomplishing the impossible. Individual services may benefit an individual unit—a person or family—but hardly a whole population or subpopulation. It takes comprehensive programs with many parts to effect change in a broad social problem. Services to individuals personally caught in these problems will help some people in their personal context. This is what is good about individual services and this is a sufficient rationale for them.

Possible explanations of particular and structural relationships among social problems

Systems theory. Society can be thought of as a *complex adaptive system* (Buckley, 1967). There are persons, groups, and environmental objects. These are linked by continuous interchanges of information. The process of interchanging information is communication. These interchanges generate meanings. They start up and continue and revise behaviors or acts. What goes on between people and what happens at home, at work, at school, in the supermarket, on the street, in court informs us about the terms and conditions of living. We interpret this information. The messages we get and give as we observe and communicate affect our self-esteem, make us angry, afraid, pleased, initiate new worries, dreams, and plans. What salary we get, the kind of house and neighborhood we live in, whether we are gassed to death by pollution, ripped off by thieves or inflation give us signals about what to think, feel, and do to ourselves and others. Meanings and behavior are maintained and altered in the medium of social interchanges. We use labels to classify and organize an understanding of interchanges: good and bad; constructive and destructive; self-defeating and self-actualizing; cooperation, conflict, and competition; neurotic and psychotic; mature and immature; appropriate and inappropriate; and so forth.

Exchange and "games" explanations. Individuals learn a certain way, not a universal way but their certain way, to map their environment. They learn to map themselves and other people. They develop self-consciousness and an orientation to past and future. People make decisions, affiliate with groups, adopt and carry out roles. Their interactions may be based on bargaining and the exchange of rewarding things and events. If cooperation is needed to get the things we need, we strive to develop complementarity of expectations. We may develop *scenarios* as frameworks for interpersonal and interpersonal-organizational *game-playing strategies*.

Deviance explanations. Problems emerge because tension and strain are ubiquitous. Tension and strain are normal, contributing to continuous reorganization, to new meanings, new technologies, new problem definitions, erosion of old problem definitions. Deviation and conformity are also ubiquitous, both representing active aspects of the social order in operation. Deviance, or whatever is so labeled at a given time in a given context, is generated by the interaction of historical and cultural structures as a result of (1) the interpersonal and interpersonal-organizational transactions of that structure and (2) the strains of everyday adjustments, bargaining. learning, and arbitrariness. Labeling (e.g., child abuser, battered child, battered wife, homosexual, drug addit) may lead an individual, group, or organization to define itself as deviant and to build a "career" based on that label.

Deviance is not likely to be typically generated within a solitary individual. It is a collaborative social activity. The collaborators in deviant acts can be the following: (1) the family or certain members of it; (2) a given social group (e.g., club, gang, circle of friends, place of employment, school class); (3) a whole subsystem or a social situation (e.g., an unsafe neighborhood or housing development, chronic poverty and malnutrition, institutionalized depreciation of women and blacks, other defeating conditions); and (4) may be, at times the system of interventions itself (i.e., unknowingly by intervenors or a result of unanticipated consequences).

Norms

Norms, values, and moral views develop in the course of making sense of the social system and organizing it to be a livable and orderly environment. Rules for the behavior of persons and the social responsibility of organizations are an interpretation of norms. Except for a relatively small number of offenses, such as homicide, normative guidelines of good-bad, well-sick, productive-unproductive vary widely among groups of people. These shifts and variations account for much of the uncertainty about whether some act or condition is or is not a deviation. Statements of norms or of moral positions strongly color what is defined as a problem or deviation.

THE RELATIVITY OF PROBLEMS

What constitutes a problem is relative (Freeman and Jones, 1970). It is possible to formulate three basic viewpoints that can be taken to define social problems and to find a clue indicating what area or condition to intervene in. Problems may be defined from a *moral* viewpoint, a *rational* viewpoint, and a *systems* viewpoint. All three viewpoints probably exist every time a problem is formulated.

Moral viewpoint

The moral viewpoint holds that all individuals are of worth and have dignity and that each is entitled to maximum self-realization (*Social Work,*

1958). This approach captures sentiments prominent in Western culture. It reflects the good aspirations of people. It is a cornerstone of the Judeo-Christian tradition and modern liberalism. Most persons in our society have acquired some belief in these moral values, which give meaning to much that they try to be and do.

The finest exposition of the moral viewpoint in human services can be found in a classic publication, *Common Human Needs* (Towle, 1945). This statement is a compassionate interpretation of the rights of people to respect and dignity, to the necessities and comforts of life. It is an assertion that practitioners and social welfare programs should preserve and extend these values of life. The moral position raises questions. Believing in the worth and dignity of all persons, how are we to define the problems of the deviant, rule breaker, exploiter, drug pusher, child abuser? What are we to do about clients whom we think are carrying out worthless behaviors, whose idea of self-realization is to exploit and attack? Can we separate the worth of persons from their acts when the only way we can know people is from what they do (Arendt, 1958)?

Referring to Joseph and Rita or to Lester (Chapter 1), the puzzles with respect to self-determination, self-actualization, worth, and dignity are baffling. Is Joseph and Rita's uncleanliness bad or pathological? Does Lester's low IQ make him unworthy? Were his parents selfish when they wanted to get rid of him? Were the school officials ruthless when they raced for a signature on the children's special education placement form, failing to find out what kind of a "Dad" escorted the children to the test?

The moral approach to defining social problems poses dilemmas not only for human service practitioners, but has also been the subject of debate among philosophers for centuries. Put into social practice, the moral approach has produced noteworthy programs to lighten the burden of old age and illness (subsidized health care), of unemployment (unemployment compensation, job training), of unsafe housing (public housing), of mental distress (public psychiatric clinics and hospitals). Programs intended to do good, however, produce undesirable results and create problems that defeat their lofty aims, including victimization of recipients (Platt, 1969; Ryan, 1971; Kittrie, 1977). Examples are gigantic high-rise slums, inadequate medical care at exhorbitant costs, public financial assistance in amounts too low for decent living, warehousing of mental patients, outpatient psychiatric ghettos, and so forth.

The moral position toward problem definitions is consistent with liberal opinion. It nevertheless contains conflicts of interpretation. It lends itself to negating the principles on which public morality is supposed to be built. One example of a dilemma in interpretation is this: if a child is removed from her parents by court order to protect her from neglect, what do we do about the injury to the parent? Such moral puzzles are widespread in practice.

Rational viewpoint

The rational viewpoint in problem definition is that a social problem consists of specifiable quantities of persistently recurring behaviors (such as juvenile delinquency) or persistently adverse social conditions (such as bad housing). The amount of these undesired behaviors and conditions in an individual or in an aggregation of individuals has to be greater than a tolerable amount. Society cannot tolerate even one incident of some deviant behavior—homicide, for example, For other deviant acts, levels of toleration vary and change. Behaviors and situations are judged to be deviant and subject to sanctions in the presence of regulatory institutions (such as a mental hospital, juvenile court, public school, child welfare agency, the Internal Revenue Service).

The rational perspective says: here is an observable quantity of unacceptable behavior or a demonstrated quantity of social hazard; therefore, to reduce these conditions, each individual's rights and interests will be compromised, to a greater or lesser degree, however it turns out. Implementation of the rational viewpoint in practice results in the existence of large numbers of involuntary clients of agency programs, of forced commitment to and release from mental hospitals, of forced appropriation of single family dwellings to make way for housing projects and highways, and other anomalies.

Issues in adhering to the rational approach are dramatically illustrated in the play *Equus* in the passage quoted on p. 23, The psychiatrist is perturbed. He has to influence a young man to give up his "delinquency" for passionless conformity to regular hours, regular work, and regular thoughts. School personnel are often troubled when they influence, drill, and control children to obey, study, turn in homework, and pass examinations at the cost of diminishing play, freedom, individuality, and perhaps creativity. One argument for the rational approach to social problems, to the extent it can be carried out, is that people need skill in conforming if they are going to survive satisfactorily, and society needs protection from some or many types of deviance. An exquisitely vague line exists between forced conformance and the debasement of personal rights, freedom, creativity, and innovation.

Systems viewpoint

A systems viewpoint toward social problem definition is no easier than the moral or rational position. As explained earlier, the systems viewpoint takes as its starting point the idea that complex human organizations can be thought of as systems. This does not mean that these systems are mechanical entities such as a computer or an automobile transmission. Applied to human social living, systems theory is an *idea* that helps us think about complex, interacting entities. *Human social systems* is a metaphor, a figure of speech. A social systems approach to thinking about social phenomena is a relatively new aid in organizing thought about complex situations in life.

A systems viewpoint toward problem definition starts with recognizing that there is a field of interactional events from which a problem definition is extracted. Moral viewpoints, values, and objective information of varying quality are parts of the system. Viewpoints, values, and information interact continuously and differently with the biological and personal individual, with environmental objects, and with other people.

Deviations from norms and values are inevitably generated in a social system. Some deviations are fed back into social processes as creative, innovative, valued changes. Other deviations become subject to deliberate social control. To define a particular social problem within a social system perspective means to scrutinize the barriers and obstacles to problem reduction and the possibilities of opportunities for alleviation Both are likely to be found in the environment and in the individual or group. Discrepancies in adaptive processes are likely to be observed in several locations in the system at the same time.

DILEMMAS OF PROBLEM IDENTIFICATION: VIEWPOINTS INFLUENCING THE KENT COREY CASE
Questions and discussion

Why was a problem definition needed?

The agency believed it had to take action to end the provision of a resource (homemaker service), to care for and protect the children, and to provide treatment for the children. The agency's action made it necessary for Mr. Corey to take a position on problem definition.

What was the problem definition?

AGENCY: Father deficient in parent role; children disturbed; children lack permanent home.

FATHER: I lack resources for child care.

CHILDREN: We lack resources for child care; we are unhappy.

On what opinions were the definitions based?

AGENCY: *Professional knowledge* from some social work, psychiatric, and child development sources suggests that children do not develop properly with only one parent. This is particularly the case if that parent behaves in an unloving, harsh, insensitive manner and does not supply a stable daily life. Under these conditions, academic underachievement, disobedience, excessive fantasizing, enuresis, and sadness in children may cause them severe present and future psychological damage. *Professional policy*, supported by public opinion and law, is that children should be reared in a stable home that is permanent for the duration of childhood.

FATHER: I as a parent have primary authority about how my children are reared, and my rights are supported by public opinion, law, and culture. Being with my own children is right and natural, and I need them for love and companionship.

CHILDREN: We have to be taken care of dependably. Leaving a parent is a terrible shock. Going to live with unknown strangers is a terrible fear.

How did personal deficiencies influence the problem definition?

The agency's purpose was to improve personal deficiencies in clients. This purpose fulfilled its view of the obligation to serve the best interests of children. A difficulty was created because of substantial disagreement between the agency and the clients over the existence and character of these deficiencies. Since the agency combined the provision of concrete services (homemaker and foster homes) with intangible services (counseling), it considered *both* in combination. The clients, however, wanted *only* the concrete resources.

Did lack of income influence the problem definition?

Yes, in the sense that a more affluent father would have been able to attract a housekeeper and pay her adequately. Not having that high an income, Mr. Corey had to seek subsidized care. If he could have afforded it, a regular marketplace transaction would have been on his terms. For a subsidized transaction, however, he had to take the agency's terms fully into consideration.

Did the times make a difference?

A hundred years ago, Mr. Corey would probably have been a farm laborer in Ireland. In all likelihood a network of kin and neighbors would have come to his rescue. Or his children might have been put in an almshouse. Fifty years ago in America, his children would have been placed in a large custodial orphanage. The problem in those times would have been "dependency"—lack of the father's own resources to provide child care. At the present time, Mr. Corey perceives his problems the way society perceived them fifty or a hundred years ago. The change is in the way agencies and society perceive the problem because of opinions prominent in present-day organizational structures, professional roles, and social objectives.

What is the social context of the problem?

The Corey family was victimized by severe shocks: death of the paternal grandmother who was close to Mr. Corey; sudden death of the child Arnold, just when Mrs. Corey was getting sick and was pregnant; debilitating sickness of the mother. This excessive stress stretched the personal resources of Mr. Corey and all the children. Then Mrs. Corey died, another wound to the family.

Then entered church people, social workers, the maternal aunt and grandmother, and homemakers. The family was inundated by demands for interpersonal interchange as well as by their own fears, hurts, and uncertainties. Everything in their world was pain and demands. Little that was good came their way. The father—under so much stress—kept his job, supported his children, clothed and fed them, paid his mortgage, started looking for a wife, kept his appointments with social workers, and was grateful to the homemakers.

Deluged by strain and not being a psychologically sophisticated person, Mr. Corey did not notice how much his children were in pain. He was powerless to get the agency to agree to indefinite homemaker placement. The agency would have been powerless to provide that service. Meanwhile, a depression in the construction industry was coming. Mr. Corey could not depend on continuing employment. He spent time ruminating about how he could get into another occupation. His age was against him. He might have to settle for low-paid unskilled work. His pride would be hurt. His skills at work were his one sure gratification in life. This might go. The neighborhood where he owned the house was deteriorating. He might have to move. Would selling lose him money? He was lonely but he understood that life meant suffering.

What viewpoints influence the problem definition?

MORAL POSITION: Mr. Corey was a person of worth and dignity and had the right to self-determination and self-actualization, *but* his apparent helplessness, stubbornness, psychological insensitivity, and clinging to the agency were offensive to normative ideals of maturity, especially because he did not want to and would not change himself. The ability to change oneself, or at least to put on a good pretense, is usually considered a sign of acceptable maturity in our culture. The children's rights were violated because Mr. Corey failed to provide a stable living plan with the normatively preferred interpersonal climate of warmth and stimulation.

RATIONAL POSITION: According to the general drift of much child development thought, these children could be considered, to some degree, to be living in a situation and behaving in a manner deemed pathological. It was the obligation of the agency to create different conditions, thought more likely to lead to normalcy.

SYSTEMS POSITION: Mr. Corey was a man who demonstrated his worth. He struggled and overcame the uncertainties of his youth. He acquired valued, expert work skills. He was self-supporting and fed, clothed, and cared for his children. He was hit by high waves of shock. He was treading water, staying afloat, but not swimming. He needed to be rescued, if that was possible.

Mr. Corey was a working-class person. He had not adopted a full set of middle-class values, psychology, or child care emphases. In fact, he did not even understand what they were and did not seem interested in them. His social workers, homemakers, and minister possessed values different from Mr. Corey's. A value conflict of substantial proportions created strife and misunderstanding between the caregivers and Mr. Corey.

The Corey children were objects acted upon rather than persons consulted. The concerned grandmother and aunt had not been involved and consulted because of a judgment indicating, on the surface, that they would have difficulty giving and making a home for the Corey children. (Years later, the older children were of the firm opinion that their Aunt Francesca had wanted them and could have made a home if she could have received financial assistance.)

The basic discrepancies follow: regularized child care was needed; parent training was needed; subsidized indefinite homemaker service was not available; relatives (paternal grandfather, maternal grandmother aunts) were too easily dismissed as substitute caregivers; the agency resources were limited to temporary homemaker service, foster home care, and adoptions; and agency services to support care by relatives were undeveloped. While emphasizing the children's problem behavior, the frequency of childhood problems such as underachievement, enuresis, rage, and suspicion as reactions to deprivation was overlooked. The plasticity of children, how much they change with improved living conditions, how readily some children's problems are reversible with minimal intervention, and how drastic intervention may create more problems than it solves were disregarded.

TASK-CENTERED APPROACH
Target problem preeminence

The task-centered approach puts the client's expression of the target problem in the central position. This position is practical because it mobilizes as much power as possible from the client's own individual, particular motivation. Concentrating on clients' own target problems is the most direct route to tapping the reservoir of problem-solving effort in clients. It eliminates endless and indefinite struggles to influence clients to want and do things they do not care about (Sucato, 1978).

This single-minded concentration on clients' target problems is consistent with the observation that intervention is usually more effective when client and practitioner agree on problem focus. To minimize dropout and increase the probability of good results, it is highly important to put and keep the focus of intervention on a problem that is defined in the same or similar way by *both* practitioner and client (Mayer and Timms, 1970, 1973; Parloff et al., 1978). An intervention contract is one way to effect agreement and commitment on problems (Stein et al., 1974). That the task-centered model demands attention to client target problems is a way to structure worker-client agreement into the focus of intervention (Reid and Epstein, 1972). In addition, concentrating effort on client target problems is consistent with a developing position that clients have a moral right to make the decisive choices about what services they will accept.

Best interests doctrine

Primary attention to client target problems, however, appears possibly inconsistent to some degree with the doctrine that interventions should be in the clients' best interests. The difficulty is that there are many conflicting opinions about what is or is not necessarily in a particular person's best interests. Different segments of the human services and different segments of public opinion hold a variety of views on this subject. The best interests doctrine is most clearly associated with intervention in children's programs (Goldstein et al., 1973). Social welfare programs have organized varying programs to implement the *best interests doctrine* with children's problems. The particular interpretation of this doctrine depends to some degree on which program a client has become associated with. It has been suggested that a preferable doctrine might be *least detrimental,* that is, instituting interventions that are probably least harmful (Wald, 1976).

With adults this doctrine has not been voiced as succinctly as it has been with children. Most discussion has focused on the situation of committed mental patients. The form in which this opinion has been stated is the *right to treatment doctrine.* That issue to some degree has been adjudicated in law. What it comes down to is this: Does an adult committed mental patient have a right to *effective* treatment? What is to be done if treatment methods are grossly ineffective, of doubtful effectiveness, or if treatment may be harmful (Brown, 1978)?

In general, the wish to carry out an intervention strategy that will be in the clients' best interests falters when faced with conflicting opinions, weak methodologies, inadequate resources, clients' specific interest in current problem reduction. It is reasonable to say that clients are best served by reduction of those current and concrete problems which they care about strongly, can and will work on, and are practical and feasible.

Practitioner-client disagreement on focus

In view of the complexities of opinion about the right problem focus of intervention, what does the task-centered doctrine of concentration on client target problems do? What is a sensible position to take where a client-determined target problem is objected to by public and professional doubts? Should the scope of the problem definition be broadened? Should we alter the client's own emphasis? Or try to alter it?

Broadening the scope of the problem can be expected to lengthen the time of intervention. It risks a high frequency of client dropout due to dissatisfaction. It incurs considerable client-practitioner negotiations about an agreed problem focus. The task-centered approach circumvents such time-consuming, frustration-inducing, and expensive interactions. In a brief time, a practitioner can state and explain to clients what problem areas they ought to consider and why, in the opinion of that practitioner. Some clients will be convinced by such explanations and incorporate a professionally recommended problem definition into their own framework. Others will not. Clients who adhere to their own formulation would then be dealt with their way. Any client target problems formulated in ways that are clearly illegal or immoral should be refused by the practitioner, unless the clients can be influenced to stay within acceptable norms.

Clients make blatantly illegal or immoral proposals rarely. The more likely occurrence is that client-determined target problems appear incomplete—too limited for professional preferences. There is often little that can be done to stretch clients' perceptions. Better a real gain from a specific problem than little or no gain from a global problem. Clients who can and will increase the scope of their perceptions pose few difficulties. The practice issue concerns clients who see their problems in a single dimension of narrow scope. It is probable that we often make too much of the client's narrow or single-minded attention. Doing so, we may miss the many opportunities at hand for effective intervention where it counts most to the client.

Mandated problems and services with involuntary clients

There are innumerable instances where a problem is mandated by an authority. The consequences of ignoring that mandate may result in severe losses to the clients' interests and well-being. Agencies cannot ignore mandated problems, for instance, those ordered by courts, without jeopardizing their public sanctions and funding. Therefore the inclusion of mandated problems is the prerogative of the agency. Normally, mandated problems are agreed to by clients on a quid pro quo basis. This means that the mandated problem is accepted by clients on the basis that the clients' own target problems are accepted by the practitioner (Chapter 8).

The enduring dilemma

The target problem doctrine embedded in the task-centered approach does not eliminate or settle the dilemmas of problem definition. There is no way to eliminte these dilemmas. They are an intrinsic part of our culture. What the task-centered approach does is to advocate a practical emphasis *that can reduce a portion of human distress.* We are not obliged to do impossible things such as change life-styles, change personality structure, cut down the incidence of broad social problems through treatment. If treatment can abate a portion of a particular individual's misery, it has done enough. Life-styles are dependent on culture. Personality evolves from living, what one does, who with, where, and when. Broad social problems have to be addressed by large-scale programs, of which individual direct services are only one small part.

Task-centered approach to problem definition: the Kent Corey case

In the Corey case there were no mandated problems. There was no court order. No laws had been broken. The clients' own definitions of target problems (lack of child care resources) could have been adopted plainly and directly. The consequences of this position for intervention strategy would have been efforts to secure indefinite subsidized homemaker service, plus influencing Mr. Corey to get training in parenting skills. If the homemaker service was not available, and in most communities it would not be, the second alternative was the maternal relatives. That strategy would have been to negotiate income supports for them (a viable possibility in many localities) and to train the aunt and grandmother in the skills of managing such a large household. This strategy probably would have been augmented by efforts to help the aunt cut down her own marital discord and her troubles with her own children.

Task-centered approach to mandated problem definition: the Andrew case

Mrs. Andrew, a black woman of 35, had four children between the ages of 2 and 9 years. She was deserted by her husband after he became unemployed. Living meagerly on welfare, with heavy child care responsibilities, lonely, without any intimate friends or relatives, she succumbed to a set of frightening fantasies. She started hallucinating; she heard voices that scared her. Absorbed with her fears, she paid little heed to her children. She thought she had become "crazy." She was reported to the child welfare authority for child neglect. Investigation showed that the children were dirty, ill fed, living chaotically. The agency feared for their safety.

Mrs. Andrew was willing to have the children placed in foster homes. She realized she was not taking care of them. She was willing to go to the local psychiatric clinic in the hope of being cured of her "craziness." With drugs and psychotherapy, Mrs. Andrew's hallucinations stopped. She felt more capable. Six months after their foster home placement, she asked for her children back. The agency's question was: Could Mrs. Andrew be depended on to provide a *safe* home for the children?

Making a clinical prediction about someone's tendency to neglect duties is an uncertain endeavor. The psychiatric clinic could not say that Mrs. Andrew would be either safe or not safe as a mother. The juvenile court preferred to re-unite the family but would not return them without a credible prediction about their future safety.

At this juncture, the agency proposed a plan that the court accepted: the children were to be allowed home on a schedule. First there was to be one full day home. Then overnight. Then two nights. Until a total of seven nights at home occurred. A homemaker would be present when the children were home. An agency worker would visit regularly. This program would take twelve weeks. If Mrs. Andrew provided adequate home safety during these visits, the agency would recommend the children be returned home.

The target problems were (1) lack of information about child safety and (2) not having child custody. The first was court-mandated. The second was Mrs. Andrew's target problem. Given the action of the agency, the psychiatric clin-ic firmed up its opinion and presented to the court their argument: Mrs. Andrew's mental condition was unstable, and it was not expected that she would be ca-pable of tending to her children properly. Continuation of foster care was recom-mended by the clinic. The court decided, however, to adopt the agency's plan.

The worker developed and proposed to the court, the mother, and the homemaker the following definition of safety:
1. Poisonous materials such as cleaning chemicals were to be put on high shelves out of the children's reach.
2. Materials would be obtained for roach extermination.
3. The small children would be watched so that they did not play with electrical sockets or wires.
4. Cooking pot handles were to be turned away from the edge when the stove was in use.
5. Plastic bags were to be stored out of reach.
6. Some educational toys were to be obtained.
7. The children's rooms were to be cleaned and curtains were to be put up.
8. The kitchen was to be cleaned thoroughly.
9. Children not toilet trained were to eliminate only in the bathroom.
10. A nap schedule for the young children was to be set up.

11. A grocery cart was to be obtained.
12. The homemaker was to teach Mrs. Andrew to schedule laundry, cooking, and cleaning.
13. The homemaker was to go with Mrs. Andrew to locate a convenient public playground and make a schedule for taking the children there.
14. A telephone was to be secured.
15. Entering the young children in a day care program and the older children in school was to be arranged.

The contract called for twelve sessions over twelve weeks. All sessions were to take place in the home with Mrs. Andrew and the homemaker during hours when the children were there. Mrs. Andrew's general task was to make a safe home. The practitioner's tasks were to get homemaker service, to report in detail to the court, to get the children transported.

The counseling consisted of setting up tasks that Mrs. Andrew would work on during each period between sessions. At each session the progress and problems in performing tasks would be reviewed and revisions made. The homemaker and agency worker consulted on the substance of parent training for the next period between sessions. The agency worker used most of each session in didactic teaching, demonstration, and practice in homemaking and child care skills.

During the contract there were normal difficulties: misunderstandings about schedule, failures in the child transportation plan, delays of various kinds. At the end of eleven weeks, the house was in order, the conditions set were in effect. The court returned the children to Mrs. Andrew. The public aid department agreed to indefinite homemaker placement on each Tuesday and Thursday mornings. The day-care center agreed to be available for special child care needed when Mrs. Andrew had an appointment at the clinic for herself.

PROBLEM DEFINITION

Practitioners are decision makers who need to have a practical plan so that they can carry it out and help people cut down their problems. The problem definition most likely to lead to effective intervention is the client's defined target problem. That problem is justified on moral grounds, on rational grounds, and is relevant to the life system in which the client is connected and grounded. The role of the direct service worker is to clarify the client's target problem definition, to put this definition within the proper social context, and to suggest and recommend the best ways to state and understand this problem. The practitioner has to define and interpret to the client what, if any, problem definitions require attention because they are authoritatively fixed or mandated. Unless practitioners have power to impose a problem definition, no power on earth can persuade a person to define a problem any way but on the clients' own terms.

Public problem definers generally do not concentrate on an individual, except as a single representative of a *class* of problem bearers or deviants. Public, including professional, problem definitions of classes of problems are negotiable. Public problem definitions, except in criminal cases, are rarely particular. A practitioner normally has leeway to negotiate problem definitions in individual cases with public and professional participants so that attention is concentrated on helping persons as closely as possible on their terms. The problems that ordinary people care about reducing are of two types: lack of resources and lack of social skills.

The preferred rationale for a particular choice of problem definition is *feasibility:* the problem defined should be one that is capable of being understood, credibly described, and observed. It should be a problem for which there is a known solution at best, or a solution that can be constructed from parts and pieces of known technology, emerging innovations in technology, and available accessible resources.

The amount of problem change that is necessary is that quantity of alteration in the environment, or in the person's habits or actions, or both *which will cut down the frequency or intensity of the problem.* The reduction has to be noticeable. It should relieve some specific stress on the person. If possible, the change should relieve stress on the social institutions or agencies that have assumed responsibility for achieving problem reduction.

When interventions fail, there are two sources of information to assess what such failure means. One source is the client. Habits and interests, state of health and socioeconomic status, individual objectives and goals may preclude change. The other source of information about failures is intervention technology. The modes and means of intervention are not developed with detailed specificity and proven effectiveness. Subjective judgments play a large part in intervention strategies and their implementation. The structures and administration of agency programs are complex and have multiple, mixed objectives. The technology used may be insufficiently relevant, obsolete, contradictory.

Practitioners and their agencies react strongly to failure, regardless of its probable source. They feel sorrow for the client's plight. They feel frustrated and fearful about their reputations. They may look for someone or something to blame: the client, the legislature, the social system, the agency administration, the practitioner. Postmortems on failed cases and failed programs are part of life in the helping professions. *The only sensible way to deal with failures is to study them:* (1) to carry out research to monitor the conditions *while the case is in process* so as to avert as much failure as possible and (2) to carry out studies to accumulate information about intervention process to be utilized in the future. *The existence of failed cases is cause for study.*

SUMMARY

1. The definition of a problem is where all intervention starts.
2. Problems are defined by particular persons and groups. They designate who are problem bearers or problem carriers. Some situations or behaviors are defined as problems by legal, moral, cultural, and professional authorities.
3. Problems become defined by a complex process of observation, interpretation, and belief organized as bodies of opinion. These problem-defining opinions reflect historical and cultural influences and special interests: they are a social construction of meaning.
4. Problems may be defined as individual personal deficiencies and as deficiencies in the structural arrangements of society.
5. Problems may be defined as objective conditions to be controlled because of a social obligation to remove personal deficiencies and alter structural conditions.
6. Conflicting theories of problem causation complicate the dilemmas of defining problems. Poverty is an example of the difficulties of definition associated with varying theories of causation.
7. The definition of a problem depends on the era: definitions change over time.
8. Problems are not firm, distinct entities. They are not the property of particular individuals. They are the product of social interactions. They have a social context of which the individual is one part only. Any or many parts may be crucial in problem identification.
9. Problem definitions are influenced by viewpoints. A moral viewpoint directs attention to individual worth and dignity. A rational viewpoint emphasizes a cutoff point beyond which individual rights could be compromised. A systems viewpoint considers discrepancies between what is judged desirable and what barriers restrict the opportunities to reduce or resolve problems.
10. The procedures of the task-centered model are based on the idea that the problems to be worked on are those of major concern to the client,

those that he or she has some control over, and those for which there are effective interventions.

11. When problems seem obscure, when adequate knowledge is not available we can sometimes invent actions to take, or we can put together an innovative rearrangement of ordinary actions. And we have to be prepared for defeat.

REFERENCES

Arendt, Hannah, 1958. *The human condition.* Chicago: University of Chicago Press.

Axinn, Irene, & Levin, Herman, 1975. *Social welfare: a history of the American response to need.* New York: Dodd, Mead & Co.

Blumer, Herbert, 1970. Social problems as collective behavior. *Social Problems 18*(3), 298-306.

Brown, Lester, & Bremer, Jeanne E., 1978. The right to treatment paradox: inadequate means to a noble end. *Journal of Psychiatry and Law 6*(1), 45-69.

Buckley, Walter, 1967. *Sociology and modern systems theory.* New Jersey: Prentice-Hall, Inc.

Freeman, Howard E., & Jones, Wyatt C., 1970. *Social problems: causes and controls* (2nd ed.). Chicago: Rand McNally College Publishing Co.

Goldstein, Joseph, Freud, Anna, & Solnit, Albert J., 1973. *Beyond the best interests of the child.* New York: The Free Press.

Handler, Joel F., 1973. *The coercive social worker.* Chicago: Rand McNally College Publishing Co.

Hofstadter, Richard, 1965. *Social Darwinism in American thought.* Boston: Beacon Press, Inc.

Keniston, Kenneth, & the Carnegie Council on Children, 1977. *All our children: the American family under pressure.* New York: Harcourt Brace Jovanovich, Inc.

Kittrie, Nicholas N., 1971. *The right to be different: deviance and enforced therapy.* Baltimore: Johns Hopkins Press.

Mayer, John E., & Timms, Noel, 1970. *The client speaks: working class impressions of casework.* New York: Atherton Press.

Parloff, Morris B., Waskow, Irene Elkin, & Wolfe, Barry E., 1978. Research on therapist variables in relation to process and outcome. In S. L. Garfield & A. E. Bergin (Eds.). *Handbook of psychotherapy and behavior change.* New York: John Wiley & Sons, Inc.

Platt, Anthony M., 1969. *The child savers: the invention of delinquency.* Chicago: University of Chicago Press.

Reid, William J., & Epstein, Laura, 1972. *Task-centered casework.* New York: Columbia University Press.

Ryan, William, 1971. Blaming the victim. New York: Pantheon Books.

Stein, Theodore, Gambrill, Eileen, & Wiltse, Kermit, 1974. Foster care: the use of contract. *Public Welfare, 32*(Fall), 20-25.

Steiner, Gilbert Y., 1976. *The children's cause.* Washington, D.C.: The Brookings Institution.

Sucato, Vincent, 1978. The problem solving process in short-term and long-term service. *Social Service Review 52*(2), 244-264.

Towle, Charlotte, 1945. *Common human needs.* Washington, D.C.: U.S. Government Printing Office.

Wald, Michael, 1976. State intervention on behalf of "neglected" children: a search for realistic standards. In Margaret K. Rosenheim (Ed.). *Pursuing justice for the child.* Chicago: University of Chicago Press.

Wilensky, Harold L., & Lebeaux, Charles N., 1965. *Industrial society and social welfare.* New York: The Free Press.

Working definition of social work practice, 1958. *Social Work 3*(2):6-9.

CHAPTER 4

People: knowing and understanding clients

What happens in social intervention is a series of transactions among clients, helpers, and their environmental and organizational context. No one section of this interlocking set of connections, communications, and conditions exists without all the others—all at the same time. For purpose of analysis, we look at the pieces separately. In life they are together. We do not know, however, how to trace all these transactions. If we put a good deal of distance between ourselves and living systems, we do better at discerning parts and connections. The discipline of history, for example, makes analyses of events at a distance, shedding light on what the events were, their antecedents, consequences, and meaning. Psychology is the discipline that concentrates attention on understanding people. The study of psychology can help to study human beings in a discerning way. Reliance *only* or primarily on psychology has produced a pronounced distortion of observation in the helping occupations. This distortion has led to an excessive preoccupation with what is inside people's heads. What is outside their heads is just as important.

BARRIERS TO UNDERSTANDING PEOPLE
Strangeness

There are barriers to understanding people because of strangeness. Clients are not our familiars. Many of us are anxious in the presence of people with whom we are not familiar. Anxiety may make us assume that our clients are inexplicable, unnatural, puzzling, unique, peculiar, odd, outlandish. Practitioners who are not troubled by unfamiliarity are lucky. They have an edge on the majority of us who feel dislocated with unfamiliar people. We want to cut down strangeness in order to proceed to intervention. Experience is probably the best antidote for strangeness. Knowledge about the people we are to help is the next best antidote to strangeness. The practical reason for studying psychology in human service work is to cut down strangeness and to emphasize tolerance and acceptance of others.

Lack of knowledge of social context

In addition to personal strangeness, we may not know what an individual's social context consists of. Since we live in a social order, all our individual lives are part of a powerful stream of social conditions. This broad environment is in flux and difficult to understand (*Daedalus*, 1978). It nevertheless directly shapes who we are, how we live, and what problems befall us.

Our lives are shaped by age and sex, where and with whom we live, our financial condition, work or school, state of health, cultural and ethnic background. A cursory review of general information about our social context suggests the nature of its influence in understanding people. Unless otherwise indicated, all statistics used in this social context section are from the 1977 *Statistical Abstract of the United States*, published by the Bureau of the Census.

Age and sex. How old we are (Table 2) and whether we are men or women, girls or boys, tells a good deal about our competencies and the roles we are expected to perform.

There are approximately 104 million men and boys and 110 million women and girls. The older the age group, the higher the proportion of women to men in the population. By themselves, these figures convey no information. However, combined with other factors such as age and sex, household arrangements, income, work, and health, they suggest the probability that some problems are expectable. For example, being older, female, and of low income will set the stage for feeling overwhelmed and unhappy, without a

Table 2. Age of the population of the United States, 1980 (in millions), estimated*

Infants (under 5 yr)	18
Preteens (5-13 yr)	30
Teens and youth (14-21 yr)	33
Adults (22-64 yr)	118
Older adults (65+ yr)	25
TOTAL	224

*From U.S. Bureau of the Census, 1977. *Statistical abstract of the United States.* Washington, D.C., U.S. Government Printing Office.

practitioner having to look any further for causes. Being one of 33 million teenagers preparing for work, competing with 118 million adults, is enough to set many a teenager's teeth on edge. At the present time the future of youth is perceived as exceedingly precarious.

Where Americans live and with whom. In 1976 there were *73 million households*, and the overwhelming majority lived in cities. The vast majority of households were traditional; that is, they were headed by men. The vast majority were white—88%. Blacks and other minorities accounted for 12% of the households. Five million white families were headed by women. Two million black families were headed by women. These are the families most prone to poverty and social problems. People living alone, another vulnerable group, numbered 15 million in 1976.

Americans move often. Forty-one percent moved at least once between 1970 and 1975.

Not everybody lives in a household. Two million people lived in institutions in 1970. The largest group of these were the elderly poor. The next largest group were in mental hospitals and residential treatment centers. Next were inmates of jails and prisons. These 2 million people are nearly always direct consumers of social welfare services, as are the estimated 300,000 children who are in foster care.

Housing conditions. In 1976 people of low income occupied over 1 million public housing units. Numbers of people with social problems live in undesirable conditions such as deteriorated buildings with inadequate plumbing on streets that are poorly lighted and unsafe.

Still, 94% of all housing units had telephones. More than half had air conditioning. In central cities about 9 million rented apartments had undesirable conditions such as noise, heavy traffic outdoors, streets needing repair, impassable roads, inadequate street lighting, personal insecurity on the street, litter, abandoned buildings, odors, and other strong discomforts. Millions of people have to put up with inadequate public transportation to and from home, inadequate neighborhood schools, and inadequate shopping.

Financial conditions. The overwhelming majority of Americans earn their keep by working for wages and salaries. A little of this income is saved. A good portion pays interest owed on charge accounts and mortgages. Most income goes out directly for personal consumption expenditures. The median yearly income of American families in 1975 was $14,000. For white families it was slightly more than $14,000. For black and other minority families the median income was $9000. Two-income families, that is, husband and wife both working, are significantly better off. In general, the more education people had, the higher their income, except that the incomes of men are greater than those of women on the average.

Twelve percent of all Americans were living below the official poverty line in 1975. There was *three times* as much poverty among blacks and other minorities as among whites. In 1974, 63% of the families in poverty received public assistance. The average monthly public grant for Assistance to Families with Dependent Children was $233 in 1975. The range was from $49 per month in Mississippi to $357 per month in New York.

Work and school. What faces young people in the world of work? In the short run, finding employment at all is a large issue. Beyond that they are concerned with the meaning and quality of work and the opportunities that open up because they work. On the average, a youth today is reasonably well educated and has high expectations. These are dimmed by fears of unemployment, underemployment, and job dissatisfaction. It is little wonder that our youth are anxious and often lacerated by conflicts.

The decade of the 1970s brought a large increase in the number of women working. The lives of working women are fraught with the pressures of fatigue, uncertain child care, keeping house, and maintaining adequate interpersonal relations. Like men, working women are consumed with the stress of coping with tedious, boring work. As with men, the intrigue among coworkers and supervisors, unfairness of wage rates, job assignments, promotions, and daily risk of work experiences take an awesome toll of energy. The husbands of working wives are better off because of the financial improvement of two incomes. But such husbands are burdened by sharing the housekeeping and child care or suffering the consequences of avoiding these burdens. The chief consequence is an overwhelmed, resentful wife. Work for women also means stimulation, ambition, new interests that conflict with the traditional wife-mother activities.

Work is the central activity of men. The relationships with fellow workers and supervisors, the struggles for dominance and competence consume their energies. Staying on top and getting ahead drain them of capability to carry out many interpersonal relationships and also provide a vital core of their existence.

Except for the ill and frail aged, older Americans confront the emptiness and terror of uselessness because they are usually not permitted to work. Deprived of work, many experience leisure as empty and an insult.

Knowing what work people do, where, with whom, with what satisfactions and what fears, all this tells us who they are in this most central area of life.

School is the work done by children and youth and by adults attempting to be retrained. In 1975 about 3 million adults were enrolled for the first time in work training programs. Almost all children and youth are in school. School life, like work, is an absolutely central, core part of life. School is not a background to interpersonal relations, self-esteem, well-being, but a crucial element. School, like work, establishes the conditions, habits, and expectations of the quality of life.

Health. Ill health, minor and major, is a source of widespread malaise. Knowing the state of people's health helps us to understand both their well-being and their distress. Poor health not only undermines activity but also influences personality traits. It impedes and undermines financial solvency. Poor health creates stress about the ability to keep going on the job, as well as about family relationships and personal aspirations. Each day almost 1.2 million Americans are hospital inpatients. Americans spend $123 million *each day* on hospital services (Piore, 1977). Like housing, income, and work, knowing the health state of people leads to getting a proper perspective on knowing who they are and what they face.

People exceptionally vulnerable

MEN: (1) They do not live as long as women. (2) They are more often than women victims of cancer, accidents, homicide, suicide, liver disease.

EVERYONE: The major cause of accidental death is explosion and fire in the home.

SUBSTANCE USERS: (1) Ninety-two thousand persons are seriously addicted to drugs, the leading problem being heroin. (2) About 7 million men and 1 million women use alcohol to excess.

CHILDREN: About 8 million are handicapped by speech impairment, learning disabilities, and other conditions.

Conclusion

The overwhelming bulk of the American people are self-supporting. For better or worse, they take care of their problems themselves with the aid of friends and relatives, teachers, ministers. Except for catastrophes, they pay for their social services by purchasing them on the open market from private practitioners and other sources.

The following characterizes the people who are the major users of the social welfare system: poverty, youth, old age, and discrimination due to ethnicity and sex. The problems of being poor, old, and discriminated against are matched by the problems of growing up in modern society. Children and youth cannot help being bewildered. The crucial characteristic of modern life is insecurity about the shape of the future. In the short run, what terrifies people most is the specter of unemployment and all the deprivations that result.

WHAT IS THE MINIMUM WE NEED TO KNOW ABOUT PEOPLE?

Most of us are curious about ourselves and others. Most of us never understand enough to satisfy our quest for knowing and mapping our world. When we are in the role of human service intervenors, *we can ordinarily perform our jobs within the limits of available knowledge if the focus of our intervention is practical.* If our focus is diffuse or on a grand scale, if our purpose is disseminating a philosophy of life or satisfying our curiosity, there is probably no limit to what we need to know. Also, it sometimes happens that our clients are baffling. In these instances, more diverse and larger quantities of knowledge may help. Specialized reference works and specialized experts may shed light on perplexing aspects of the clients we deal with. In the normal course of events, however, *we need to know some basic attributes of the individuals* seen in a particular case load: *we need to know what material resources* they possess or can readily acquire, and *we need to know what social skills they have.*

"Sizing up": a mode of understanding people

We need processes to size up clients—to form an impression, an image of them. We need enough of an impression, but no more, for a particular purpose. This purpose is to make a decision about *selection,* or *classification.* Selection means to accept them or not for particular interventions. Classification means to make a hypothesis (clinical diagnosis or personal and problem assessment) that places the person in some service classification (public aid recipient, foster care recipient, residential institutional care recipient, psychotherapy client or patient, etc.).

We *size up,* or *assess,* people according to what goes on in our own heads when we confront the stranger. We bring to bear our past experiences with people to construct a mental *"working image* or *model* of the client or person . . . This image is *a set of hypotheses about the person and his situation, or potential situations"* (Sundberg, 1978). First impressions are powerful and hard to change even in the face of contradictory later information. Hence rushing from the working image to selection or classification is unwise. It can be unfair. It can lead to premature and unyielding classification, which is *stereotyping* or simplistic labeling. In normal practice, unless case loads are low, a broad theory about a specific person is neither obtainable nor necessary.

Descriptive generalization: knowing who a person is

What is normally needed is a *descriptive generalization based on data and observations, with the minimum necessary amount of conjecture from scanty evidence.*

The basic content from which to construct a descriptive generalization of a person follows:

1. *Identifying information:* Name, address, phone number, sex, age, persons in the family
2. *Socioeconomic status information:* Occupation, income, amount of education, housing resources
3. *Life-style information:* Cultural and ethnic situation; major attitudes toward life and problems in living; major personal interests such as recreation, avocations, friendship circles; obvious power and communication style of the family
4. *Personal traits:* Intelligence, articulateness, appearance, moods, preferences, sexual interests, substance use, aggressiveness, friendliness, health, social skills; if necessary, a gross estimate of observable mental and behavioral handicaps

Example: descriptive assessment of Ron

Ron is an 11-year-old boy living with his divorced mother and 9-year-old sister. The family is at poverty level, subsisting on public aid. The mother graduated from grammar school. Ron is in fifth grade in an alternative school. His sister is in the fourth grade in a regular school. The family, of Jewish origin, is close knit. All members have good health. The mother dominates her children, who are attached to but somewhat fearful of her. The mother and children are present oriented, without long-term objectives, tending to be responsive to things that happen but hopeless about influencing how they live. None of them has any intimate relationships outside the immediate family. There are no aunts and uncles. The grandparents are dead. Aside from an occasional card game, the mother has no recreational interests except TV.

Ron is above average in intelligence, well spoken, neat, fearful, 40 pounds overweight and extremely sensitive about being fat. He believes his overweight causes other children, especially girls, to make fun of him and avoid him socially. He is passive. He is eager to be friendly but a nuisance to people because he tries too hard.

The family live in meager circumstances. The mother has no work skills. Their life is restricted by these circumstances. Their available fun is eating high-calorie food. The mother would like to marry. That would probably lift them out of abject poverty.

Ron is opposed to the mother's having boyfriends. He lacks a grasp of his mother's personal and financial needs. He does not understand the probable benefits for him if the mother marries. Ron lacks elementary skill in how to approach peers for friendships. He lacks an understanding of and control over his food intake. His study habits are erratic. He has little control over his bowel movements. He jiggles, jumps up and down, and makes faces. Peers shun him for such behavior. He has been diagnosed *hyperactive* and is given drugs. It is not known to what extent they are effective.

PSYCHOLOGY AND ITS RELATION TO UNDERSTANDING PEOPLE

For formal knowledge with which to understand people, we look to psychology. The kind of psychology prevalent today is a product of the twentieth century. It reflects the contemporary emphasis on empiricism, or concentration on observation and experimentation. It strives for formal organization of its ideas into self-contained thought systems. Its findings and conclusions are most likely to be practical when they are constrained to limited areas of behavior. Psychology is less practical or impractical when used to explain total areas of real life personal experience. It is such a young science that it must develop much more content in the future compared to what knowledge it currently has.

The field of psychology will be described according to three broad basic subdivisions: personality theories, developmental psychology, and social psychology. A fourth field, *psychobiology,* is emerging and is at present a source of controversy.

Personality theories

When working with individuals, groups, families, and organizations—any way professional activities are concentrated—persons are the basis of the practitioners' attention. It has become the custom to look to personality theory for ways to understand and appreciate people.

A personality theory is a set of assumptions about human behavior. The assumptions are intended to lead to rules for explaining behavioral phenomena believed to be significant. Thus a personality theory is ordinarily intended and put forward as a *general theory of behavior*. Personality theories attempt to account for a broad range of varied behaviors. A good theory of any type is supposed to lead to systematic expansion of knowledge. It is supposed to suggest ideas, hypotheses, and predictions that can be subjected to empirical testing. Theories are not predetermined by nature or data. They are constructed by *theorists* in a creative and arbitrary manner, developed out of their experience, interests, and circumscribed perceptions. All theories are temporary. They are not "revealed truth." None is infallible. Theories become obsolete and are revised. The empirical knowledge they lead to is partial and it, too, becomes altered with the passage of time.

The test of a good theory is its *usefulness*. A theory is useful if it can generate predictions of propositions that turn out to be verified, that is, true. A theory is useful if it generates research or new forms of practice. A theory is useful if it has a reasonable degree of consistency with, or similarity to, known empirical findings (from research and observations).

A theory is particularly useful to practitioners if it cuts down the strangeness and complexity of disconnected observations made in real life. Many behavioral events can be identified and described in a wide variety of ways. A useful theory should organize observations, instruct us about what to concentrate on, and suggest what things hang together. In perceiving ourselves and other people, we *always* use a theory as a guide. We use theories that are formal and explicit and those which are informal, personal, and vague (Hall and Lindzey, 1978).

Personality theories vary along many dimensions, depending on how they stand on the issues that are unsettled. Included in the controversies among theorists are the following:

1. Is behavior purposive or created by the particulars of some event or series of events?
2. Is behavior the result of pleasure seeking, rewards and reinforcement, needs, consequences?
3. Is behavior primarily learned? How much can be attributed to heredity? To developmental processes?
4. Are developmental processes continuous, discontinuous, a mixture of both?
5. Can behavior be understood only in terms of total functioning? Or can it be understood by concentrating on particular segments?

6. Is self-regulation to maintain a state of equilibrium essential? Or are learning and change more important?

7. Is it necessary to emphasize self-concept as a way to organize personality theory? Or are cultural and social influences and transactions paramount?

8. What is motivation and what has this idea to do with a theory of behavior?

9. Is deviant behavior the source of knowledge about behavior? Or normal behavior?

10. Is it necessary to posit an unconscious state?

11. What is personality structure?

12. How much does one's past determine the present and predict the future?

These twelve questions are stated in exaggerated form. They do not cover all the issues of personality theory in its present state, but they suggest the range of controversy and the extent of the unknowns. The test of a personality theory for scholars is: Does it spur research so that the present state of uncertainty may be reduced eventually? *The test of a personality theory for a practitioner is: Does it enlighten understanding of client-persons? Does it reduce strangeness? Does it suggest things to do?*

There are approximately fifteen to twenty major personality theories in modern psychology. They overlap but are distinctive, or unique, in some aspects. None of them adequately meets the usual scientific criteria for explicitness and thoroughness of their statements and definitions. Two broad schools of psychological thought have captured the attention of those who provide and plan human services and of the public: (1) psychoanalysis with its derivatives and revisions and (2) "behaviorism," a loose term applied to a variety of differing approaches. Both sectors have generated substantial research. We are, nevertheless, far away from any thoroughgoing, empirically based, unified theory of behavior.

Strong personalities and powerful ideological commitments have arisen among the disciples and followers of leading theorists. The names of Freud, Skinner, and Piaget are known worldwide to people who never read a word of their writing. These three and probably a few others such as Eric Berne and Fritz Perls have become folk heroes. Their followers are divided into schools, subschools, and "sects." Claims have been made or implied that a particular theory is "revealed truth," and "heretics" are punished. All this may be simply a part of the state of affairs in psychology and among human service practitioners who think they are dependent on psychologists. At the same time, this atmosphere is hardly conducive to reason and logic in the conduct of study and practice. Since no single position seems to have a convincing superiority over all others, it is wise to consider a variety of theoretical positions. We must use whatever is reasonable, particularly if the ideas match what is observable and what has been subjected to research scrutiny. In the present state of personality theory, eclecticism is preferable. Theorists themselves have a tendency to merge theories, parallel to what practitioners already do.

What does all this tell us about guiding practitioners as they try to reduce strangeness between themselves and their clients, understand them, size them up, and become informed of their social context? It tells us that there is a wealth of insight about human nature available in the literature on personality, that this literature is worth studying. It tells us that *no single theory is best or most helpful.* Much of the literature is irrelevant for immediate use in practice. Some of it is so dramatic and lopsided that it increases, rather than decreases, strangeness.

If someone should say, for example, that Ron (to whom we return again) is engulfed in an oedipal entanglement with a seducing mother, that his jiggling and jumping symbolize attempts to externalize his sexual wishes toward his mother, all we can conclude is that Ron is bizarre, crazy, obscurely pathological, sick, must have "treatment." What that "treatment" is, however, no one knows for certain. We could also conclude that the statement about Ron is "crazy." If we use some common sense addressed to Ron's target problems, we have a chance to teach Ron successfully to lose weight, do homework, be toilet trained. This is quite a lot. If we could also do a thorough study of the effects of the drugs he takes, we could get some hard information about whether these drugs are increasing or decreasing the jiggling. If we could track his jiggles, we might find out what events set them off so that we can start to rearrange these events to be less disturbing.

Developmental psychology

Another large segment of psychology assumed to be helpful in understanding people is developmental psychology. Many personality theories and considerable empirical research have gone into the study of biological, psychological, and behavioral capabilities as they change over time. The basic notion is that there are stages, which ought to be definable, that help us to understand what people go through as they age. This basic notion is plausible, has been around for centuries, and has given rise to ideas about age-appropriate behavior, life cycles, maturity, behavioral deterioration, developmental crises and tasks, and so forth. The literature on developmental psychology is vast but unduly concentrated on childhood. Regardless of the particular focus of the theorist or researcher, the basic life cycle stages are self-evident: childhood, adolescence, adulthood, and old age.

Potentially, developmental psychology has more to offer human service practitioners than does personality theory in its present state. The field of developmental psychology seems less imbued with "theological" arguments, more tied to facts, and possessed of relevant substance in its research. The central core of developmental psychology is relevant to a major concern of social welfare: helping people to become independent; to exercise restraint in their actions; to be rational, organized, and planful. There is a virtual consensus that independence, restraint, and rationality are the characteristics that describe maturity (Kagan, 1978). If our general objective is enhancement of maturity, we need information about what lack of resources and what lack of social skills inhibit development. Memorizing a list of desirable attributes has appeal but does not have any power to predict or repair a developmental trend. For example, it would seem best for resource staff in agencies dealing with depressed older people to find out from studies—or from common sense—and specify the resources older people need and want to be able to keep going, as well as to find out the effectiveness of various resource packages provided to keep them from going under. The sadness of approaching death, the loss of deceased loved ones, and the loss of health can be taken as natural and universal aspects of life.

Developmental psychology contains some solid information about all stages of life. There is, however, need for such information to be organized so that it is available for practitioners to use. This field of psychology has immense potential for practical application in social welfare programs. The nature of the knowledge—and a strength—is that its theories deal with limited areas of life and its research is specific to particular persons or groups of similar persons under certain conditions. That body of knowledge, however, is not readily accessible to practitioners. At this stage it is necessary for agencies to organize in-service training or to assign resource persons to collect, present, interpret, and adapt particular knowledge areas to fit the problems of the case load. This knowledge organization, now done on a small scale, would have to be expanded if practitioners generally are to benefit from developmental psychology.

Although most information produced in developmental psychology has concentrated on childhood, this situation is changing. Perhaps as a response to the aging of the population, the conditions of adult living, changing, and aging have become of interest to theorists, researchers, and practitioners. It is heartening to open a new book and read that "the realization of adult potential has become the sign of our times. . . . Rapid social change, pluralistic and equalitarian values, and an aging population have shifted our attention to the dynamics of the processes by which adult life unfolds" (Knox, 1977).

When reviewing cases of adults, it could often be concluded from the case reports that grown persons are the children that they were, bigger in size and with larger or smaller spots of "residual psychopathology." This narrow-minded viewpoint is an affliction of the helping disciplines, brought about by inadequate knowledge of adulthood. The real life of adults, however, only tangentially connects to childhood. Adult concerns are work, status, friends and enemies, the community and neighborhood, intellectual interests, the welfare of children and spouse, and how to take care of aged parents.

The stereotyping of older adults is the most glaring demonstration of deficiencies in knowledge about adult development. These deficiencies are being rectified (Butler and Lewis, 1977). Probably the changing structure of the economics of aging will alter the mandated uselessness of late adulthood. As the costs of governmental and private pensions go up, the need and willingness of society to permit older people to work and live productively will change the stereotypes.

Social psychology

Social psychology, too little developed for use in social welfare programs, is another promising area that can increase understanding of clients. Social psychology addresses the interactions between individuals and their environment. To avoid the trap of stereotyping and increasing strangeness, knowledge about how people are socialized is pertinent.

Especially pertinent is understanding social class characteristics and how they affect child-rearing and adult roles and status. The importance of socio-economic status is that *inequality* is closely linked to belief systems, interests, life-style, and problems. This relationship, although central, is not linear. A person's adaptation to life is not completely determined by status. Different components of status are differentially related to adaptation and problems in living. For example, the work satisfaction of employed women is likely to be affected by more factors than is the case for men (Hodge, 1970). The difficulty with knowledge from social psychology is that it has not been related to practice: it cannot be readily applied to practice problems. Hence at present its usefulness is unfortunately limited.

Psychobiology

At present information is being generated in the various biological sciences that may, in time, expand our knowledge of people significantly. Studies of animal and human brains suggest immensely interesting possibilities for understanding that people become, in part, what their brain physiology makes them (Meredith, 1973; Thompson and Wilde, 1973). The subject is both too technical and too controversial to be elaborated on in this book. The topic, however, will not go away. It will be interesting to find out how this field will unfold. At present it cannot be related to practice in social welfare intelligibly.

A PERSPECTIVE ON UNDERSTANDING PEOPLE

In preparing to see clients, every practitioner to a greater or lesser degree faces *strangeness*. No amount of formal study of psychology (individual and social) or biology will reduce this strangeness. That reaction is a condition peculiar to and unique to a practitioner. Genetics has confirmed what practice wisdom has assumed: every person is unique and different. But every person is also quite the same as every other, particularly in the same or similar socioeconomic status. It is perfectly plausible and legitimate to assume that if the practitioner makes the effort to imagine himself or herself in the client's shoes, some strangeness will abate. Also, if the practitioner can suppress for the moment the fear of failing to master a new situation and attend to the fact that the client is the powerless one in this dyad, the basic structure of the working relationship can be rationally set. The techniques of the task-centered model for establishing a concentration on client target problems and for focusing on the social context is designed to help reduce strangeness and to equalize (somewhat) the power imbalance between client and worker.

At present, neither the disciplines of psychology or biology can provide direct or certain methods to understand or assess people. It is rare to find a practitioner who is fully expert in even one of these disciplines. It is more common to find practitioners saturated with small or large quantities of *abnormal psychology*, especially in its medical adaptation in psychiatry. There can be little doubt that a solid general education in psychology is an aid to a practitioner. This aid is not in providing immediate payoff about what to do. The payoff is in providing the practitioner's mind with sets of organizing themes to interpret *several reasonable possibilities* for understanding the client. What is of immediate practical use is specific knowledge, especially research-based knowledge about the features, forms, characteristics of the particular problem and circumstances. This kind of information—case and problem specific—can be obtained by self-study and by access to educational resources (courses, in-service training, expert consultation).

High emphasis on psychopathology is not warranted. What psychopathology is depends on prevailing definitional conventions. For many situations thought to be psychopathological, there is no known treatment. For some of these identified conditions, however, there are interventions considered to be relatively effective. If a case load contains persons with conditions for which there is a treatment, this information should be acquired and cherished as gold. Except for acute breakdowns, people with chronic psychopathological conditions are candidates for financial support, housing, learning social skills, reduction of loneliness.

Preoccupation with psychopathology is the surest way we know of to overlook the many activities that can be carried out to lighten a person's burdens.

However, if such concrete problem reduction is not enough, that is the time to switch to the intervention system based on the medical metaphor, psychiatry and psychotherapy. Some people will be helped by therapy and some will not. Some people will have to be institutionalized for their own sakes or to preserve the ability of their relatives to carry on. Many programs of therapy can be strengthened by parallel attention to providing resources and enhancing social skills to shorten therapy and make it possible for people to reenter community living. Many programs based on psychotherapy already do that.

Some people pose a special problem if they seem to be, or have proved to be, dangerous. When a person induces real fear in our image of him—fear for his safety, our safety, the safety of relatives or even strangers—this fear is a signal. This information tells us to gather special resources: to convene a conference or make a referral. In such instances, we call on those who have special knowledge in a particular area and the necessary authority and responsibility for effective protection.

Expert advice is often useful also when a person impresses us as having much more potential than is being realized at present. The social welfare system provides many resources to augment the knowledge we may have alone. We should not hesitate to use these resources. We should not expect experts, however, to know more than the knowledge base possesses. Clients are sometimes puzzling people. They get into awful scrapes that defy effective intervention (as do we all, incidentally). Administrative policy ought to contain provisions for calling the shots about what an agency can and will do, based on available knowledge and skill.

What practitioners can use in the absence of a firm psychological base is a pragmatic set of practice guidelines. This is the purpose of the task-centered approach. From a practical standpoint, clients can benefit from a courteous, respectful, and open-minded attitude and from interventions that seek to provide them with necessary resources and social skills. The study of personality, development, and social psychology can offer a practitioner an intellectual climate, selected usable ideas and facts, and a sophisticated understanding of the complexities of behavior. These can cut down on strangeness. There is, however, no known substitute for common sense, certainly not in psychology.

A SPECIAL CASE OF MISUNDERSTANDING: "THE MULTIPROBLEM FAMILY"

Certain people come to prominence, at given time periods, as a heavy focus of attention in social welfare. The so-called multiproblem family contains persons about whom the social welfare system is greatly concerned and who regularly seem to defeat practitioners. People from these families compose a great many of the involuntary clients. Following is a hypothetical example.

Mother held after seven boys found unfed and filthy

The mother of seven children, who were found abandoned Thursday night in their rat-infested home, was being held in City Jail Saturday after her arrest in a public aid office. Mrs. Hernandez, who came here from California eight months ago, had gone with her sisters to the public aid office to ask help in locating her children who had disappeared. She learned that, in response to a neighbor's report, police had taken the children to a hospital. The Court had already assumed guardianship and was planning foster home placement. Mrs. Hernandez had failed to confer with social workers about her older children's truancy from school. She had left the children alone for at least one night.

The boys, ranging in age from 11 months to 9 years, were in fair condition, suffering from rat bites, cuts, and malnutrition. Mrs. Hernandez told authorities she needed a larger sum from public aid to take care of her children. She said the children were from two marriages and she didn't know where the fathers were. The Board of Health has sealed the apartment with a sign, "Unfit for Human Habitation." Mrs. Hernandez has been charged with child abandonment.

This is a multiproblem family. It has the usual characteristics: people especially disadvantaged, such as ethnic and cultural minorities who are poor; female-headed family; children dirty, malnourished, not being educated; home dirty. By implication the mother is *sexually promiscuous* and *neglectful*. She has not cooperated with social welfare personnel. How can she be understood? What is to be done? Why should it be done? What will be the outcome?

There is a view that a substantial portion of the case load are multiproblem families. It is often stated that these families will not accept and use the services offered. Multiproblem families are considered to have an obdurate tendency to avoid or discontinue contact, to be interested only in concrete services, to drift, to behave erratically. These tendencies seem to frustrate objectives to *rehabilitate* families and *prevent* more breakdown. Practitioners become overwhelmed by such families.

In attempting to deal with multiproblem families, it is common to make comprehensive inventories of problems, collecting various kinds of more or less trustworthy information. The inventory approach to defining social problems is based on the idea that a social problem is an objective condition that is untypical (Chapter 3). By cataloging a large list of problems, it seems as if their aggregate constitutes a problem definition—multiproblem family. Persons designated by the multiproblem family label are often explained as the product of faulty personality development that has led them to psychopathology, frequently classified as *character disorder*. Agencies and staff may assume responsibility for ambitious intervention plans going far beyond clients' statements, theoretical understanding, and the capability of intervention methods.

What is a multiproblem family?

The notion that there are multiproblem families with patterns of social malfunctioning arose in its present form following the close of World War II. One definition of these families states that they are "presenting an abnormal amount of subnormal behavior over long periods with a marked tendency to backsliding" (Hare, 1973). The term *multiproblem family* seems to have been introduced by the Family-Centered Project of St. Paul, Minnesota (Geismar and LaSorte, 1964).

Contemporary depictions of the multiproblem family are descended from nineteenth century concerns about an "underclass" and the "undeserving poor." Serious scholars have raised fundamental questions about the merits of the multiproblem family classification. Meyer (1970) suggests that this classification represents a "wrong turn," affixing a label thereafter misconstrued as a "diagnosis." Perlman (1968) believes the term is "not a concept at all. . . . It has no specificity, nor has it a diagnostic or classifying value. On the face of it, it says that a family has many problems."

The assumption that a small number of families absorb an excessive amount of agency time and funds without benefit is probably spurious. What is more likely is that the presence of a particular program in a community results in case finding that matches or even exceeds the program's capability. The degree of taxpayer concern and the interests and beliefs of social welfare professionals can elevate the degree of public attention to a problem. Concentration on multiproblem families may reflect patterns of service rather than incidence and type of social problem (Lukoff and Mencher, 1962).

The main traits and conditions of the families likely to be designated as multiproblem seem to be lack of cleanliness of the persons and their homes, mental and physical illness, impoverishment and dependence on public aid, delinquency and crime, alcoholism and drug abuse, sexual promiscuity, child neglect and abuse, truancy from school, mental retardation, husband-wife conflict, parent-child conflict, single-headed family structure (Schlesinger, 1970).

Many of these behaviors are offenses against normative ideals that often exist as mythical expectations of the human condition. Some represent offenses against a minor type of legal proscription, for example, truancy and "victimless crimes" such as public drunkenness. Others represent complex, widespread social problems such as poverty. Still others are misfortunes, general afflictions of the human condition, such as mental conflict.

The multiproblem family is usually described as:

1. Of public concern because of their presumed social and economic cost to the community
2. Pathological, in the sense that some of their behaviors can be subsumed under some diagnostic system pertaining to psychological or

behavioral "disease," especially parental inadequacies or destructiveness toward children and parental "emotional immaturity"

3. Failing to respond to help or treatment offered

What is wrong with this definition is obvious. "Public concern" is often a political matter. It results from a prevailing social policy or conflicting social politics at any given period of time.

Defining a condition as a social problem because the identified problem carriers do not respond to the "treatment" proffered is poor logic. It is not reasonable to label a person and family deviant because they have not responded to some interventions. Such a characterization does not tell anything useful about the person or family. Generally speaking, treatment technology in psychiatry, psychology, and social work is in a state of tension due to the recognition that it is ineffective in many of the conditions where it has been applied (Chapter 6). Treatment technology is in a state of flux as practitioners and researchers study methods for arriving at more explicit formulations of problems and intervention techniques.

The definition of multiproblem families, as previously explained, puts the primary focus of efforts to control deviance on an individual deemed to be deviant. The inference that so-called multiproblem families are necessarily pathological is not warranted. There is no empirical basis for positing the existence of a multiproblem family entity. What we are left with is (1) a pervasive and ancient concern with nonconforming family units; (2) knowledge that modern society produces severe inequities in the way that opportunities are distributed; and (3) knowledge that the social conditions under which some families live—their neighborhoods, housing, schools, health and occupational conditions—constrain their access to social resources. No treatment technology of any kind has the capability of addressing itself to, managing, or controlling influences so vast.

How many multiproblem families: extent of the problem

There is no information about the incidence of the multiproblem family. No counting mechanism could be designed to collect statistics about an entity whose definition and parameters are so elusive. The existence of substantial literature simply tells us that the subject is of interest to professional authors, but we do not know the actual incidence of the problem itself.

Authors have been meticulous in pointing out that the multiproblem pattern appears in only a portion of poor families, but there is no way of identifying that portion. The multiproblem designation tends to be affixed more to black families and ethnic minorities than to white families (U.S. Department of Labor, 1965). However, most black families in most communities of any size meet the test of stability (Herzog and Sudia, 1973).

How have we understood and treated them: dominant practice themes

There has tended to be heavy emphasis on formulating how the problem came to be (cause, or etiology), how the problem should be classified (clinical designation), and how the problem is played out in the present ("dynamics"). The assumptions are that the present condition was caused by the family history; the clinical "pathology" created undesirable behaviors and attitudes; and the present problem condition consists of ineffective capacities for problem coping, of environmental stress, and of distorted perception. It has been thought that diagnostic data will indicate the treatment objective. Treatment, it has been believed, will sufficiently alter the developmental deficits and clinical pathology so that social functioning can acquire the desired (i.e., normative) characteristics. A further assumption is that lifting away any quantity of real environmental stress will help. If the stress is intractable, the recipients of treatment may nevertheless acquire enhanced understanding of themselves, of significant others and their world, possibly as a result of finding a trustworthy, kind, concerned practitioner.

The objectives of treatment of the multiproblem family have usually been stated in global terms such as helping families to meet the expectations of the community. Projects that attempted programs to influence multiproblem families have been thought of not only in terms of "rehabilitation" but also in terms of "preventing" worse conditions. Obstructing the "contamination" of the children who may grow up to propagate generational pathology—breaking the vicious circle—has been the ideal objective. The projects report the following kind of observations: "The families tended to view—at least at the outset of treatment—their family problems in terms of financial difficulties and lack of employment" (Geismar and Ayres, 1958). This observation has usually been interpreted as meaning that dealing with needs for concrete resources such as money, housing, medical care, homemakers, day care, baby-sitters, transportation is "less threatening" than dealing with problems of family conflict and child neglect.

Clients' lack of response to social workers' overtures led to the philosophy of outreach. This position was based on the belief that social welfare had a responsibility to enable families to fulfill their duties concerning child care and development. It was clear from the beginning of the contemporary movement to treat multiproblem families that "usually, what the families want is the relief of immediate pressures. . . . If a family can see that we can do something besides talk . . . they will trust us with other matters needing attention" (Overton and Tinker, 1959). Thus the principle of "goal stretching" developed, which means providing immediate concrete resources *as a technique* of securing client trust. The hope was that when trust is established, clients would undertake work on more esoteric matters. The hope was vain.

Another discredited explanation for multiproblem families is the idea of a "culture of poverty": a self-perpetuating subsociety with a defective structure. This once popular notion has been exploded by the realization that complex societies such as the United States contain a multitude of variations in life-styles, many of them adaptive, even when they fail to conform to the expectations of others. Nonconformance with a dominant life-style causes problems, to be sure, but they are as likely to be due to lack of knowledge, value commitments, cultural history as to "pathology" (Valentine, 1968; Hobbs, 1975).

The present impasse concerning the amelioration of the multiproblem condition has powerful historical roots. The ideology of social welfare is saturated with it. The pervasiveness of the idea at least partly accounts for agencies and practitioners recognizing something that signals them: here is the multiproblem family. They have been prepared to identify multiproblem families retrospectively, with hindsight, to judge that a "pattern" has existed all along; to diagnose (or "denounce"); and to negotiate with the client to adopt the definition of pathology ascribed to him (Szasz, 1971; Schur, 1973). These ideas have placed a harsh burden on practitioners with large case loads and on public agencies with social responsibilities.

Understanding the multiproblem family

It is advisable to cease using the term *multiproblem family*. This term interferes with thought, conjuring up all kinds of fanciful and incomplete applications of psychological theories, especially personality theories. It might be better simply to refer to families with special hardships. The criteria are *poverty* and the presence of one or more of the following conditions: (1) being, or in clear and present danger of becoming, the object of authoritative intervention by courts and the correctional system; (2) inability to secure appropriate education and work training; (3) dangerous housing; (4) untended, life-threatening ill health or disabling physical or mental handicap; (5) lack of necessary or basic child care and self-care provisions. These criteria indicate a threat to life and to reasonable life goals, the absence of life-sustaining and life-enhancing resources. Interventions flowing from these criteria are of two basic types: (1) provision of resources and (2) provision of opportunities for acquiring social skills to use resources. Conflict among family members and personal unhappiness are likely to abate with acquiring or working toward adequate life conditions. If they do not, they could be attended to with whatever techniques are available.

Closely related and a part of the multiproblem dilemma are parents accused or suspected of *child abuse* or *child neglect* and the children affected. A parent becomes labeled "child abuser" and simply "abuser," and children become classified as "victims." Public and professional concern about child abuse seems to have surfaced in the early 1960s. Attention to it became a concentrated movement. State laws were passed, funds allocated, projects begun and expanded. Neglect, a related phenomenon, has long been an ongoing focus of attention. Except at the extreme end of the continuum (child homicide and manslaughter), the dividing line between neglect and abuse is unclear. An uncertain area of *psychological abuse* and neglect is also of concern in many quarters.

The fact is that, despite the publication of "scare" statistics which are estimates variously arrived at, the incidence of child abuse is not known. The lowest estimate of incidence per year is 6600; the highest, 4 million (Steiner, 1976). The various state reporting systems lack uniformity and contain vague definitions. There is no way to know how much of this problem goes unreported. Studies of child-abusing parents have been based on small samples. The conclusions about parent personality pathology, parents' own upbringing, and characteristics of mothering behaviors lack credible empirical foundations. There is credible evidence from medical sources that some children are indeed maimed, deformed, and murdered. Parents can be and are charged with criminal offenses and sentenced (Nagi, 1977).

Many adults whose children are neglected are in poverty, suffer consequent distress, and manifest bad, sometimes unpardonable, behaviors. They tend to be female heads of families who are deprived of basic resources and adaptive social skills. Overintervention, often resulting in placement, is probably the costliest mode of intervention if used on a large scale. Foster home placement is also an uncertain intervention, capable of causing harm as well as affording child protection. Concern about escalating the antichild abuse movement has caused the Carnegie Council on Children to urge reform: institution of due process proceedings to restrain extreme remedies from being employed if not clearly necessary, abiding by a presumption in favor of children remaining in their own home or with the extended family (Keniston, 1977).

SUMMARY

As helping persons we want to understand people, stigmatized and offensive as they may sometimes be. We cannot eradicate strangeness or grasp who the people are by distancing ourselves from their *social context*, which explains them more fully than does reliance on narrow, incomplete selected pieces from any psychological theory. Socioeconomic factors, housing, education, social supports tend to be enlightening because they fill in both the foreground and the background of particular individuals. Relevant information, gleaned from psychology, can then fill out and enhance understanding of who the people are, real flesh and blood, in a harsh, risky, and at times fascinating world.

REFERENCES

Butler, Robert N., & Lewis, Myrna, 1977. *Aging and mental health* (2nd ed.). St. Louis: The C. V. Mosby Co.

Geismer, Ludwig, & Ayres, Beatrice, 1958. *Families in trouble*. St. Paul, Minn.: Greater St. Paul Community Chest and Councils.

Geismar, Ludwig, & La Sorte, Michael A., 1964. *Understanding the multi-problem family*. New York: Association Press.

Hall, Calvin S., & Lindzey, Gardner, 1978. *Theories of personality* (3rd ed.). New York: John Wiley & Sons, Inc.

Hare, P. M., 1973. *The social services of modern England*. In P. Seed, *The expansion of social work in Great Britain*. London: Routledge & Kegan Paul Ltd.

Herzog, Elizabeth, & Sudia, Cecilia E., 1973. Children in fatherless families. In *Review of Child Development Research*. Chicago: University of Chicago Press.

Hobbs, Nicholas, 1975. *The futures of children*. San Francisco: Jossey-Bass, Inc., Publishers.

Hodge, Robert W., 1970. Social integration, psychological well-being, and their socio-economic correlates. In E. O. Laumann (Ed.). *Social stratification: research and theory for the 1970's*. Indianapolis: Charles E. Merrill Publishing Co.

Kagan, Jerome, 1978. *The growth of the child: reflections on human development*. New York: W. W. Norton & Co., Inc.

Keniston, Kenneth, & the Carnegie Council on Children, 1977. *All our children: the American family under pressure*. New York: Harcourt Brace Jovanovich, Inc.

Knox, Alan B., 1977. *Adult development and learning*. San Francisco: Jossey-Bass, Inc., Publishers.

Lukoff, Irving I., & Mencher, Samuel, 1962. A critique of the conceptual foundation of community research associates. *Social Service Review 36*(4),436-437.

Meredith, Howard V., 1973. Somatological development. In B. Wolman (Ed.). *Handbook of general psychology.* Englewood Cliffs, N.J.: Prentice-Hall, Inc.

Meyer, Carol, 1970. *Social work practice.* New York: The Free Press.

Nagi, Saad Z, 1977. *Child maltreatment in the United States.* New York: Columbia University Press.

Overton, Alice, & Tinker, Katherine H., 1959. *Casework notebook.* St. Paul, Minn.: Greater St. Paul Community Chest and Councils.

Perlman, Helen H., 1968. Casework and the case of Chemung County. In. G. E. Brown (Ed.). *The multiproblem dilemma.* Metuchen, N.J.: Scarecrow Press.

Piore, Nora, 1977. Health as a social problem. In *Encyclopedia of Social Work* (17th issue, vol. 1). Washington, D.C.: National Association of Social Workers.

Proceedings of the American Academy of Arts and Sciences, 1978. *Daedalus 107*(1):entire issue.

Schlesinger, Benjamin, 1970. *The multi-problem family.* Toronto: University of Toronto Press.

Schur, Edwin M., 1973. *Radical non-intervention: rethinking the delinquency problem.* Englewood Cliffs, N.J.: Prentice-Hall, Inc.

Steiner, Gilbert Y., 1976. *The state of welfare.* Washington, D.C.: The Brookings Institution.

Sundberg, Norman D., 1978. *Assessment of persons.* Englewood Cliffs, N.J.: Prentice-Hall, Inc.

Szasz, Thomas, 1971. *The manufacture of madness.* New York: Dell Publishing Co., Inc.

Thompson, William R., & Wilde, Gerald J. S., 1973. Behavior Genetics. In Benjamin Wolman (Ed.). *Handbook of general psychology.* Englewood Cliffs, N.J.: Prentice-Hall, Inc.

U.S. Department of Labor, Office of Policy Planning and Records, 1965. *The Negro family: the case for action.* Washington, D.C.: U.S. Government Printing Office.

Valentine, Charles H., 1968. *Culture and poverty.* Chicago: University of Chicago Press.

CHAPTER 5

The social welfare system: its relationship to practice

Human services are dispensed in the social welfare system, a vast sprawling conglomeration of people, things, and institutions. This system contains laws and organizations. It is surrounded by different and conflicting public beliefs, intentions, and expectations. People who act and react in the social welfare system are *users* or service *consumers* (clients), *practitioners, administrators* and *supervisors, politicians, sellers* of goods and equipment, *maintenance* persons, and others. The network of working people and business and industrial concerns who supply and maintain the system's physical plant is enormous. Think of the buildings (plant) used as headquarters and branches; the phones, computers, file cabinets, typewriters, and dictating machines; the fleets of cars; and the millions of reams of paper whose production starts in the forests to the north and northwest of the country. Think of all the newspaper, magazine, and television workers who monitor the social welfare system, who interpret it to the public by using industrial products—electronic, paper, transportation, and communications equipment—to do so. Think of the high schools, colleges, universities—of their buildings and their faculties, research people, and students at work studying social welfare and producing findings, conclusions, and recommendations. Think of the army of consultants who are knowledge shapers and suppliers for the social welfare system. Think of 148,602 persons employed by the United States Department of Health, Education, and Welfare (in 1976) to organize, plan, and monitor social welfare.

To a practitioner handling some case problem it often appears as it all parts of this system are awry: the laws governing social welfare are a poor fit with the case; the organization implementing the law (the agency) requires, imposes, and expects actions that may hinder good service delivery; the public is suspicious, hostile, and prying; the clients are often angry, dissatisfied, demanding, and hurt; and they disappear and reappear. In any particular instance, all or some of these may be true. *Discrepancies within the system, lack of sequence and coherence, and discontinuity are widespread and to a great extent inevitable.*

DISSONANCE IN SOCIAL WELFARE

Dissonance in social welfare practice is a product of the fact that welfare is a vast social system in a political context. Its components, that is, its constituent agencies, people, and laws, developed historically in an uneven manner. Parts of the system are archaic and redundant, kept in place by habit, by connections to other parts, and by vested interests. The parts are continuously changing in response to development and change in power arrangements, social norms, numbers and distribution of population, distribution of income, type of industrialization, and other factors.

We search in vain for stability and order, for sweet reasonableness in the processes of social improvement. In 1519 Thomas More coined the word *Utopia*, an ideal state to be founded on reason, an imaginary place of perfection. More was beheaded by Henry VIII of England in 1534, beatified by Pope Leo XIII in 1886, and canonized by Pius XI in 1935. The longing for benign norms to rule social conditions and relationships has a long, lasting, and bloody history.

The state of affairs in the social welfare system in the United States, sometimes called the "welfare mess" and other nefarious names, is shaped directly by social welfare legislation and administration. Some social welfare services in this country are *universal.* They cover all citizens—the affluent and the poor. Public education, social security, the police, and the United States employment service provide universal coverage without resort to an *eligibility (means) test.* The bulk of the social welfare system is *"residual":* services are provided to particular individuals who have been screened to make sure they qualify. A good deal of attention is paid to formulating and reformulating these qualifications.

If people are deemed eligible, the services are provided at the discretion and according to the judgment of the particular agency and its agents, the direct service professionals. These judgments are made in accordance with law, regulations, codes of professional standards, styles, and principles. The objective is that these judgments be fair and informed by social science, psychological, and medical knowledge.

Despite a multitude of regulations supported by supervision and consultation, individual practitioners retain considerable independence and latitude for their actions. The quantity of manuals, directives, and consensuses arrived at in staff meetings tends to obscure the substantial areas in which independent judgment can be and is exercised. When all is said and done, direct individual services are provided in a private meeting (an interview) between a client and a worker. Usually no one else is present at the critical point of service delivery. A worker is surrounded by co-workers and supervisors only a short distance away and is influenced by regulations and practice theory; nevertheless, at the point where the most important decisions are transmitted to clients, the direct service practitioner is a solo entrepreneur. The client recognizes the power that goes with this role. It is too bad that many practitioners do not realize how much capability they have to be influential.

Social welfare programs. Social welfare programs are sets of resources, policies, and practices. They are contained in particular formal organizations. These organizations have social auspices: they are sanctioned by law and custom. Social welfare programs normally do not operate for financial profit. Their funds for staff salaries, space, equipment, and tangible resources dispensed to clients are provided by government from tax collections. A small amount of social welfare costs is provided by private, nongovernmental sources. Professional private, fee-for-service practice provides some services similar to those of social welfare (primarily psychotherapeutic counseling, medical and psychiatric treatment, or legal services). Many fringe benefits provided to employees in industry and government include social welfare benefits, for example, pensions and medical insurance. Tax credits, shelters, exemptions, and deductions are social welfare benefits obtained by middle- and upper-class persons (Wilensky and Lebeaux, 1965; Kamerman and Kahn, 1976).

Social welfare programs can be pictured by dividing them into six sections: *education, health, financial assistance, housing, employment,* and *personal services.* All six sections have both a public and private sector, as in the accompanying diagram. The public sector is the services operated by governments, sanctioned by laws, and funded from taxes. The private sector is of two types. There are the private, or voluntary, agencies that are funded in part by moneys supplied through charitable contributions and grants. Grants to private agencies come from government and from private foundations. In addition, the private sector consists of social services provided by employers alone, or as a result of employer-union contracts, such as fringe benefits that cover medical care and pensions.

Outline of the Major Social Welfare Programs

Sector I	Public education	Private education
Education	Preschool Elementary Secondary College and university	Preschool Elementary Secondary College and university

Sector II	Public health services	Private health services
Health (physical and mental)	Hospitals Outpatient clinics Community care Medicare (social insurance) Medicaid (public assistance grants)	Hospitals Outpatient clinics Community care Commercial insurance

Sector III	Public financial programs (distribute money and material)	Private financial programs
Income maintenance	*Insurance types* Old Age, Survivors' and Disability Insurance (OASDI), or social security Unemployment Compensation Workmen's Compensation for industrial accidents *Grant types* Supplemental Security Income (SSI) for the aged, blind, totally disabled Aid to Families with Dependent Children (AFDC) General Assistance (GA) for those not fitting elsewhere Food: food stamps, school lunches, milk	Insurance Fringe benefits Income tax shelters and deductions

Sector IV	Public housing	Private housing
Housing	Low rental units Urban renewal Rent supplements	Open market: rental and sales Urban renewal

Sector V	Public employment services	Private employment services
Employment	Job placement Vocational counseling Vocational rehabilitation Job training	Job placement Vocational counseling Vocational rehabilitation Job training

Sector VI	Public personal services	Private personal services
Personal human services	Counseling and psychotherapy: individual, family, small group social adjustment Child welfare Neighborhood service centers Social care: the handicapped, frail, retarded Individualized services for youth and the aged Information and referral	Counseling and psychotherapy: individual, family, small group social adjustment Child welfare Neighborhood service centers Social care: the handicapped, frail, retarded Individualized services for youth and the aged Information and referral

HISTORICAL PERSPECTIVE

The history of social welfare helps to explain some of the present conditions that at first glance appear to be less than logical. This history can be divided into three distinctive periods of time: (1) pre-1930—before the Great Depression; (2) the 1930s—the New Deal; and (3) 1964 to the present—the War on Poverty, leading to the present welfare reform era.

Pre-1930

Before the 1930s the primary policy followed in social welfare owed its origins to the Elizabethan Poor Law, codified in England in 1601. This law and the way it was enforced were imported by the American colonists. Although conditions in the colonies were vastly different from those in England, the basic philosophy of the poor laws was adapted to the new society. Unemployment was not a problem in the colonies. Rather, there was a scarcity of labor. The social problems dealt with involved people unable to work: the sick, the disabled, widows with children, and those seasonally and temporarily unemployed. Such persons were aided right in the immediate locality where they lived. There were not any other sources for help. However, the financial resources of the colonial towns were extremely limited. The goal of welfare at that time was to minimize the costs, to return the recipients as soon as possible to self-dependence so that they would make a contribution to the economy.

This period of social welfare history is long. It is much more complicated than can be covered here. What is important is that the objectives set in the colonies continue to this day to influence welfare policy, although the practices have changed immensely. Despite continuance of the original colonial emphasis on self-dependence and personal deficiency, in the modern social welfare system the attention is shifting. Today, emphasis is on malfunctions in the structure of society for which an individual is not usually personally to blame.

As the United States became a nation, its population and territory expanded, and it began to become industrial, the social welfare programs had to address new problems. Urban poverty became the central concern. It was then called "pauperism." The prevailing opinion remained fixed on the idea that poverty could be abolished by reforming individuals.

For example, in 1818 one John Griscom write a report (Axinn and Levin, 1975) to the New York Society for the Prevention of Pauperism. He listed the causes of poverty in New York City as (1) ignorance, due to "inherent dullness" or lack of opportunities for self-improvement; (2) idleness, an "evil" that was either "inherent" or habitual; (3) intemperance, "the crying and increasing sin of the nation"; (4) failure to save money; (5) imprudent and hasty marriages; (6) gambling; (7) pawnbrokers; (8) houses of ill fame, and (9) charity, which undermines "wholesome anxiety to provide for the wants of a distant day."

The first half of the nineteenth century, starting about the time Mr. Griscom had his say, saw the emergence of a reform movement that started to develop social programs to increase equality of opportunity: trade unions, universal male suffrage, and public education, for example. Humane and professional approaches to deviant and sick individuals started to emerge, opposed by Griscom and those for whom he spoke.

The 1930s

The economic collapse of the 1930s brought the struggle between reformers and conservatives to a head. With millions of unemployed, the problem swamped the local cities and towns. The federal government became the crucial developer of policy and the provider of large sums of money. The modern social welfare system was born. The New Deal, roughly 1930 to 1940, saw the emergence of the social insurance principle, intended to cushion people over the worst economic crisis. This perspective was already in existence in Europe and was adopted in England. With the entrance of the federal government into mass unemployment relief and the start-up of social security, the local governments became a partner with the federal government in administering welfare. The partnership was and still is an uneasy one, the responsibilities and funding being divided. The New Deal coincided historically with the development and dissemination of modern psychotherapy approaches to substitute for the harshness of older measures to reform the poor.

The War on Poverty and welfare reform

By 1940 America was the modern industrial, urban nation we know today. Although involved in worldwide military conflicts, beset by continuing poverty of a substantial number of people, and developing industrial and political conflict, America was also affluent. It possessed sophisticated technologies of all types and a body of social science that might be effective in the planning and implementation of new programs. The War on Poverty and the subsequent programs, begun in the mid-1960s, signified a change in welfare policy. The programs started under the War on Poverty slogan attempted to emphasize reforms in the opportunity structure of society. The intention was to build economic and social conditions that provided all people with adequate work, decent housing and neighborhoods, good health, well-being. The social welfare system turned attention to (1) increasing the scope of social insurances, (2) setting up businesslike management of the huge public assistance programs, and (3) modernizing and expanding personal help with individual problems.

Solutions to the poverty of individuals and families were planned through employment training, work incentives, and counseling. In legislation and administration of programs there developed a reliance on an expanded, professional cadre to correct such social problems in individual cases as illegitimacy, neglect and abuse of children, blatant conduct problems of children. In response to pressures from civil rights activists, programs sought to involve community participation in the development of services and repair of neighborhoods. At the same time, new dissonance in social welfare emerged as amendments to the Social Security Act, now the major governing statute, legislated restrictions of access to services and resources. The conflict between those wishing to punish the poor and deviant and those seeking reform and social betterment continued.

The effects of the War on Poverty and the subsequent revisions of social welfare are extremely complex. The results are affected by social conditions such as the rise and fall of unemployment related to recessions in the economy. The problems of reducing poverty and upgrading personal well-being remain with us in full force. Nevertheless, we are more sophisticated today about the composition of these problems and less inclined to be naive. According to the analysis of the University of Wisconsin's Institute for Research on Poverty, the practices since 1965 are more uniform and fair than they used to be. Progress has been piecemeal but real (Plotnick and Skidmore, 1975).

It is the policies and practices of this modern phase of social welfare history that concern present-day practitioners. Despite nobility of intentions, what has been learned is that good intentions do not spell success in the social welfare system. Modern social welfare does help people and society. The problems, however, are vast, and firm solutions are evasive.

THE "WELFARE STATE"

The broad scope of social welfare today has been characterized as the welfare state. This term refers to universal coverage for all the normal and expectable crises and stresses of modern urbanized life. We do not, of course, have universal coverage. Some European countries come closer to inclusive coverage than does the United States. Conservatives today support the preservation of the basic human services. No conservative politician would seriously propose that social security, child welfare, or mental health clinics be abolished. The necessity to maintain social welfare for humanitarian reasons and for internal stability in the social order is obvious and deeply rooted in the social structure.

What is at issue is not whether social welfare should exist, but *how it is to be conducted.* This is where opinions vary and where conflict occurs. Liberals, conservatives, and professionals are to be found throughout the entire range of opinion. In modern democracies there is a strong consensus, in the abstract, about the objectives of human services. This consensus holds that the aim is the provision of well-being for the whole population. Among other attributes, it is believed well-being means that individuals possess the highest possible degree of self-determination. In theory but not always in practice, individual autonomy may be curtailed only to respect the appropriate rights of others and the basic stability of the social order.

SIZE OF THE SOCIAL WELFARE SYSTEM

The numbers of citizens using some type of human services have increased vastly in the last two decades. Some of the increase is accounted for by population growth: from 151 million in 1950 to a projected 224 million by 1980. Some types of poverty have become less extreme, but the appearance of improvement in the poverty statistics obscures some basic and pernicious faults. One of these is inflation, which reduces the purchasing power of the funds allocated for welfare purposes. Another fault is the use of a mechanical, unrealistic poverty line figure of $5500 per year for an urban family of four, as of 1975. To be financially solvent, a family must consist of two parents, both employed. Problems of family management, relationships, and child care develop readily when both parents work. The number of families headed by single women has risen sharply, and a third of them are absolutely impoverished. Sixteen percent of the aged are in extreme poverty. Women heads of families and elderly widows are among the poorest people in our population.

There is a huge apparatus trying to respond to social problems. The quantity of social welfare programs has expanded massively in the last several decades. Government expenditures grew from $3.9 billion in 1929 to over $331 billion in 1976 (Axinn and Levin, 1975; U.S. Bureau of the Census, 1977).

Taking together *all* public expenditures (federal, state, and local combined) for 1976, the highest sums went for income maintenance: $147 billion for social security and $49 billion for public aid grants. Next in order was education—$86 billion. Public expenditures for health and medical care were $19 billion; for veterans' benefits, $19 billion; for housing, $3 billion; and $8 billion was allocated to personal social services, child welfare, individualized counseling and planning for older people and youth, psychotherapy, and so forth (U.S. Bureau of the Census, 1977).

In America, in contrast to most European countries, there are private expenditures for social welfare. In the United States the welfare state is a unique blend of private and public spending. In comparison with $242 billion in government funds, private philanthropy in 1976 amounted to only $29 billion. Most of this sum was individual, tax-deducted contributions, the bulk of it allocated to religious organizations (U.S. Bureau of the Census, 1977).

Social welfare is big business. Income maintenance, education, and health care are the largest sectors of social welfare. The personal social services are the least financed by local, state, and federal governments, augmented by a portion of the funds available from private philanthropy. What emerges from this survey of the size of social welfare reveals that the system is in fact pouring resources into basics: income supports, education, health care. The system is, in fact, trying to take care of the worst scourges, lack of income and illness. Educating children and youth ranks as a top priority also. How well the system takes care is another matter.

POVERTY: THE CRUX OF SOCIAL WELFARE

The existence of poverty and programs intended to reduce poverty are at the heart of social welfare policy and practice. It is mostly the poor who are the mental patients, the children in foster care and residential treatment, the juveniles in custody, the adults in prison, the aged throwaways. Poor people are more prone to have ill health; to live in tough, sordid, and dangerous neighborhoods; to be overwhelmed and hopeless.

WHAT IS WRONG?

With $331 billion and 4.5 million human service workers, why do we seem still so poorly off? For three reasons. *First*, there are deeply complicated political problems involved in changing the structure of American society to reduce inequality of opportunity. *Second*, the most profound and chaotic changes have been and still are occurring in the fabric of social life, changes not yet understood and not really capable of being controlled. *Third*, the quality of services provided in the welfare system (and related systems) has not kept pace with the expansion of this system. Although the sums allocated to social welfare are large, they are not sufficient. There are large gaps in knowledge available to construct and operate these programs. Major research projects have been carried out to generate knowledge that could hopefully improve programs. However, often available knowledge is not used or is used ineffectively. Research utilization is arduous and lags behind program operations by a long period of time. Research tends to be put to use in an erratic fashion.

There is much uncertainty and disagreement about how to design programs that will have the desired impact on poverty. For instance, Steiner

(1971) advocates cash assistance benefits high enough "so that clients are not half housed, half clothed, or half fed." On the surface this is a straightforward and logical recommendation. Plotnick and Skidmore (1975) concern themselves with additional issues. They stress the powerful public opinion that distrusts the poor, fearing poor people will be idle "layabouts," draining the public funds, buying nonessentials. This view persists despite factual evidence indicating that adequate benefits do not restrain the ability to work, that the spending habits of the poor are much like those of the nonpoor. The problems of the *working poor* call for remedies such as earnings subsidies. The AFDC program allows for great variation in benefits among the states and lacks a correction feature to adjust benefits adequately for inflation. There are anomalies in the schedules for calculating benefits that can cause a person who goes to work to be considerably less well off. The financing structures—federal matching grants to states, as in public assistance and Medicaid, and payroll taxes, as in social security—are developing large trouble spots. There is an enormous amount of work to be done before poverty is brought under control.

HOW PRACTICE IS SHAPED
Bureaucracy and professionalism

The social welfare system is run by formal organizations, or bureaucracies. Only a few exceptions exist: small agencies and, sometimes, new agencies whose hierarchies have not yet "jelled." Bureaucratic organization shapes practice through staffing patterns, regulations, and public relations.

Every agency has staff with varied backgrounds and skills. To mobilize and coordinate effort, a hierarchy of authority is established. This hierarchy also creates a pattern for staff careers, the steps of advancement. The fact that social agencies are guided by laws, boards of directors, and internal hierarchies necessitates rules to reduce as much of the work as possible to routines. These routines structure the relationships with clients and also the relationships between staff members. The formal relationships of bureaucracy conflict with the personal relationships encouraged by professionalism. However, bureaucracy and professionalism live together in social agencies, they can hardly be pulled apart, and their characteristics merge.

Agencies with old and strong bureaucracies tend to create firm divisions of labor based on their definition of technical qualifications. Work acquires particular jurisdictions. In new agencies or where reorganization is taking place, these jurisdictions are not so firm or may be almost nonexistent. In established agencies the rules and regulations mold the behaviors of staff and clients firmly.

Hierarchical arrangements demand special communication procedures: paperwork, recording, supervision, conferences. Formal communications take up time. They usurp time that could otherwise be spent with clients. The formality of an organization cuts down its ability to respond to staff and clients in instances of urgency, although it can, and sometimes does, enhance the reliability, continuity, and fairness of the enterprise.

Bureaucratic shaping of practice. Bureaucratic regulations in agencies of any size—excluding small, fluid, innovative, entrepreneurial settings— generally prescribe the methods of intervention. Sometimes details are prescribed: where clients are to be seen, how often, the hours for client contact, what family members are to be involved, the objectives of the service. It is not uncommon for agency regulations to establish a style of practice that creates the form for discussion with clients and the theory or theories of intervention. Departures from these norms are often questioned and may even be prohibited (Briar, 1968).

Agency regulations that set strict rules for the substance and manner of intervention are not usually intended to be rigid or counterproductive. Regulations are set in order to control practice in the interests of public accountability, uniformity of service, and smoothness of operation of a large organization. These regulations tend to be based on some selection of social and behavioral knowledge and some theories of intervention. The large size of these organizations and the existence of upper-echelon cadres with considerable seniority have a tendency to solidify the knowledge base of the practice. This may, and often does, inhibit the introduction of new information and changes in practice. The tendency for bureaucracies in social welfare to become rigid is a substantial hindrance to encouraging individualized services and change in service delivery patterns.

Public relations shaping of practice. How a particular agency is related to other community institutions shapes direct practice. Agencies are dependent on a variety of publics. Adverse media publicity can threaten them. Commendatory publicity can win friends, support, funds, and other resources. Some agencies live in a goldfish bowl of media scrutiny. They can see their errors and prejudices exposed on TV, sometimes correctly but sometimes punitively and with prejudice. The particular interests and constituency of local and federal legislators, who vote the funding allocations, cannot and should not be ignored. Legislative oversight can be good or can cause difficulties. Federal government officials, exercising proper oversight, bring their own interests to bear. The various professional disciplines and other agencies are the sources for raising or reducing the reputation of the agency and status of its staff, as well as influencing the agency's goals for clients.

Is the system perverse?

All these influences can be perceived as perverse. It needs to be recognized that such influences are inevitable. Every single agency unit is in a good or bad position to deliver services, depending on how its services are understood, respected, and supported by publics. It is not so much that the agency watchers are watching us. Rather, we service workers are not private entrepreneurs. In our small offices, in the client's home, in a staff meeting we are—like it or not—agents of a basic social utility that everybody is interested in.

Client influence on shaping of practice

One constituency, however, is generally ignored—the consumers (clients). Clients cannot "shop around" for services unless they are able to go into the open market and purchase services privately. Many social agencies are *one of a kind* and essentially monopolize the resource. Customers may not appreciate their dealings with the telephone company or the electricity company, but they have no other place to go. Clients may not appreciate their dealings with a state mental hospital, but unless they are millionaires, they have no other place to go. Client preferences do not have the weight they would have in a competitive market, and clients do not pay, or pay little, for the services. The one way clients do have to threaten the agency's operations is by dropping out and otherwise failing to respond. And this they do, if they can get along. But some cannot get along. And some are prohibited from dropping out, such as prisoners and committed mental patients, children in foster care, and other *captive clients.*

The last decade has seen the development of a heightened appreciation of the ethical issues involved in dealing with clients as objects of intervention. The value of client participation has long been a tenet of the faith of agencies and workers. All too often, however, the attempt was to gain participation on the agency or practitioner's terms. This is changing, at least somewhat. Examples of this change are seen in such developments as formal feedback from clients through questionnaires and research interviews; obtaining their views about service; putting clients on planning committees; developing structures in closed institutions to encourage client participation with staff; and structuring intervention so that clients possess as much information as possible and are the ultimate deciders of their participation.

THE TASK-CENTERED APPROACH WITHIN THE SOCIAL WELFARE SYSTEM

People who come on their own and who are referred or required to get help from social welfare agencies are not all "sick." Their degree of deviance is generally mild or moderate. Only a small portion are seriously disturbed in their lives. Clients of agencies can be roughly divided into three groups: they are seeking *resources;* they are seeking *advice and guidance to solve problems;* or they are *suffering special or extreme hardships.* These groups are described in more detail in Chapter 6 (Perlman, 1975).

The direct and straightforward procedures advocated in the task-centered model are designed to provide immediate *linkage* between clients and resources to the extent available. Eliminated is any requirement to make obtaining resources contingent on broad explorations of life-style. The only exploration needed to provide resources is to ascertain whether the resources exist and can be obtained and whether the client meets eligibility requirements. Most eligibility requirements are directly observable. Clients' incomes or other financial resources either do or do not fall below the cutoff line set by regulations; that is, clients do or do not have the income deficit that makes them eligible to receive the resource free of charge or on payment of a stipulated and regulated fee. Some eligibility requirements stipulate other conditions, which are also straightforward. For instance, to get homemaker service, a client may have to demonstrate a prescribed degree of physical disability, the absence of a child caretaker, or the incompetence of a child caretaker. To get treatment for a mental illness, the client may be required to qualify because of a particular diagnosis. To get job training, a client may have to be of a certain age and physical condition. Most eligibility requirements can be made operational specifically, making determinations about resource provision straightforward. By cutting down explorations not necessary or not related to resource provision, the task-centered approach cuts down waste motion, increasing efficiency and client satisfaction.

Clients wanting advice and guidance can be productively handled by directly giving them appropriate advice and instructions. The advice and guidance can be monitored over a short period of time to test out their usefulness and to make necessary revisions. For example, a young adult who is dissatisfied with a job or who does not know what direction to take can benefit directly from close attention to what is wrong, what she or he would like, what talents or impediments exist, what opportunities there are. A parent distressed about an erring child can be guided toward new understanding of the child and be provided with better child management skills, or the child can be given corrective counseling if wanted.

Most clients are resource seekers, problem solvers, or both. If this distinction is made in an ordinary case load, a goodly portion of the work can be regularized, systematized, and scheduled and be relatively productive. The remainder will be the clients with special hardships (Chapter 3). A case load management scheme that deals with resource seekers and problem solvers in a direct fashion would allow for the greater time needed to manage clients with special hardships.

The task-centered model has another feature that can help to organize case practice—the setting of feasible goals (Chapter 6). Adherence to practical and clear goals is coming to be a primary requirement in practice. There are many issues, largely unresolved, about what are goals and how to formulate them. Nevertheless, the present trend toward goal specificity is a significant step in the right direction. Goals are a first step toward developing performance measures that can discover what is being done well or poorly so that program and practice revisions can be intelligently designed. Task-centered practice offers procedures for setting goals. Such practice is *measurable,* provided the procedures for measurement are developed and staff time is allocated to it.

How the social welfare system shapes practice, an example: Christine

Client problem directs agency practice

Christine is 31 years old, unmarried, white, a public health nurse, which is a civil service position. Four months ago she became severely depressed. Although characteristically a person given to sad moods, as well as a "worrier," this time she could not pull out of her depression.

Special interest of the agency shapes selection

Christine went to a psychiatric outpatient clinic of excellent reputation, known to have a long waiting list. She was lucky to be selected for treatment right away.

Her rapid selection was due to the fact that the clinic is a training center for psychiatrists. Her diagnosis fit the type of case looked for by the clinic as appropriate for the training program.

Eligibility restrictions of the resource shape the amount of service

Christine's depression was so deep and her suicidal ideas so frequent that she was hospitalized. She made good progress and was *released when her medical insurance ran out.* The insurance was a private plan, paid for as a fringe benefit by her employer, the public health service. At this point, on her release, Christine had no income. The sick pay from her job had expired. She gave up her small apartment and moved back to her parents' home. The parents were elderly, living on social security, and owned their own home, which was now free of mortgage payments.

•   •   •

Christine was a lonely person. She had no close women or men friends. Her depression hit when she arrived at her thirty-first birthday and contemplated the high possibility that she would never be married. Not only was being single a lonely state, it was also humiliating. She believed there must be some mysterious thing wrong with her that she could not attract men. Christine was a pretty woman, frail, wispy, unaggressive, quiet, bright. To her patients on the job she was unstinting in her effort, kind, sensible, and sensitive. She worked exceedingly hard. She was always anxious about whether her work would be approved by her superiors. She was exhausted on her return from work and on weekends. She took her holidays at home alone, having no one to travel with. She was twice passed over for promotion.

Treatment preferences of the agency shape the substance of service

In the psychiatric clinic and later in the hospital, Christine was provided with *therapy services that were typical of that facility.* Her life history was reviewed and a central pathology was defined. Christine was thought to suffer from dependence on her parents. Both of them worked during her childhood and thus did not give her enough emotional support to build self-confidence. She was encouraged to revise her low estimate of herself.

Uncoordinated service network shapes the client situation

Out of the hospital and without funds, she was again dependent on her parents, including financially. With new insight and a wish to get back in the world,

Christine was constantly agitated by being at home and taking a small allowance from her parents. Not strong enough to take up her demanding job, from which she was on sick leave, she was attending a day center.

Preferred practices of the agency shape service

The center's typical program protected clients from stress; guided them into social interaction with other similar persons; provided practice in talking with people, asserting themselves, and sizing up people; furnished an opportunity to learn recreational skills; and gave therapy focused on getting clear about self-esteem. There Christine practiced necessary social skills. She was learning pottery making and was getting her better self-image strengthened. The day center was satisfied with Christine's performance within *the program they believed in and operated. They thought she needed two to four months with them.*

Eligibility restriction impedes client well-being

Christine applied for public assistance at the suggestion of her day center therapist. Public assistance would enable her to move into her own apartment and start relearning how to take care of herself alone. *She was rejected for public assistance* because she had a few thousand dollars in the public health service's pension fund. The only way she could get this money would be to resign. If she resigned, she would later have a hard time looking for another job. Before she went to work for public health, she had worked as a hospital nurse which nearly "drove her mad."

Service of a specialized agency is sought to overcome the first agency's rule

Christine, again at the suggestion of her therapist, went to a *legal aid service* to ask them *to represent her in an appeal* of her rejection for public assistance. The attorneys advised her that she had little chance for appeal.

Client is referred forward to a third organization to overcome limitations of the specialized agency

The attorneys did say they thought that forcing persons to jeopardize their jobs was unfair. Hence *it was recommended that her case be discussed with a civil liberties organization* to consider a lawsuit challenging that regulation.

Christine was to think about this action and let the legal aid service know if she wanted to go ahead to get the regulation brought up for judicial review. Christine failed to keep her return appointment and was not heard from again.

CONCLUSION

The social welfare system is huge. It is a product of all the institutions of society. It is political, often less than rational; it is essential, expensive, not expendable.

There are important gaps in the structure of social welfare delivery systems, as well as in the policies set by statutes and by administrative regulations. Direct service staff are usually acutely aware of inconsistency and discontinuity stemming from problems with legislation and administrative policies. Doing an efficient job on a direct service case load has little effect on changing social policy or agency structure. This is not its purpose. Present policies and structures are outmoded in some respects. Systems erected to deal with social problems prevalent in the 1930s and 1940s, according to the social science knowledge then available and the political forces then existing, are today in a process of change. Institutions do not change rapidly, but they historically always change in order to respond to new conditions. It therefore pays to be moderately optimistic that necessary change in social structures will evolve. And while this evolutionary process takes place, positive efforts to provide rational specific services directly to clients can accomplish only benefits. *Appropriate services to clients are a good in themselves.*

REFERENCES

Axinn, Irene, & Levin, Herman, 1975. *Social welfare: a history of the American response to need.* New York: Dodd, Mead & Co.

Briar, Scott, 1968. The casework predicament. *Social Work 13*(1), 5-11.

Kamerman, Sheila B., & Kahn, Alfred J., 1976. *Social services in the United States.* Philadelphia: Temple University Press.

Perlman, Robert, 1975. *Consumers and social services.* New York: Wiley & Sons, Inc.

Plotnick, Robert, & Skidmore, Felicity, 1975. *Progress against poverty.* New York: Academic Press, Inc.

Steiner, Gilbert Y., 1971. *The state of welfare.* Washington, D.C.: The Brookings Institution.

U.S. Bureau of the Census. *Statistical abstract of the United States,* 1977 (98th ed.). Washington, D.C.: U.S. Government Printing Office.

Wilensky, Harold L., & Lebeaux, Charles N., 1965. *Industrial society and social welfare.* New York: The Free Press.

CHAPTER 6

Intervention

goals, technologies, effectiveness

Intervention means coming in between something. Providing a social welfare resource, such as residential care for a child or financial assistance to a single mother, comes between the child's lacking proper care and having proper care or between eviction and being at home. Psychotherapy in any of its varieties comes between drinking oneself out of a job and keeping that job, between depressed loneliness and a modicum of reasonable companionship. Intervention is an interference in a state of affairs. One of its purposes is compelling actions to occur. Other purposes are to restrain, control, cause, or hold back certain actions; to maintain or alter a condition; or to permit or encourage actions to occur.

Interventions have intentions, objectives, and goals. The goals are powerful instruments for determining the substance of the intervention. Goals are not the only factors that determine the substance of intervention programs, for example, in a mental hospital, a juvenile court, a welfare agency. Public outcry in the newspapers and decisions of a professional conference shape intervention goals. The present and particular interests of a single client and groups of clients shape intervention goals. Because of influences coming from different directions, goals become ambiguous. The conflicts among them may be muted, yet the conflicts remain. This is why goals should be explicit. Unstated, vague, hidden goals are powerful but elusive.

WHAT ARE GOALS IN SOCIAL WELFARE SERVICES?

The idea of a goal is straightforward. It is the end toward which effort is directed. A goal is a point beyond which something does not or cannot go. A goal is not a wish. A wish is something desired. A wish is the same thing as a goal *only* if it is attainable. Therefore a goal is an *attainable wish.* A wish is made attainable by resources and social skills. For instance, to say that a goal is "personal maturity" is rhetoric. Rhetoric serves a purpose. It encour-

125

ages communication about a subject. From communication may or may not come useful ideas. Rhetoric can be a shorthand way to clarify or obscure a subject. The notion of personal maturity is shorthand for expressing a wide variety of attitudes about being a desirable type of person. To be loved, be employed, live in a nice place, be promoted, graduate, have a good income, have healthy children, all these are understandable as goals because they refer to conditions in the commonsense real world. They are not abstractions.

The notion that social welfare services have goals is old and commonplace. What is new is the attempt to make goals concrete, finite, measurable. Since the mid-1960s a climate of thought has developed, putting high value on social welfare programs that could demonstrate "payoff." Results were wanted in accordance with defined objectives, produced by methods that were efficient, economical, and accountable. The payoffs from using goal-directed interventions were expected to be that (1) clients would benefit from direct, rapid action to cut down a problem; (2) collecting information about goal achievement (results) could be used to improve service by distinguishing between better or worse interventions; (3) staff could be rewarded and their morale improved by seeing client change; and (4) potential improvements in program management could come from the accumulation of information, shedding light on the characteristics of problems and interventions. Using older approaches with broad or nonspecific aims and the modern goal-oriented approaches has been compared to "the difference between playing a football game without or with goalposts and a scoring system" (Davis, 1973).

Goals are not a panacea

Goal-oriented interventions are not a cure-all for the ills of the social welfare system. Intervention methods to reach goals have to be constructed. They have to be learned, which takes time, energy, and money. Issues of values emerge and create conflict among staff, agencies, and the public. Some goals seem better and more important, depending on one's viewpoint, habits, and beliefs. Techniques have to be constructed to monitor outcomes and effectiveness of interventions, that is, to measure the performance of clients, staff, and agencies. The results of studies of outcome, whether for a single case or a total agency clientele, have to be interpreted. These interpretations can be complex, inconsistent, contradictory. The complexity of economic and social problems often retards straight-line goal achievement.

Incomplete and inadequate goal achievement raises questions about how much goal attainment is enough. Because today's perspective on goals is a change from that of the past, resistances to change develop and make an innovative process bog down.

It has been an ideal to *maximize* help to clients. To this end, the tendency developed to formulate goals that were broad, inclusive, and multiple (Siporin, 1975). Such an ample approach, however, cannot be put into practice. Maximization is an ideal that seems logical and desirable. What interferes is lack of resources and technology to achieve these ideals and often lack of consensus about definition of an ideal. The present trend to simplify, reduce, make concrete, and put practical limits around intervention reflects the practical meaning of goals, an end set of client behaviors and conditions in the environment. Goals should be achievable in a reasonably short period of time, as economically as possible. They should result from relatively specific actions that the client and practitioner can and do take to alleviate a specified target problem.

Why goal-oriented interventions?

Cost and efficiency. In the last decade the numbers of persons receiving social services increased markedly, along with total numbers of staff and total costs. As of December, 1975, over 2.6 million children and adults received public social services (*Social Services U.S.A.*, 1975). The size of public expenditures aroused intense scrutiny, debate, and considerably acrimony among many influential sectors of the public. In general, the various publics want to know what is being accomplished by social welfare expenditures and whether the results are worthwhile. These questions disturb everyone. To deal with these questions, there arose plans to collect detailed information with computerized information systems (Reid, 1974). Problems exist in starting up and maintaining these systems. For instance, the size and diversity of the population involved in information collection are large. Also, administrative units collecting information are dispersed among many legislative and political domains. Data collections may not be uniform and comparable, leading to conflicts about what information is collected, from whom, to what end. The subject is sensitive. The information-gathering technology is relatively new, and there are many technical problems to be solved.

Administrative and policy problems. It is believed in some important quarters that methods of administering the social services have lacked clarity, tightness, and systematic attributes. Suspicions have been voiced that "sloppy" administration may be responsible for poor goal attainment (Comptroller General, 1973). Questions have also been raised about the policies that are administered.

There used to be assumptions that providing social services could (1) rehabilitate and train social welfare beneficiaries for economic self-dependence, (2) reorganize and enhance family relations, (3) minimize and prevent problems in family life and in the relations of individuals and society. These ideas were the basis of the 1962 Amendments to the Social Security Act and the War on Poverty. That stretegy is now deemed unsatisfactory, since it obviously failed to achieve its ideal goals (Wickenden, 1976). Emerging innovative practices directed at goal-oriented actions are today seen as potentially capable of reducing limited, specific problem conditions and behaviors. This policy may develop programs that can be better administered and more effective.

Congruence between agency and client interests

A present objective of social welfare is that client services be congruent with the wishes of client-consumers, specific, concrete, and as brief as possible and that the client receive the available services. A client ought not have to take a forced course of counseling. Counseling wanted should be available. Many of the specific services provided in social welfare, such as day care, job training, foster home placement, and protection of children, youth, and the frail aged include counseling. A minority of clients need psychiatrically oriented treatments available from both public and private social agencies of various types. Planned short-term interventions that are specific and systematic have been shown often to produce reasonably good outcomes. It is therefore not only justifiable but also proper that these newer methods be substituted for old-style interventions. It is also necessary that newer methods not become stabilized as eternal verities. The techniques for providing services should be changed from time to time as their consequences are observed and as revisions appear necessary.

Issues about goals

The view that goals should be specific creates problems in practice. It conflicts with historical tendencies in public and professional beliefs. There is a deep (unjustified) belief in America that human beings are perfectible. Many practitioners seem to share this belief. They have evolved or seek to find methods of practice intended to perfect humans. This effort is doomed.

Some public figures and authorities want workers to achieve unlikely or impossible results, especially with segments of the population who are identified as deviant or dangerous or who must be provided with financial assistance and resources. Publicly acknowledged attributions of deviance change over time. Predictions of what may be dangerous are extremely difficult to make. Nevertheless, the social welfare system and its professions are charged by society to make an impact on these hard-to-define and often seemingly intractable situations. Dissonance between the possible and the desired creates stress on agencies and practitioners. This stress is good when it serves to push for better knowledge and better policies. It is bad when it propels agencies to adopt fads and make promises they cannot fulfill.

The setting of specific goals often raises troublesome questions in a practitioner's mind. These questions also arise in discussing cases with colleagues, supervisors, judges, doctors, teachers, journalists, and others. Practitioners and their associates in cases get very concerned about the "right or wrong" of some goals, especially about whether the goal is large enough or important enough to be meaningful. These are important questions. Dealing with individuals and families in their social context, however, the "goodness" of a particular goal or set of goals can only be answered by testing in the realm of practicality.

Although it is clear that social policy, research, and common sense support goal-oriented services, there are unresolved issues, for example, how to deal with a public opinion habituated to viewing public social services as panaceas. Another example is how to deal with the control of dangerous behavior, that is, severe misconduct that clearly victimizes others, a function often assigned to social welfare. Hostile and spectacular publicity that occurs about actions of public welfare agencies creates tension in staffs. They may behave as if every case may land them in headlines, but threatening publicity occurs around only a few. Most cases proceed uneventfully. While special measures need to be taken by agency administrations to deal with publicity, these measures ordinarily do not have to be invoked in regular day-to-day service.

WHO SHOULD RECEIVE GOAL-ORIENTED INTERVENTIONS?

It would be immensely valuable if a reliable technique existed to classify the problems of people who receive welfare services. Many classification schemes have been devised, but their usefulness is limited. Numerous classifications of services are used in the mass public welfare agencies, but these do not show what the client problems are. They show what categories of service were provided. It is possible to infer from service classifications what client problems are. However, by the time the service provided is checked off on a form, vital information about clients' opinions is lost forever.

A classification scheme adapted from Perlman (1975) was introduced earlier (Chapter 5). The types of cases within this classification scheme may be voluntary or involuntary. They may also be quasivoluntary, meaning the clients may come to an agency under duress but they may be open minded, even hopeful, that acceptable help will be forthcoming. To shed light on the probable connection between client-perceived problems and practical goals, some examples of the classification adapted from Perlman are given.

Classification of client problems connected to goals

Client problem	Goals
Resource seekers	
People lacking adequate resources to solve a present problem	Day-care provision
	Financial assistance
	Care for aged persons
	Homemakers
	Job training
	Employment
	Admission to public housing
	Special education
	Other
Seeking problem solving	
People lacking information to manage personal and interpersonal conflicts, hazards, dissatisfactions or to make decisions about a course of action	Parent training education
	Marital counseling
	Training in job seeking
	Training in skills to keep jobs, to get promoted
	Counseling to clarify alternative courses of action
	Training in problem-solving skills
	Other
Seeking relief of a multiplicity of extreme hardships	
People experiencing poverty	First two types of goals, putting together various combinations, according to priorities
Female-headed family composition	
Untended ill health	
Mental and physical handicap	
Dangerous housing	
Inability to care for vulnerable family members	

Using this classification as a rough guide can be helpful in making *distinctions* that guide goal setting. The ideal of maximization of services and an unwarranted assumption that most clients are multiproblem can lead to unrealistic goal setting. Clients and practitioners become inundated with massive and frustrating expectations and unproductive actions.

A GOAL-ORIENTED DELIVERY STRATEGY
Types of goals

The contemporary emphasis on goal-directed intervention means that selecting and stating goals will constitute a major strategy (or planning) element in designing the set of actions (interventions) in any case.

If goals are thought of as end states to a particular timed sequence of activities, it is implied that a *change* is intended to occur during the stated course of intervention. Two types of change are feasible: (1) an *increase* or (2) a *decrease* in environmental conditions and resources, client behaviors, and behaviors of significant other persons. Concentrating on resources, behaviors, and conditions is the most direct way to convey humanistic concern for people in distress and to demonstrate respect for their feelings, attitudes, and well-being. It is also a direct way to set specific goals.

Agency goals. Agency goals are those established formally by the organization. These chart a direction for administration and accomplishment of a whole program: an aggregation of services provided according to legislative mandates and public responsibility. *Agency goals cannot be directly applied to individual cases because they are too abstract. Their accomplishment depends not on a single individual case, but on the results of large collections of cases.* Agency goals determine case goals *indirectly*. There is usually no straight-line, discernible connection between broad, abstract agency goals and individual case practice or service delivery. There is no technology for carrying out broad agency goals applied to individual clients. There are only intervention techniques for individual cases. To intervene with large aggregations of individuals requires macrosystems interventions: community organization, social planning, and so forth. A direct connection between agency goals, intervention at a case level, and results is normally not discernible. Agency goals are normative. They express convictions about ideal abstract intentions. They express intentions that are required by laws and custom. They reflect political aims.

For example, an agency is operating to carry out a law to protect victims of child abuse. The agency goal may be stated as protection of children, rehabilitation of disorganized families, prevention of multiple problems. No individual case goal can be visualized to carry out such lofty aims. An individual case goal would more likely be to eliminate physical abuse of Bill; to place Bill in a foster home; to teach the parents how to control their rage; to get the father a job; and so forth. The accomplishments of individual case goals can be measured. Bill's mother either does or does not stop beating him with an electric cord. She does or does not stop taking out her rage on her son. Her husband does or does not get a job. Bill either does or does not go to a foster home. He either does or does not thrive in the foster home.

Agencies need to evaluate achievement of their broad goals. Did the number of reports of child abuse go down? Or up? Are there fewer dirty, scared kids in the local public schools? Is an agency carrying out the law? The problem of how to design and conduct evaluations of agencies is different from evaluating outcomes of single cases. There are many techniques for agency program evaluation. That subject, however, is not the concern of this discussion. Here the emphasis is on direct practice, not administration.

Professional goals. Professional goals are opinions of what actions are good, effective, and valuable to further the well-being of people and society. They may be abstract or specific and, if espoused by powerful leaders such as supervisors and teachers, may exert substantial power over the opinions and actions of practitioners. Professional goals, like expert opinion, vary over time, vary from one locality to another, and rarely offer a firm consensus to guide individual case action. Professional techniques can guide action. Professional goals tend to be long range and philosophical.

Personal practitioner goals. Personal practitioner goals reflect the private opinions of individual workers, their own view of life and their own biases. These may be highly individualistic and unexpressed; they may also reflect the cultural and socioeconomic background of the practitioner.

Client goals. *These are the only practical way to carry out a goal-oriented strategy for individual case action.* Dissonance or lack of close congruence between practitioner goals and client goals sets up a struggle that disposes a case to failure. Client-directed individual case goals are usually capable of being consistent with agency and professional goals. They usually do not reflect the entire range of agency and professional goals at any given time or in any specific case. The client goal is normally a segment of the whole agency or professional array of goals.

Individual case goals can be constructed from the techniques of the task-centered approach, which is discussed in Section two. Briefly, this means starting with the client's expressed target problems. The only exception is in situations where focus on a problem is mandated by legislation or influential authority. The alleviation of the target problem is the goal. When the target problem is specific, the goal can be constructed specifically. The goal will then be tied to the target problem. Connecting target problem and goal increases the likelihood of problem reduction. *Individual case goals are the direct representation of a goal-oriented delivery strategy.*

• • •

In operating a goal-oriented delivery strategy, it is essential that these four types of goals be separated: agency, professional, practitioner, and client goals. One type of goal—client individual case goals—is likely to lead most directly to good outcomes, provided resources exist and are provided. If these distinctions among types of goals are not made, the benefit of the goal strategy may be lost. Case goals would be overwhelmed by the quantity and complexity of goals of different types. Agency, professional, and personal practitioner goals are never out of sight or out of mind. They provide a general climate of opinion and requirements. However, so long as clients goals do not seriously contradict vital segments of the broader goal structure, they should determine the individual case goals. Should there be contradiction, that is the time to discuss the contradiction with the client, to influence the client to alter his or her goals, if possible.

Examples of the classifications and case goals
RESOURCE-SEEKER, MRS. A
Request 1: Temporary foster care for the children

CONTEXT: Mrs. A just learned she should have a biopsy. She is separated from her husband. She has not heard from him for three years. She has two young children whom she supports from her salary as a secretary. She expects to be hospitalized. She may need surgery because of cancer. Her baby-sitter will not be able to manage during Mrs. A's hospitalization. She will need comprehensive child care if she decides to have the biopsy and possible surgery.

Request 2: Information about how she can become a foster mother

CONTEXT: If she is unable to resume her secretarial employment after surgery, Mrs. A will want to obtain income from work at home. She thinks that becoming a foster mother will serve that purpose.

Target problems

1. Lack of child care during illness
2. Possible incapacity to leave home to work
3. Lack of income if work incapacity is protracted

Goals

1. Child care
2. Income plan

SEEKING PROBLEM-SOLVING SKILLS, MRS. B
Request: Placement of 12-year-old son

CONTEXT: Mrs. B, a widow, has only one child. She receives public assistance. Her son's early childhood was uneventful. Within the past year he began hitting her occasionally. Once he cut himself by punching a hole in a window. Mrs. B is dismayed by his interest in sex. His academic achievement is poor.

Target problem

Her son is not controllable.

Goals

MRS. B.: Place the child in an institution that will teach him self-control.
WORKER'S RECOMMENDATIONS:
1. Secure psychiatric evaluation.
2. Secure intelligence and academic evaluation.
3. Select a course of action to change the son's behavior, based on information from the evaluations.
WORKER-CLIENT AGREEMENT (CONTRACT)
1. Secure worker-recommended evaluations.
2. Plan for Mrs. B's son in accordance with evaluations.

SEEKING RELIEF OF EXTREME HARDSHIP, MRS. C
Request: Mrs. C wants custody of her 16-month-old child

CONTEXT: The child was made a ward of the court on a neglect complaint six months ago. The complainant was a local businessman who had received $100 worth of bad checks from Mrs. C. Mr. and Mrs. C were notorious in the small community. They had lurid fights on the street. Both were seen in local bars often—intoxicated. Sometimes Mr. C left home for months and returned. The child was in good health. At times he was left alone when the parents were out on the town. The house doors were not locked. Neighbors and relatives kept an eye out for the child. They would go and sit with him or take him to their homes. Mr. and Mrs. C were employed erratically and were not receiving public assistance. The child was made a ward of the court and placed in a foster home out of the state. The parents could not visit because of the distance and lack of transportation.

Target problem

Does not have custody of own child

Goal

Return of child to mother

Goals for individual cases: summary

Individual case goals should be logically connected to the target problem. They should be specific, feasible, attainable. The details of the process of goal setting with clients is described in Chapter 9.

TECHNOLOGY
Defined

To produce results in a goal-oriented intervention approach, there needs to be a technology. An intervention technology is a set of specific and described actions, taken in a relatively specific sequence, to reduce a client target problem. The map of the task-centered model (Fig. 1) depicts an intervention technology. Technology is the bridge between client problems and outcomes. The idea of technologies for the human services is new but rapidly gaining acceptance.

Formerly we spoke of "methods." The idea of methods is based on statements of principles. Methods principles are formulated broadly and normatively. They consist of ideas that are consensually agreed on by many practitioners, but not all. Principles are given public voice by leading practitioners. They may take on the attributes of fundamental truth, law, or doctrine. Methods principles become settled through discussions, primarily at conferences, and through publication. Methods principles are derived through a process of many impressionistic observations, by different people, in different places and times, under different conditions. When put into texts, principles, like theories, take on the particular coloration and slant of an author or group of similarly minded authors. Methods are developed through thought about observed or inferred phenomena.

Technologies differ from methods in some ways and are similar to methods in other ways. Technologies are being developed at present as a result of recently emerging social science research applied to the processes of intervention. This means that systematic observations are made of some defined and bounded sector of intervention. There is a *design* that states and describes what is to be observed, when, where, and with whom. The design is the product of thought, just as methods are. There is always something in the mind of the practitioner-researcher that tells what should be looked at and why. The observations are recorded according to some structured data collection paper, an *instrument*, or *form*, or by taping interviews. Data thus collected are analyzable according to social science methods. The result is a statement about *findings* and conclusions, including implications for practice. As small pieces of data are studied, they tell something about the studied intervention and its pros and cons. Over time, these studies produce a shape or structure of the interventions. That structure becomes guidelines for practice. This way of developing intervention procedures is different from the way treatment methods were developed before social science research techniques were available.

Technologies today are incomplete, as are methods also. Technologies depend for usefulness on a reservoir of methods ideas to fill them out and adapt them to real life conditions. If technologies are worth their salt, the research they come from will be replicated by others than the original developers, as well as by the developers themselves. Technologies will be revised as indicated by their results and the difficulties identified. Conventional methods go through no such systematic process. Nevertheless, methods change and are affected by research. Knowledge developed through research is selectively added to established principles as addenda and revisions. The revision of technologies should be more systematic than the revision of methods. However, any development of intervention processes needs a group of people committed to the endeavor, and its needs financing. Development of intervention process is not going to occur by itself. The commitment of practitioners, researchers, agencies, professional schools, and funding sources is a prerequisite.

The difference suggested here between methods and technologies may be illustrated by an example of an almost universally accepted principle: "start where the client is." There are also the principles of *acceptance, self-determination, treatment relationship,* and so forth. The methods orientation assumes that techniques for carrying out the principles are numerous and varied. The methods take varying forms, depending on many differing conditions. The variability of "methods" is shown in the standard response of a teacher or supervisor who is asked specific questions about how to apply a principle. The usual response is: "It all depends." Often, the number of things the answer depends on is long. The different "things" interact in a tangle of past and present events, as well as hunches about the future. What the "things" are is subject to varying interpretations. The idea of self-determination gives as much credit as possible to clients for pursuing their own lifestyle. The treatment relationship idea in the various methods is almost impossible to make operational at this point. This idea refers to the well-known belief that there is something intrinsically beneficial in the covert interactions between the one who helps and the one who is helped. Almost no one in the helping professions doubts the importance of this relationship, yet no one can describe it succinctly.

The incomplete and unfinished state of emerging technologies reflects the difficulties of conceptualizing, describing, identifying, and testing the labyrinth of activities involved in interventions. At least this work has begun. In addition, work to test the efficacy of techniques has also begun, together with revisions of technique to take account of what testing shows.

Eclecticism

Intervention practice cannot get along without developing and using technology. Real practice, however, must be *eclectic*. (For an excellent discussion of eclecticism, See Fischer, 1978.) This does not mean a hodgepodge. It means *reasoned selection* from a number of sources of what seems or is judged best at a particular time under specific circumstances. What is best obviously depends on a viewpoint, a philosophy of practice. It is our persuasion that *best* means those techniques that (1) have been developed from empirical testing or research, (2) are most closely connected to the target problem, (3) have a published record of effectiveness, and (4) make sense.

Making sense as a criterion for eclecticism needs an explanation. One way to try to make sense of a set of interventions is to fit them into an intervention theory. This means that if the interventions can be explained and justified by the theory, they can be viewed (by some) as making sense. Ordinarily, this does not work out. Intervention theories, when they exist at all, tend to be a partial application of a theory of behavior, such as psychoanalysis, ego psychology, Perls' gestalt psychology, Berne's transactional analysis psychology, and so forth. What such intervention "theories" suggest is that if good personality or good behavior is to come out of bad, then the person should be induced to obtain or be provided with certain conditions and attitudes. The conditions and attitudes often recommended by a personality theory and its practice frameworks are loosely defined attributes such as love, sharing, independence, mutuality, self-actualization, responsibility, and the whole shopping center of ideal norms (Chapter 4).

The nature of practice is the construction of temporary feasible actions, to be taken within a given time period, treading an uncertain line between divergent interests and compelling stresses. Currently a few general statements of purpose and content can serve to organize thought about the nature of practice (Smalley, 1967; Roberts and Nee, 1970; Goldstein, H., 1973; Pincus and Minahan, 1973; Gottman and Leiblum, 1974). No one of these can or does claim general applicability. Each one is valid only where its particular assumptions fit case or program circumstances. The search for grand theory does not seem to be urgent. Much more urgent and badly needed are frameworks to guide practice activities. This means techniques. Making sense about selecting interventions comes down to whether the practitioner can understand what can be and is being done, whether clients and their social networks can understand, and whether there is some obvious comprehensible value to the undertaking.

EFFECTIVENESS

The modern emphasis on specificity of goals requires technology to produce these goals. Assessment of effectiveness then becomes possible. There is no point in designing and carrying out relatively complex processes, at considerable cost, without checking into what the results are.

For more than a decade the opinion has been developing that there is a high degree of ineffectiveness in the results of interventions carried out in traditional practices. An impressive body of research makes this opinion credible. Criticism of the helping occupations is widespread in government, legislatures, the press, and among professional workers themselves. One opinion is that the practitioner is the source of ineffectiveness in handling individual and family cases. This opinion implies that practitioners do not follow the traditional rules of practice (Strean, 1976; Wood, 1978). It is also implied that practitioners are not trained to follow the traditional rules properly. This argument does not hold up.

The intervention rules and techniques suggested by traditional methods, as discussed earlier, are vague, complex, contradictory, and subject to a wide range of interpretation. Practitioners are hard-working people under stress. They often find traditional rules not only difficult but also impossible to apply and, more important, a bad fit to their conditions of work. Practitioners try hard to conform to the expectations of their agencies, supervisors, and teachers. Their practice problems lie not so much in themselves as in the guidelines they have been provided. This is not to assert that there are no stupid, foolish, or insensitive practitioners. However, gross incompetence is easy to spot. All cannot be that bad.

Take, for example, a recent survey of research. This effectiveness survey reports on twenty-two projects conducted since 1957, involving 2696 experimental cases and 2303 controls, a total of 4999 cases (Wood, 1978). It is a bit much to conclude that the poor showing of desired outcomes in such a large number of instances is the result of failure to follow the traditional rules properly. Furthermore, in these and other studies the absence of information that portrays what the interventions were cannot be attributed to poor practice. To a considerable extent, these studies, rough as many are, can be more reasonably understood as appropriate representatives of traditional practice. It is possible to argue that practitioners do, relatively well, what the methods guidelines tell them. The guidelines and the programs in which these guidelines are embedded have problems. Defective guidelines and programs are the reasons why the current revisions in practice are developing.

The revision of guidelines and programs is at this time a priority in all the human services. The difficulty of this endeavor should not be minimized. It has only begun. Today's practitioners are working in a time when questions are legitimate, innovation is justified, and research in the long run can help. There is a huge literature dealing with studies of the effectiveness of intervention. The problem with using that literature is serious. The reports are distributed throughout many journals and books. It is impossible to retrieve this mass of information of varying quality and timeliness without aids. There are large-scale and small-scale studies. They have been made over the last two decades. Results depend on the sample used, the research methodology employed, and the designs of the studies. Only recently are there starting to occur distilled collections of this information potentially usable by practitioners (Rothman, 1974; Fischer, 1978; Maas, 1978; Mullen, 1978; Wood, 1978).

One of the values of the task-centered guidelines (Section two) is that it is based on research findings, as well as on analysis of experiences. The task-centered approach has attempted to state guidelines that have been developed from tests for effectiveness. Techniques being developed in behavior modification, based on research, lend themselves to coordination with task-centered guidelines (Brown, 1977; Rossi, 1977). Because task-centered practice is a product of mainstream casework methods, it can also be combined with principles attached to psychoanalytically oriented treatment methods (Ewalt, 1977).

What is known about effectiveness

Studies of effectiveness have taken place in social welfare programs and in psychotherapy of many varieties. Psychotherapy studies use patients of mental health settings as their sample. Both social welfare programs and mental health settings deal with the same or similar people as clients or patients. There is, however, a highly significant difference between these two sectors of studies. That difference is *organizational context*. Typically, the goal of psychotherapy in a mental health clinic is thought of as a change for the better in the *person's self:* his attitudes, inner well-being, interpersonal relationships, personality. The goal of intervention in a social welfare agency may be exactly the same as that in a mental health clinic. Typically, however, the social welfare service gives priority or equal importance to reduction in *public deviance* of some sort: for example, juvenile delinquency, being a welfare recipient, being afflicted with gross family disorganization, being institutionalized. This distinction between private and public deviance means that two partly different sets of goals and techniques have to be evaluated. It is therefore questionable to lump the products of these studies together as one thing.

On the other hand, much intervention practice in social welfare agencies looks very similar to practice in mental health clinics. Therefore it is reasonable to assume that the findings from mental health practice are informative about social welfare practice. This is probably correct up to a point. At any rate, we have now little choice about combining these two sets of research because of the paucity at present of studies of the influence of settings on practice. Since psychotherapy studies and studies of social welfare seem to be addressed to the same or similar concerns, both are informative. And both types of studies are informing us about many of the same things.

What is effective practice?

The effectiveness studies in mental health outnumber the social welfare studies. Reasonably good quality studies of psychotherapy number in the hundreds while social welfare practice studies are numbered in the dozens.

Research that has studied the effectiveness of social and psychological treatment indicates that its effectiveness *in general* is doubtful. Available evidence reveals *little solid support that the usual and ordinary interventions result in changes* caused by the interventions. There is evidence that some clients deteriorate in treatment, although it cannot be said that the treatment itself caused deterioration. There is no convincing evidence that any one traditional method is superior to any other (Mullen et al., 1972; Fischer, 1976; Bergin and Lambert, 1978). However, a series of findings reveal that *satisfactory to excellent results occur* in social-psychological treatment in a portion of cases.

Attributes of effectiveness. Following are the general characteristics likely to lead to good outcomes.

Structure. Structure means *arrangement* of a set of interventions according to the dominant goals (Phillips and Wiener, 1966; Reid and Shyne, 1969; Reid and Epstein, 1972, 1977; Reid, 1978).

Interventions can be seen to have structure when the strategy pins down the particulars of the start-up, problems that will be worked on, terms and conditions under which the work will be done, specific interventions to be used or which evolve in the course of an intervention sequence, end product sought, end point, and results obtained or not obtained.

Specificity. Specificity means exactly and sharply *defined goals and actions*, to be taken by any or all the participants, that are *demonstrably connected to the targeted problem and the goals* (Gambrill, 1977; Reid, 1978).

Practitioner-client congruence. As explained previously, practitioner-client congruence means *correspondence* between client and practitioner on the problems and interventions to reduce the problems and to *cut down dropout rate* (Mayer and Timms, 1970; Goldstein, A., 1973; Epstein, 1977; Wexler, 1977; Bass, 1977; Bergin and Lambert, 1978).

Summary of effectiveness attributes. *Based on current knowledge, the big three characteristics of interventions most likely to be effective are structure, specificity, and congruence.* These are the characteristics on which the task-centered approach are based. They are advocated currently in the literature (Siporin, 1975; Gambrill, 1977; Loewenberg, 1977; Fischer, 1978; Wood, 1978). These characteristics are becoming incorporated, in lesser or greater degree, in the conventional methods approaches. These three characteristics represent qualities of good practice based on a distillation of available research, translated for practice use. This conclusion, however, is not to be taken as "revealed truth" or as a permanent statement of the best conditions. New developments are going to occur. The revision of practice to fit contemporary conditions has only begun. No one can say exactly where it will lead.

Effectiveness of task-centered intervention

Various studies of the task-centered model have been conducted since 1970 in an effort to evaluate its effectiveness. The model was designed to be developed and tested through empirical research. The initial studies indicated that the approach was indeed promising, that interventions carried out according to task-centered guidelines resulted in demonstrable improvements. Subsequent more sophisticated research enhanced the credibility of the earliest findings. Task-centered methods have been shown to be capable of important problem reduction and are superior to no treatment. The effectiveness of the model is, at least in part, attributable to its adherence to the three decisive characteristics—structure, specificity, and congruence (Reid, 1978).

Techniques that may be related to effective practice

A number of characteristics of intervention are studied continuously. Some things about them are known and are reasonable. These aspects, however, do not have as firm a research base as do the "big three." In view of the uncertainties in practice, they should be given consideration as appropriate to the particulars of cases and settings.

Practitioner personal traits. The question of matching the practitioner with clients has not been adequately studied. This refers to which practitioner is likely to do best with which client. It is not known whether matching of races does or does not affect outcomes and how. The same uncertainty exists about matching clients and practitioners for social class and sex. This is not to say that these factors are insignificant, only that we do not know their significance for effective intervention. Also lacking research substantiation is the idea that a practitioner's personal therapy improves practice. It is not at present known how to test the importance of many of the personal characteristics of practitioners that are often cited as important. The exception is that attributes of *warmth, genuineness,* and *empathy* have been subjected to much research. The findings on their importance and relevance for practice is simply not clear cut (Parloff et al., 1978). However, the most up-to-date, comprehensive research literature review available concludes that practitioner personal factors "are crucial ingredients even in the more technical therapies"; that "trust, warmth, acceptance, and human wisdom" are indispensable (Bergin and Lambert, 1978).

Organizational influences. On the surface it would seem probable that outcomes in many social welfare programs would have a close dependence on the features of the setting: high-low caseloads; availability-unavailability of needed material resources, high-low "red tape"; high-low social control demands; loose-tight bureaucratic arrangements; high-low educational attainments of staff; high-low staff morale and turnover. Despite its obvious importance, study of this subject has been scanty. The evidence to date does not allow for any conclusions. The commonsense assumption that obviously bad organizational conditions will hamper effectiveness probably needs no proof.

Client traits and environmental conditions. There is general consensus in the research literature, supporting often expressed practitioner impressions, that the client's traits and the environment, separately and in interaction, affect satisfactory outcomes. Agencies and practitioners, if they can, screen intake to "cream off" the "good" treatment candidates. The criteria used to discover a good candidate are usually experience and a "gut feeling," as it is called. The research literature supports the idea that client traits and environment make a strong difference in the results obtained. Unfortunately, we do not know which traits or which environmental qualities are the decisive ones.

There is a new emphasis in current literature on the characteristics of clients' *cognitive states*. This means psychobiological processes such as vision and hearing. It also means thoughts, beliefs, and problem-solving skills. The idea of cognitive state includes all of what traditional methods referred to as "feelings"—but with a difference. This difference is that the newer ideas analyze "feelings" into more distinct parts. Examples are what the client says and believes, the errors of judgment made in coming to these beliefs, what thinking skills are lacking, what emotional "charge" is put on the beliefs. The emphasis in cognitive approaches on overt client statements, lurking unclarity, and illogic is similar to the emphasis in traditional treatment methods on "feelings." The newer ways, however, do not require any assumptions about an unconscious realm of being. Therefore they eliminate possibly wasteful exploration, as well as the emergence of impasses and "resistance" to be dealt with. Training clients to improve their cognitive skills, including problem-solving skills, is a promising development (Brown, 1979; Mahoney and Arnkoff, 1978).

Evaluation of effectiveness

Interventions can be evaluated many ways. *Evaluation* means finding out the following: What did the intervention consist of? Did the intervention have the intended effect? What effect did it have? Finding out the effects of an intervention has two purposes: (1) to enable the practitioner to correct the interventions while the case is active and (2) to collect information from many cases to judge the effectiveness of the practices as a whole.

It has been common in the past to study groups of clients, monitoring their condition before and after intervention. It is necessary to account for changes that occur but are due to factors other than the intervention. Control groups that do not receive the intervention are needed. Control groups for social treatment studies are hard to come by. It is often uncertain exactly how much they are the same as the experimental group. Such studies on a large scale are extremely expensive and very difficult to conduct. Their results are difficult to interpret.

One of the important problems in interpreting evaluation studies is disagreement about and plain lack of firm, credible measurements of performance and results. For an exercise, try to state in simple, plain language what a satisfactory result is. Then try getting a consensus among several practitioners. Ask a researcher. It is possible, however, to find out how much goal achievement occurred, provided the goal is concrete and specific. Measurements can be devised to ascertain whether or not a client looked for a job or got one, whether or not a practitioner provided job-seeking resources. It is very difficult to devise measurements to ascertain the level of a client's self-actualization and whether or not the proper resources for self-actualization were provided. It is also difficult to be certain that the interventions caused the job to be found or the feeling of personal satisfaction to occur.

At present, the idea has developed to find relatively simple research methods that can be applied to single cases. Possibly information accumulated systematically from a series of single cases would be of value. Such single-case research requires observing and recording the observation in a structured log or on a graph. Usually what is recorded is the problem frequency and intensity before, during, and after the intervention. It is still necessary to take into account the problem that factors other than the intervention are causing either improvement or lack of it. If my client's target problem is "poor job performance" and later he is promoted, does this mean his improved job performance was due to my treatment? Or could it mean he was transferred to a different supervisor with different expectations? Or his health improved? Or his wife left him? Or he had some generalized nonspecific change in self-image because he was "seeing a therapist"? Or a new boss took over the company and shook up the whole plant? Or what else? If his job performance does not improve, does that mean I failed to teach him properly? Or is he sick? Stubborn? Or is he so worried about the mortgage or his child's trouble with the police that he cannot concentrate? Or is his supervisor disagreeable?

To take account of the effects of the interventions and other events, several types of research designs have developed. Statistical tests need to be used for increasing the credibility of the findings (Hersen and Barlow, 1977). These kinds of procedures are not now normally known and available in social welfare agencies, with rare exceptions. They could become available if agencies were to decide to invest time in training, allow practitioners time to do the studies, and employ researchers to assist the practitioners. A few professional schools of social work have begun programs to prepare practitioners of the future to conduct such research. Clinical psychologists trained in behavior therapy have already prepared practitioners in the use of single-organism design research. The *Journal of Applied Behavioral Analysis* is devoted to publication of their studies.

There are important questions about single-case research. Some of these questions are technical. A broader issue is whether the results of single-case research can be generalized to make judgments about an agency program, a practitioner, a collection of clients. Nevertheless, these methods "offer considerable advantages over traditional, one-shot clinical case studies where a poorly defined intervention is applied to a nebulously defined problem with inadequately defined outcome criteria" (Fischer, 1978). Although single-case research is promising, its applicability to ordinary practice is not a simple matter. There are differences and conflicts between practice and research that are inevitable. A variety of tactics have to be planned in order to preserve the integrity of both practice and research (Thomas, 1978).

Can anything be done to develop more objective measurements of case effectiveness or lack of it in agencies that do not provide necessary research resources? Without agency support, a practitioner who is stimulated to do so can certainly devise a system for orderly recording and graphing of changes, querying clients, and making gross judgments about progress or lack of it. Given high caseloads and work pressures, such entrepreneurial attempts can be expected infrequently. Agency programs that check up on client goal attainment and rate practitioners according to how much or how little occurs take a risk, under present conditions. Their staff will soon learn to concentrate on recording those goals (possible trivial or peripheral) which are easily identified as pluses. It takes more than a do-it-yourself approach to measurement to get statistics that are relevant, mean something, and are fair.

Even such a limited device as structured recording needs administrative support. An agency that hands a practitioner a ten-page recording outline sends a clear message: write an article covering all 200 items in the outline. Recording outlines are a major device for shaping agency practice. Structured recording means that an agency administration has to pare down its recording outlines so that the staff will be free to eliminate diffuse writings and concentrate on simple systematic information known or believed to have a connection to goals. Many agencies have adopted simplified and focused recording practices. Where these exist or can be installed, recording can enhance the ability to do periodic checks on progress and make midcase corrections. In a gross manner the product of such recording gives a better idea of the activities in a case load or an agency that does discursive, unanalyzable narrations. Such practices, worthy as they are, do not substitute for technically competent evaluation studies. Fortunately, there is now a small cadre of professional people who can be obtained to help set up and monitor evaluation, and the number will increase.

REFERENCES

Bass, Michael, 1977. Toward a model of treatment for runaway girls in detention. In W. J. Reid & L. Epstein (Eds.), 1977. *Task-centered practice.* New York: Columbia University Press.

Bergin, Allen E., & Lambert, Michael J., 1978. The evaluation of therapeutic outcomes. In S. L. Garfield & A. E. Bergin (Eds.). *Handbook of psychotherapy and behavioral change* (2nd ed.). New York: John Wiley & Sons, Inc.

Brown, Lester B., 1977. Treating problems of psychiatric outpatients. In W. J. Reid & L. Epstein (Eds.). *Task-centered practice.* New York: Columbia University Press.

Brown, Lester B., 1979. *Client problem solving in task-centered social treatment.* Dissertation in progress, The School of Social Service Administration, The University of Chicago.

Comptroller General of the United States, 1973. *Report to the Congress, social services: Do they help welfare recipients achieve self-support or reduce dependency?* The Social and Rehabilitation Service, Department of Health, Education, and Welfare.

Davis, H. R., 1973. Four ways to goal attainment. *Evaluation 1*(2), 43-48.

Epstein, Laura, 1977. *How to provide social services with task-centered methods: report of the Task-Centered Services Project* (Vol. 1). Chicago: School of Social Service Administration, University of Chicago Press.

Ewalt, Patricia L., 1977. A psychoanalytically oriented child guidance setting. In W. J. Reid & L. Epstein (Eds.), *Task-centered practice.* New York: Columbia University Press.

Fischer, Joel, 1976. *The effectiveness of social casework.* Springfield, Ill.: Charles C Thomas, Publisher.

Fischer, Joel, 1978. *Effective casework practice: an eclectic approach*. New York: McGraw-Hill Book Co.

Gambrill, Eileen D., 1977. *Behavior modification: handbook of assessment, intervention, and evaluation*. San Francisco: Jossey-Bass, Inc., Publishers.

Goldstein, Arnold P., 1973. *Structured learning therapy*. New York: Academic Press, Inc.

Goldstein, Howard, 1973. *Social work practice: a unitary approach*. Columbia, S.C.: University of South Carolina Press.

Gottman, John M., & Leiblum, Sandra R., 1974. *How to do psychotherapy and how to evaluate it*. New York: Holt, Rinehart & Winston.

Hersen, Michel, & Barlow, David H., 1977. *Single case experimental designs*. Elmsford, N.Y.: Pergamon Press, Inc.

Loewenberg, F. M., 1977. *Fundamentals of social intervention*. New York: Columbia University Press.

Maas, Henry S. (Ed.), 1978. *Social science research: review of studies*. Washington, D.C.: National Association of Social Workers, Inc.

Mahoney, Michael J., & Arnkoff, Diane B., 1978. Cognitive and self-control therapies. In S. L. Garfield & A. E. Bergin (Eds.). *Handbook of psychotherapy and behavior change* (2nd ed.). New York: John Wiley & Sons, Inc.

Mayer, John E., & Timms, Noel, 1970. *The client speaks: working class impressions of casework*. New York: Atherton Press.

Mullen, Edward J., Fall 1978. The construction of personal models for effective practice: a method for utilizing research findings to guide social interventions. *Journal of Social Service Research* 2(1), 45-64.

Mullen, Edward J., et al., 1972. *Evaluation of social interventions*. San Francisco: Jossey-Bass, Inc., Publishers.

Parloff, Morris B., Waskow, Irene Elkin, & Wolfe, Barry E., 1978. Research on therapist variables in relation to process and outcome. In S. L. Garfield & A. E. Bergin (Eds.). *Handbook of psychotherapy and behavior change* (2nd ed.). New York: John Wiley & Sons, Inc.

Perlman, Robert, 1975. *Consumers and Social Services*. New York: John Wiley & Sons, Inc.

Phillips, E. Lakin, & Wiener, Daniel N., 1966. *Short-term psychotherapy and structured behavior change*. New York: McGraw-Hill Book Co.

Pincus, Alan, & Minahan, Anne, 1973. *Social work practice: model and method*. Itasca, Ill.: F. E. Peacock Publishers, Inc.

Reid, William J., 1974. Developments in the use of organized data. *Social Work* 19(5): 585-593.

Reid, William J., 1978. *The Task-Centered System*. New York: Columbia University Press.

Reid, William J., & Epstein, Laura, 1972. *Task-centered casework*. New York: Columbia University Press.

Reid, William J., & Epstein, Laura (Eds.), 1977. *Task-centered practice*. New York: Columbia University Press.

Reid, William J., and Shyne, Ann W., 1969. *Brief and extended casework*. New York: Columbia University Press.

Roberts, Robert, and Nee, Robert (Eds.), 1970. *Theories of social casework*. Chicago: University of Chicago Press.

Rossi, Robert B., 1977. Helping a mute child. In W. J. Reid & L. Epstein (Eds.). *Task-centered practice*. New York: Columbia University Press.

Rothman, Jack, 1974. *Planning and organizing for social change*. New York: Columbia University Press.

Siporin, Max, 1975. *Introduction to social work practice*. New York: Macmillan Publishing Co., Inc.

Smalley, Ruth, 1967. *Theory for social work practice*. New York: Columbia University Press.

Social Services U.S.A., 1975. Social and rehabilitation service. U.S. Department of Health, Education, and Welfare, Pub. no. (SRS) 76-03300.

Strean, Herbert S., 1976. Is the psychoanalytic model obsolete? In J. Fischer (Ed.). *The effectiveness of social casework*. Springfield, Ill.: Charles C Thomas, Publisher.

Thomas, Edwin J., 1978. Research and service in single-case experimentation: conflicts and choices. *Social Work Research and Abstracts 14*(Winter), 20-31.

Wexler, Phyllis, 1977. A case from a medical setting. In W. J. Reid & L. Epstein (Eds.). *Task-centered practice.* New York: Columbia University Press.

Wickenden, Elizabeth, 1976. A perspective on social services: an essay review. *Social Service Review 50:*570-585.

Wood, Katherine M., 1978. Casework effectiveness: a new look at the research evidence. *Social Work 23*(6), 437-459.

Section two

PRACTICE GUIDELINES

This entire section describes the start-up phase and each of the four steps of the task-centered model. (See the map of the task-centered model, Fig. 1.) Illustrations will be given throughout the descriptive discussion. These guidelines can be read from start to finish to get a complete picture of the normal flow of work. For ease in reference or review, particular steps or sub-steps can be looked up separately.

The phases and steps of the task-centered model follow:

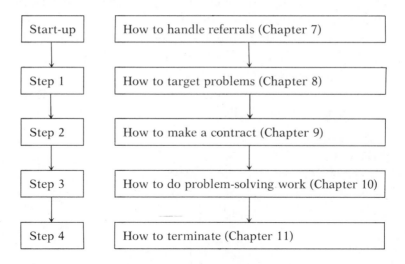

Start-up	How to handle referrals (Chapter 7)
Step 1	How to target problems (Chapter 8)
Step 2	How to make a contract (Chapter 9)
Step 3	How to do problem-solving work (Chapter 10)
Step 4	How to terminate (Chapter 11)

In describing these guidelines, every attempt is made to take into account the real world of practice: its contradictions, pressures, and anxieties; the harsh, discordant, and sometimes repellant conditions in which many clients live. However, this book is intended to bring a reasonably high degree of or-der into a complex, fluid field, and so it is sometimes necessary for the sake of clarity to simplify. The objective is to concentrate on how to organize practice. Nevertheless, an agency and its practitioners always have to use informed judgment. They have to add, subtract, and rearrange the preferred order to accommodate the realities of their lives.

One additional caution applies to guidelines: their steps are not exclusive of one another. The steps cross over and merge. Because systematic practice is necessary for effectiveness, the steps should be a firm outline for the sequence of case events. However, clients and client situations are an interacting whole. Therefore similar actions will be observable throughout the steps. The guidelines serve to point up priorities of actions. These priorities should be changed to fit the special logic of each individual situation. However, they should not be changed whimsically. Research findings obtained from study of this model of practice indicate that satisfactory results are associated with the whole package of procedures (Reid, 1978). This finding suggests the advisability of adhering to the basic guidelines without veering too far off course. When the order does have to be changed, the steps should be reordered as soon as possible and as completely as possible.

These guidelines are based on several reasonable conclusions drawn from practice research into the question: What processes have the probability of producing good outcomes? (See Chapter 6.)

The processes that probably produce good outcomes follow:

1. Carrying out interventions that are *structured*
2. Contracting for *specific goals*
3. Being *congruent* with the clients' own stated and demonstrated expression of their problem

REFERENCE

Reid, William J., 1978. *The task-centered system.* New York: Columbia University Press.

CHAPTER 7

Starting up: receiving referrals

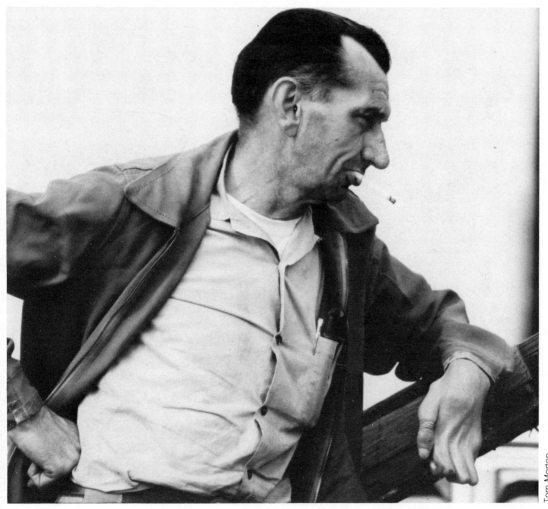

Tom Morton

Start-up	Client referred by an agency source	Client applies independently and voluntarily

	FIND OUT
	  Source's goal
	NEGOTIATE
	  Source's specific goals
	  Source's resources to
	    achieve goals
		Not needed for voluntary clients

WHAT IS A REFERRAL?

A referral is sending or dispatching a client from one agency to another in search of resources. Arrangement for transmitting or transferring the case from one agency to another may be by letter, phone call, or conference. The client can sometimes be sent in person without prior arrangement.

A referral is an *exchange*. One agency exchanges the client with another (Kirk and Greenley, 1974). A referral is also a *linkage* between people and resources. The referral connects a person with a resource. If possible, it makes a bond between the person and the resource: this means the referral "takes" (Pincus and Minahan, 1973). Referrals may result in a client's receiving a resource. Another result is a "runaround." When agencies accept, reject, or lose referrals, their supply of resources is affected. Their funds, staff, time, and position in the social welfare system are diminished or augmented, depending on whether resources are used, used well, used up, or wasted.

Table 3. Outcome of a hypothetical cohort of 100 people referred for service*

	Result		
Action taken	**No service**	**Service**	**Contact**
Do not contact the agency	32		
Contacting the agency			68
Receiving service after contact		48	
Not receiving service after contact	20	—	—
TOTAL	52	48	68

*From Weissman, Andrew, 1979. *Linkages and Referrals.* Doctoral dissertation, University of Maryland at Baltimore.

A review of published studies of referrals between 1955 and 1974 (Table 3) suggests the probable outcomes of referrals.

The fate of clients referred to an agency varies. A portion, perhaps one third, will drop out of the process. They will give up, forget the matter, get help from informal channels or channels that do not report into the statistical bank. Another portion, about half of those who make contact, will be accepted.

In any year it is likely that hundreds of thousands of persons will pass in and out of the referral mechanisms. No one knows exactly the frequency and scope of referrals or why about one half fail to receive service. Attrition of the total number seeking service has been attributed to various causes. Lack of practitioner skill and lack of total resources in a community have been suggested as two explanations of attrition. Organizational processes, however, affect the rate of acceptance of clients. A client or potential client can be an asset or a liability to an agency. Clients are an asset if they commit their time and effort and pay a fee, as well as if the agency receives reimbursement from the referring agency. Clients are a liability if they consume staff time, occupy room in a scarce facility, fail to change in the desired ways, expand the case load to an extent that lowers staff morale, or affect the agency's public reputation in a negative manner.

An agency's organizational objective to accept asset clients cannot usually be attained fully. There are social and legal obligations to accept referrals from agencies that have formal authority to impose an intervention program on the agency and the client. Agencies develop traffic patterns to stabilize and regularize the flow of clients within certain networks of the welfare system. These networks evolve over time as a result of habit, preferences, legal mandates, and reimbursement arrangements, known as *purchase of care*. Barriers to the flow of referrals are created by budget allocations among agencies. For instance, problems defined as "mental health" tend to be referred to a department of mental health. Those defined as "child abuse" tend to go to a department of child welfare. "Financial support" problems go to a department of public aid, and so forth.

RECEIVING REFERRALS
Fields of service

In each community there exists a formal division of labor and responsibility among agencies. The idea of fields of service, in a general way, demonstrates this formal division of labor, shown in Fig. 2.

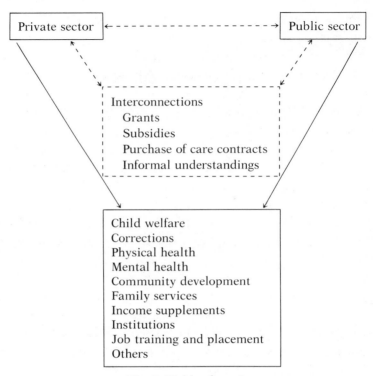

Fig. 2. Fields of service.

These divisions are, in some instances, highly stable. A particular agency or a sector of a field may have a tradition of certain service provisions. It may be sanctioned by law and custom to monopolize a particular service. It may be funded to provide a particular service. The supplementation of earned income, for example, is exclusively the domain of public welfare agencies. Funds doled out elsewhere in the system are petty cash "nickels and dimes."

Some of the divisions among fields of service are less stable or highly unstable. Ever-changing funding patterns, trends of public attention, and practice innovations create flux. It is difficult to keep up with new agencies, extinct agencies, new programs added or deleted. In this fluctuating domain traditional agency boundaries meet, cross over, solidify, and liquefy again. Agencies initiating a referral are often uncertain how that referral will be received. Agencies receiving referrals are ordinarily not prepared to give a quick response. The referral has to be *evaluated*, that is, judged in terms of the current position of the agency.

Why referrals are made

Referrals, or exchanges, are made for many practical reasons:
1. Lack of sufficient staff
2. Lack of staff with necessary skills
3. Clients or their problems outside the normal and usual mission or function of the agency
4. Presumed superiority of the quality of some other agency's resources
5. Presumed quantity of services available in another agency
6. Assumption that another agency has been vested with responsibility for certain classes of clients and problems

For example, when Lester (Chapter 1) was *referred* for vocational training, he was in this sense exchanged. The practitioner lacked time and expert skills in vocational assessment and knowledge of the labor market. The agency had no training program itself; another agency was funded to develop and provide these resources.

Problem definition and referrals

Behind a referral there has been a problem definition and identification—explicit or implicit. This problem definition can have been made according to many criteria. Problem definition means the description of the *class* of problem, such as "marital conflict about money." *Problem identification is a concrete problem definition.* It means the behavioral and situational details that individually characterize the class of problems such as fighting for six hours each weekend about what bills to pay, what purchases to make, and who will get control over the money.

Problem identification practices vary according to the style of work prevailing in an agency. Practices vary also according to particular professional, agency, and public interests (Chapter 3). No matter how soundly or vaguely based, a referral agency will have made its problem definition. Its referral assumes (correctly or incorrectly) that the receiving agency can or should alleviate the problem identified by the source.

Task-centered approach to referrals

In the task-centered model, in order for a receiving agency to collaborate with a client on a target problem that the client will choose, it is absolutely necessary to pin down what problem has been defined and identified by the referral agency and what goals it seeks. Incongruence between target problem identification and goals of the referral source, the client, and the receiving agency has to be negotiated. Also to be negotiated—and, if possible, contracted for—are the resources possessed by the referral source that can or should be supplied to the client. These resources can be tangible (goods and services) or intangible (attitudes and skills). Some problem identifications passed on to a receiving agency from a referral source are, to varying degrees, nonnegotiable. These are mandated problems.

The receiving agency, dealing with referred clients who are involuntary, that is, required to apply or appear, secures these referrals usually in writing by a letter or a written order from a court. Sometimes such referrals are made on the phone or result from a case conference. The crucial first step is finding out the referring agency's reason for the referral, that is, its *particular* reason, not only its general reason.

Goals. When a referral is made, there are implicit assumptions about the goals (Chapter 6). If the goals are only implicit and are not concrete and particular, they are subject to excessive ambiguity. Ambiguous goals are a hindrance to systematic intervention procedures and a source of dissonance between the agencies and the client.

Example: Ron

The receiving agency is a public child guidance clinic. The referral was received from a teacher and the school social worker in a conference. The teacher said that Ron (Chapter 4), 11 years old and overweight, was well behaved. His problem was wanting other children to praise him for being good and soiling his pants in school. The social worker said that Ron was "clinging" and "bizarre." She believed the mother was the chief problem. The mother should be helped to focus on her own problems and learn how to allow Ron to be independent.

Analyzing this referral, one can make a chart, as follows:

Ron: identified problems by source and goals

SOURCE	IDENTIFIED PROBLEM	GOAL
Teacher	Ron wants praise for good behavior.	Not stated
	Ron soils himself.	Not stated
Social worker	Ron is clinging.	Not stated
	Ron is bizarre.	Not stated
	His mother has personal problems.	Not stated
	His mother keeps Ron dependent.	Not stated

In view of the absence of specific goals stated by the referral sources, there has to be an analysis of the possible implicit goals. (See below.)

Without pinning down, or specifying, the concrete goals of the referral source, a practitioner could get the idea that the goals were to deliver Ron in two to three months as an independent, nice 11-year-old who is self-confident and modest, neat, and clean and whose placid, comfortable mother takes joy from having an independent son. Undoubtedly the referral sources are not so foolish, but without specific understandings on the objectives and an evaluation of their feasibility, who is to know?

Once goals have been put in feasible terms, a referral source will be able to suggest or respond to such practical things as making detailed observa-

Ron: analysis of assumptions about goals

ASSUMED GOAL	INTERPRETATION
1. Reduce Ron's praise seeking	How much reduction does the teacher want? In what explicit praise-seeking actions? What exactly are the praise-seeking actions that are obnoxious? Since most of us enjoy and seek praise, why should such a usual and ordinary characteristic be eliminated? What would be the result?
	Might the teacher be misstating what is obnoxious? Does she mean that Ron lacks appropriate self-esteem?
	What specific behaviors does the teacher want changed?
2. Stop his soiling	This one is obvious.
3. Reduce his clinging	We all cling. What's special about Ron's clinging? What would be the desirable change?
4. Stop Ron's bizarre behavior	In what way is Ron bizarre, meaning odd, extravagant, eccentric, incongruent? When and how often?
	What would absence of this quality look like?
5. Reduce his mother's problems	All mothers have problems. What particular problems does the social worker think Ron's mother has?
	What do they have to do with Ron?
6. Stop his mother from keeping Ron dependent	What does she do and how does she do it? What would the desired independence look like?

tions and getting detailed information about Ron's praise seeking, soiling, clinging, bizarreness; his mother's problems and her keeping him dependent; getting medical information and medical care; availability and accessibility of supplies of clean pants; and assessment of Ron's capabilities and worth.

Negotiating interagency understanding. When such explorations and negotiations are plainly conducted with a referral source, they tend to restrict the open-ended and anxiety-producing scope of the work, at the same time increasing the confidence of the referral source because of the practicality and obvious realism of expectations. A good initial negotiation, however, has to be continued by follow-up reports to the referral source. There has to be follow-up collaboration as new conditions emerge. The payoff expectable from ongoing contact is worth the time, even when it means letting some other things go (Rooney, 1978).

Problems in negotiating inevitably arise, and some are not so solvable. The primary problem is a referral source adamantly requiring that another agency make massive changes in the life-style, culture, basic personality, and intellect of the client. A reasonable explanation of the practical limitations often reduces this kind of demand. But it is not unknown for a referring agency to hew to the line of unreasonable or impossible goals. This situation will create a conflict that may have to be borne stoically. It is better subjected to debate and compromise by upper-level agency administrators.

In follow-up conferences (by phone or in person, or perhaps by letter), one additional area may have to be negotiated: the client's own target problem, which is the center of intervention. Normally, the referral source has a long list of problems, and the client has a short list. The referral source should know what the focus of the intervention is—the client's list. The referring agency should be shown the practical value of connecting the client's list and its own. To the greatest extent, its cooperation should be secured to put its concentration on the target problem for the most germane reason possible: increasing the possibility of a good outcome.

Negotiating conflicts with other agencies. It would be ideal if the social agencies in a community all had reliable knowledge about what is best and what works best. They do not. Furthermore, the individual histories of agencies, along with the aspirations, community relationships, and staff caliber of each, make for different viewpoints and interagency conflict. Nevertheless, since service components are spread out unevenly among several agencies, coordination at some level is necessary in order for clients to receive needed packages of service.

The typical interagency discord that needs negotiating occurs when (1) a case is referred with a specific service request (really a recommendation) and (2) the client's target problem is not consistent with what the referring agency wants. For example, a teacher refers a child who is underachieving, fearful, insufficiently aggressive, and has family problems. The child's target problem is singular: only to work on raising grades in math and social studies. The parents' target problem is singular: they will work on helping the child raise grades in math and social studies. If that fails, they want to transfer the child to another school.

The negotiating strategy called for here is to persuade the referral source: (1) that the child's and family's position is reasonable and (2) that the clients are probably capable of good achievement on problems of high importance to them (learning in this case). Reasonably regular reporting back to the referral source normally alleviates this kind of dissonance. If this process is repeated several times with the same referral source and if they see some satisfactory results, conflict tends to disappear or be cut to a low level (Epstein, 1977; Ewalt, 1977; Rooney, 1978).

Some interagency discord is more complex than that in the example just cited. More actors are involved, or highly charged aspirations are involved.

Example: Myra

A prestigious private psychiatric institution for residential treatment of children referred Myra, a teenaged girl, for placement. It named a long-term residential treatment institution as its preferred placement. The referring institution's policy was to provide care for no longer than three months.

The following analysis shows the objectives of each of the actors in the situation:

Myra's target problems

1. Mother antagonistic to her
2. Cannot live with mother
3. Will not agree to further institutional placement

Her mother's target problems

1. Afraid of her daughter
2. Distress about her own personal circumstances (nature of distress obscure)
3. Heavy indebtedness (reason obscure, since income from employment average for working-class woman)

Referral agency objective

It wants to place this girl in a long-term institution of its choice on the grounds that psychotherapy is needed for a borderline psychotic condition.

Institution selected by referral agency

1. Would consider Myra if referred by public agency on purchase of care contract but had no immediate vacancy
2. Not sure if it could provide treatment

Public welfare agency

The policy is to place in institutions as a last resort; the agency is not convinced that the girl is psychotic. This diagnosis is not confirmed by a public mental health consultant. The agency knows that a maternal aunt is interested in the girl's living in her home with the aim of eventual return to the mother. The agency is willing to consider foster home placement also.

Negotiating strategy

The public agency has a firm opinion. It must be prepared, in this case, to take a solid position against institutionalization and for placement with the aunt. It must offer counseling services to the girl to help her learn to cope with her distress about being rejected by her mother. It must be prepared with a backup plan for institutional psychotherapy in case the ominous diagnosis of the referral agency proves accurate.

In general, a negotiating strategy can be conducted along a continuum from (1) explanation to referral source; (2) explanation, plus mutually agreed participation of referral source on its services and actions; (3) explanation, plus solid position statement; and (4) explanation and solid position, plus plan for available backup and alternatives.

Issues in dealing with referral sources. Earlier in this chapter two examples were described. The case of Ron illustrated the unnecessary technical complexity that could be caused by a failure to clarify the referral source's goals. The second case, Myra, illustrates the extreme complexity of deciding on goals where there are many actors who have an interest in the referral. The greater the number of actors, the greater the likelihood for conflict among agencies in setting agreed-on goals. In Ron's case there were only two referral sources, working in tandem: the teacher and the school social worker. In Myra's case there were three powerful agencies, one of which was the child's legal guardian. Each of these agencies had at least a service worker, a supervisor, and a consultant. At a minimum that makes nine actors in the referral process. The large number of participants and their high power created a pronounced conflict over the objectives for the case and the intervention strategy. The presence of that many actors tends to overpower the client's own personal focus unless care is taken to preserve the client's rights.

●　●　●

The example of Sally Roscoe, which follows, illustrates another type of issue: difference in focus between agencies about who is the identified client.

Example: the Roscoe family

An 8-year-old girl, Sally, was referred to a multiservice community agency. The referral was made by a schoolteacher because Sally was underachieving in her schoolwork, seemed agitated, and was not clean. Following normal procedure, a practitioner interviewed Sally briefly, explaining the reason for the referral. The child acknowledged doing poorly in school and was willing to work on improving her grades. She did not speak of any other problems. She gave permission for the practitioner to talk with her mother, a necessary step required by the school. An appointment was made to visit the home.

At the first home visit the practitioner found a timid young mother. Mrs. Roscoe was tense and worried, troubled about her child's school problem. She knew no details of the school problem, had not conferred with the school. She thought it likely that Sally was not doing her homework but had done nothing to schedule homework time for Sally. The mother showed concern but no interest in taking any action. If the practitioner wanted to get Sally some extra help at school, that was alright.

Because of such a weak response about her daughter's school problem, Mrs. Roscoe herself was asked if there was something that she wanted help with. That question caused a flood of problems to emerge. The father, Mr. Roscoe, had failed to pay the rent for three months. After several weeks of threats, the landlord had now obtained a court order permitting the authorities to evict the family. There was no money to rent another apartment. Mr. Roscoe was not looking for another apartment. He became enraged when Mrs. Roscoe said she would look. In addition to Sally, Mrs. Roscoe had a 3-month-old infant to care for. Mr. Roscoe was bringing in food, but no rent money and no moving money. Desperately and strongly, Mrs. Roscoe asked for help with *her target problem—eviction*. Exploration of how this problem came about brought out the story.

Mr. Roscoe was a painter. His work was seasonal and erratic. Sometimes he made good money and sometimes he made nothing. Before the infant was born, Mrs. Roscoe worked on an electrical parts assembly job. Her steady income took up the slack when her husband was not employed. She was no longer able to work because of the young child's care. She could not afford a baby-sitter. Her relatives were in another state. Her husband's relatives were not friendly. There was just no one to care for the child. Mr. Roscoe did not want her to work anyhow.

Mr. Roscoe was at home while this decision was taking place. Asked to join, he refused, although he was obviously listening at the doorway. Lowering her voice to keep him from hearing, his wife explained that he was sick and so was she. He had no company group medical insurance. Her insurance lapsed when she quit her job. They could not afford medical care.

To Mrs. Roscoe's relief, the practitioner contracted with her on the target problem of eviction. The goal was to prevent the eviction, if possible, or to help her find, rent, and move into another apartment. The other target problems—the ill health of the parents and the school situation of Sally—were put into a pending status, to be resumed or not, depending on the outcome of the eviction problem.

Discussion. The child, Sally Roscoe, did indeed have a serious school problem. Sally had shown a low but definite interest in working on that problem. The referral source expected action to reverse Sally's underachievement. Tutoring her on her schoolwork had a reasonable chance to improve Sally's grades. However, here was a mother who could not participate in the reduction of Sally's problem because of a real and imminent threat to her and the family's survival. Mrs. Roscoe could work on solving her problem and would have to let Sally's problem go.

There is said to be a Chinese proverb that holds: when the house is burning down, you do not stop to wash the curtains. Figuratively the Roscoes' house was burning down. The referral source, the school, had no difficulty in agreeing to a delay in taking up Sally's problems so that the necessary time could be spent with the mother on safeguarding the home.

It is a frequent occurrence that a referral is received which deals with a *peripheral problem.* Interviewing the identified client and the other significant persons involved brings out a problem condition that is closer to the client's interests than the problem identified and defined by the referral source. Getting these facts and reporting them allow for sensible decisions on target problems; these decisions are convincing and gain necessary support from referral sources. In the Roscoe case, Sally's school problem was attended to in a *second* contract, much later, after the housing crisis was solved; after public assistance was obtained, including medical care for the parents; after Mr. Roscoe joined in the effort; and after the family settled in a new apartment. There were fourteen interviews in all over four months. The issue—the seeming neglect of Sally's problem and the delay in taking up the school's interests—was false. To have ignored Mrs. Roscoe's plight would have been cruel. To have worked with Sally on her schoolwork while her family life was a shambles would have been ineffective.

THE GIST OF THE MATTER
The main points about receiving referrals

1. *Referrals received are of two types.* (a) Potential voluntary clients may be routed forward to an agency and (b) involuntary clients may be required to use the services of an agency.

2. *Voluntary clients pose little difficulty.* Unless they are lost in the complexities of being sent and transferred from one agency to another, the work consists of deciding. The decision has two parts: deciding what the client's target problem is and deciding whether the agency possesses the resources for having some reasonably effective impact on it. Normally, whether or not the agency can bring effective resources to bear on a problem is a straightforward "yes" or "no." Sometimes, the answer is not obvious so that the decision is "maybe." In maybe instances the practitioner should clearly explain to the client what is uncertain and make a contract to explore possibilities.

3. *The majority of referrals are, to a greater or lesser degree, mandated.* The essential actions are to find out as neatly, specifically, and concretely as possible what the source's goals are; to negotiate with the source directly to reach an agreement on feasible goals and on what resources, if any, the source will provide to get these goals in place; to make explicit to the source what resources the receiving agency can apply; and to negotiate the strongest possible support for reducing the *client's target problem.*

4. When a referral is received, *the receiving agency is likely to feel that it is being required to do that which the referring agency is asking.* What the referring agency wants represents its best judgment at the moment. Referring agencies are obviously within their rights to ask, particularly if they can give a reasonable explanation about what they want and think is best. However, a receiving agency may find out from its client or may understand situations differently because of its particular perspective. Given the extrusion of differ-

ences about a referral, the receiving agency can surreptitiously pursue its own opinion and wait for a conflict of interests to emerge. Or the receiving agency can impose the referral agency's opinion and wait for an impasse to take place with the client. The best action is to explain, interpret, and reach agreement with the referring agency.

REFERENCES

Epstein, Laura, 1977. *How to provide social services with task-centered methods: Report of the Task-Centered Services Project* (Vol. 1). Chicago: School of Social Service Administration, University of Chicago Press.

Ewalt, Patricia L., 1977. A psychoanalytically oriented child guidance setting. In W. J. Reid and L. Epstein, (Eds.), *Task-centered practice.* New York: Columbia University Press.

Kirk, Stuart A., & Greenley, James R., 1974. Denying or delivering services? *Social Work* *19*(4), 439-447.

Pincus, Alan, & Minahan, Anne, 1973. *Social work practice: model and method.* Itasca, Ill.: F. E. Peacock, Publishers.

Rooney, Ronald H., 1978. Prolonged foster care: toward a problem-oriented task-centered practice model. Doctoral dissertation, School of Social Service Administration, The University of Chicago.

CHAPTER 8

First step: target problem identification

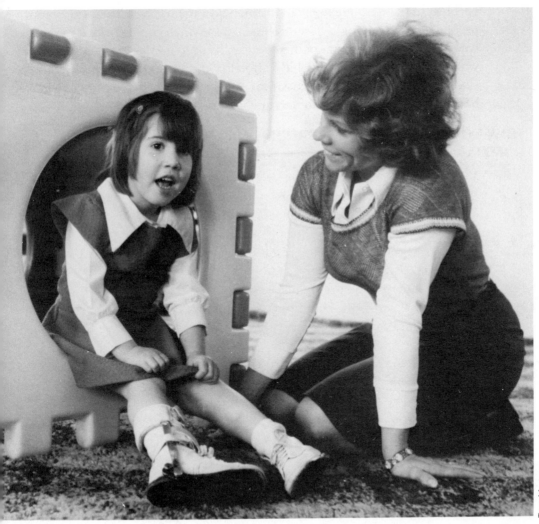

Step 1	**Client target problems identified**
	FIND OUT
	Problems defined by client Client priorities (hold to three) Referral source priorities (mandated problems)

This chapter will describe how to make a target problem identification. It will point out some of the most frequent practice problems of targeting a problem and offer guidelines for dealing with them. These frequent practice problems are deciding whose problems and which problems are the focus, what are the various standpoints that can be used in making these decisions, what to do about clients who have difficulty stating an explicit problem, possible ways to use a problem classification, what kind of explorations to make, how to set priorities, how to handle mandated problems.

HOW TO SPECIFY TARGET PROBLEMS: SUMMARIZED OUTLINE

A. Purpose of identifying target problems
    1. To name, state, and describe the target problem(s) (not to exceed three)
    2. To establish the center (focus) of intervention activity
B. Basic actions
    1. To establish the actual presence of a problem acknowledged by the client
    2. To describe the problem specifically
    3. To determine the conditions or behaviors to be changed
    4. To state the goals, that is, what the desired changes are to be
    5. To get information about the social context of the problem
        a. Client social and physical environments (social context)
        b. Client characteristics and mode of functioning
    6. *Optional:* To get information about the history and developement of a problem, if needed, and only to the degree needed

PROBLEMS DEFINED BY CLIENTS

Analyzing a problem situation in order to come down on a focus (Whose problems? Which problems? How important?) is one of the most crucial steps in task-centered work. Given the amount of uncertainty in the social sciences about defining *problem* as a concept, it is little wonder that there is confusion about how to pin down or operationalize this concept in professional practice (Chapter 3).

There is almost a universal consensus in the helping professions that human services are a problem-solving enterprise.

Some practitioners speak about helping clients to become *self-actualized* or to *potentiate themselves*. These expressions refer to influencing personal attitudes or feelings, creating a condition of good internal feeling, and creating a sense of personal satisfaction and control over one's circumstances. Self-actualization is an attractive viewpoint to present-day Americans. Many people are making reasonable or better salaries. They have leisure to contemplate art, architecture, and decoration of themselves and their homes. Self-actualization seems a reasonable preoccupation in the face of rapacious inflation, astronomical prices, strangling red tape, and physical dangers of fire, theft, mugging, catastrophic illness, old age, desertion of loved ones, and waste of people. It has been suggested that basic social forces in modern society are turning our attention inward, to our inner selves, as an exclusive priority (Hardwick, 1978). But the most adamant believers in self-actualization tend also to be problem solvers. They may prefer rapping about "feelings" (meaning attitudes), but they do help their clients get public aid, better housing, jobs, child care. They help clients repair all the thousand mean and destructive deficits that real people have.

GENERAL ORIENTATION TO THE ELEMENTS OF A PROBLEM

In order to get a problem into focus, we need a general orientation. We need to perceive the problem in relation to the persons involved, the environment in which the problem is occurring, and the knowledge available to describe and explain the problem. Four orienting perspectives can be identified. These perspectives are used by practitioners and clients and are ways to become acquainted with and arrange the terrain of the problem. The four orienting perspectives are needs, personal deficiencies, lack of social skills, and classification. These perspectives are *not* mutually exclusive. However, adopting one or another as a major approach to a problem tends to shape what problem will be emphasized and how this emphasis will influence intervention.

Needs

The needs viewpoint makes assumptions that a person's *needs are a deficit in social and personal resources*. The problem is thought to be the client's need for certain material goods, skills, personal attitudes and relationships, and services.

Examples of needs
"Mrs. A needs day care."

This means Mrs. A does not have the resources to care for and teach her children during the day *and* does not know where to get day care and probably does not have funds to purchase day care.

"Mr. B needs a psychiatric evaluation."

This means Mr. B is thought to lack normative interpersonal skills, and he lacks the knowledge, will, and funds to procure an expert opinion from a mental health professional.

"John needs treatment."

This means John is thought to lack normative interpersonal skills, and he lacks the knowledge, will, and funds to procure advice and *guidance* from a mental health professional. This statement assumes that treatment has the capability of improving his interpersonal skills and well-being.

A needs viewpoint may be the result of reliable information about clients' concrete deficits. Examples of presumably reliable information on needs deficits are intelligence test results; measurement of quantity and type of malnutrition; economic status above or below a poverty line; quantity and quality of rooms in an apartment; sufficiency of a welfare grant; and so forth. *Needs may be consensually held beliefs about what is good for people to have:* loving and caring parents and spouses, personal self-sufficiency, fulfilling work, ability to give love and to care, flexibility of attitudes and responses to other people, and so forth. *Needs can be converted to social welfare service categories:* day care, protection, health service, family planning, foster care, and so forth.

Needs are an indirect way of stating a problem. Although subject to inaccuracy, they also have a commonsense basis. Issues in basing a general orientation to a problem on needs are illustrated in the following vignettes:

Mrs. Elly

Mrs. Elly is living in a rat-infested flat, without any heat in the winter. Furniture is very sparse, window shades filthy and torn. An assessment of "needs proper housing" is absolutely sensible.

Mr. and Mrs. Chris

Mr. and Mrs. Chris, both in their eighties, were brought by the police to the emergency room of a local hospital. They were weak, their bodies and clothes covered with coal dust. They spoke incoherently.

The weakness was diagnosed as malnutrition. The coal dust was accounted for by their living in a basement amidst the furnace and coal bins. Because they were incoherent, a social worker attached to psychiatry was called in. Because of the incoherence, the social worker could not find out anything. The couple were hospitalized, bathed, fed.

The next day Mr. and Mrs. Chris were coherent. It was learned that the malnutrition was the result of their trying to live on the husband's meager social security. They did not know they were eligible for an additional public assistance sum. A neighbor who used to give them food had recently moved away, and so they were more hungry than they used to be. They had lived in that particular coal bin fifteen years. The landlord let them stay rent free because they watched the coal. He was—he thought and they thought— befriending them. The couple had no children. They loved one another. They were not stupid. They were old and their lives were restricted.

The social worker offered them an emergency nursing home placement. The couple blew up. They eagerly accepted intervention to get them an increase in their social security and help them apply for public aid. But they would only return to their accustomed living quarters—the coal bin! No place else. The question of whether they did or did not need housing has no single answer.

A needs viewpoint is both a moral and rational accompaniment to understanding the social context of a client's target problem. Identifying needs helps a practitioner to be specific about the particular resources and social skills in which the client and his situation are deficient. However, the needs viewpoint must be tailored to match the particular target problem. Otherwise, it may do harm to aggressively fulfill some "need" that is not real to that client. The harm may come about because a practitioner and the agency impose their own standards of what the client should have or should do, disregarding the client's individual appraisal of what she should have or do.

Personal deficiencies

It is difficult to separate personal from broad social problems. It is conventional to think that a client's or a family's specific problem consists of the deviant behavior of individuals and that the deviance is revealed by the part of their conduct which departs from consensual norms. Deviant behavior is *objective* in the sense that it can be observed and verified, and it is *subjective* in the sense that judgments about what constitutes deviance are often based on unverifiable inferences and a variety of moral judgments (Chapter 3). The personal deficiency framework is useful in the task-centered approach only if it is *not* seen as the most important or the only area to be addressed.

Lack of social skills

Ordinarily the following social skills are needed for carrying out a reasonable life-style:

- Providing child care (minimum basic parenting skills)
- Maintaining reasonable personal hygiene
- Maintaining a home
- Learning subject matter from school or special training courses
- Perceiving relatively accurately the intentions and expectations of other people, especially parents, close friends, siblings, spouses, authorities, and peers
- Communicating understandably to other people, especially parents, close friends, siblings, spouses, authorities, and peers
- Earning a living, especially finding and doing a job, getting along with fellow workers or bosses, and getting the rewards of work
- Planning problem-solving steps
- Taking problem-solving action

Deficit in social skills is another way to organize thought about needs and personal deficiencies.

• • •

There is, however, a potentially important difference in the direction and structure flowing from each of these three ways to formulate a viewpoint. The logic of needs is to provide what is missing as directly as possible, for example, a clean home, a father figure, a mutually satisfying marital relationship. The logic of the personal deficiency approach is to provide therapy that is intended to develop a mature person. The logic of the lack of social skills approach is to educate, teach, and train a person how to do necessary things.

Classification of problems

A broad classification of problems affixes a name or label to social problems that are collective, aggregated troubles judged to be afflictions of sizable groups of individuals. Examples are delinquency, crime, illegitimacy, school underachievement, unemployment, female-headed families, child abuse, child neglect. This kind of labeling has a role in organizing information about different conditions in social life. However, broad labels are useless as guides to understanding individuals or particular social situations. They give no information usable in planning interventions on a case basis. A more useful problem typology is one that can capture salient features of problem conditions and behaviors. The task-centered model has this kind of a problem typology. It will be described later in this chapter.

CLIENT TARGET PROBLEM

Another way to classify problems is to start with client target problems. This approach concentrates primarily on those problems explicitly acknowledged and stated by the client. The idea of target problem to get a general orientation to a problem includes needs, deficiencies, lack of social skills, and broad classifications. *Its tilt, however, is on those problems the client cares about most, in the way he cares, and which he can alter, with help if necessary.* The task-centered approach emphasizes this orientation as being efficient, capitalizing on client interests and capabilities, and being most likely to start service toward an effective outcome (Chapter 3).

Clients who cannot state their target problems

Sometimes there is difficulty with clients who cannot or seem not to be able to come forth with target problems.

Extremely fearful persons. Extremely fearful people cannot state their target problems. There are all kinds of fears. *External fears* usually come from experience. A client may have learned that he is taking too much of a risk to reveal himself to a representative of an agency. His relatives or friends may have told him of negative consequences brought about by too frank statements to persons in authority. The client may have experienced negative consequences firsthand. Some clients have learned to transfer fears from teachers, police, physicians, or other officials to all or most helping persons. Clients may have suffered punishments or reprisals from unsympathetic relatives and peers. It is difficult, perhaps impossible, to risk exposure with a strange worker when a client's experience suggests caution.

Internal fears are probably also learned from experience, but they seem to have become a permanent part of an individual's character. Some people are afraid and suspicious even when the evidence is that no harm will come to them in reality if they say what they mean. They have become so habituated to being suspicious that almost no amount of checking out will convince them to come out of their protective shell.

Some fearful people can take the risk of stating a target problem with a reasonable amount of encouragement. Some will not do so at all.

Confused persons. People may be confused because of real deficiencies in cognitive ability. They lack experience in sizing up situations. Young children may misperceive an offer of help because of limited experience in deciphering the intentions behind the offer. Some people, adults and children, may be intellectually handicapped because of low intelligence or disordered thought processes.

Experience with the task-centered model for elementary school children reveals that, with rare exceptions, children of school age can develop clear and cogent target problems (Epstein, 1977). Many mentally handicapped and ill persons make relevant statements of their problems (Brown, 1977).

Resolving an impasse in stating a target problem

When clients cannot come up with target problem statements, *the practitioner must make suggestions.* The practitioner must explain the reasons behind the suggestions and give the client ample opportunity to consider them. The practitioner should, if necessary, suggest that clients try out the suggestion tentatively so they may decide whether to commit themselves to it or alter it. Should this process fail to result in agreement, the basis for further work needs to be changed.

It is unheard of, in our experience, for a voluntary client to be unable to produce reasonable, relevant target problem statements. The difficulty arises when an agency is obliged by law or custom to introduce interventions and when a parent or other responsible relative wants help with someone else such as an erring, ill, or incapacitated person. Techniques for these difficulties will be discussed later in this chapter.

Practitioners worry about what to do if a client should propose a target problem that is unrealistic, trivial, or involves illegal or immoral activities? There is no question about such an occurrence. The practitioner should not participate. However, this is exceedingly rare. Usually it is possible to alter obviously wrong or bad target problems.

It is not proper to assume that confused or unskillful people do not know their trouble and cannot state it. Most clients know, or can develop in a discussion, what they think their problem is. Clients who are distrustful of agencies and cautious about expressing themselves may give studied and stereotyped responses. They may speak in what they hope is an acceptable manner.

Problem search. One means of helping clients establish a target problem when they cannot do so is the *problem search* (explained in more detail later in this chapter). This is a one- or two-interview special phase. The client is informed exactly what the subject of the interview is: to come up with a notion of what the client's problem is from his viewpoint. A client who gets involved in this process can be expected to develop for himself and for us background and contextual information that helps get hold of an understanding of his predicament. If this effort is not successful or sufficiently successful to start up intervention, the case can be terminated. Sometimes it is not possible to terminate. That means that the practitioner must confer with the referral sources and the client's close relatives to help them start on a course of action to affect the problem.

Problem search is a procedure that can be initiated in the start-up phase, the Step 2 phase, or both. The problem search is to be used with clients of two types: (1) those who are referred by an authoritative agency but acknowledge no problem and (2) those who apply to an agency for a specific service, but the agency would like the client to expand the request. With a client of the second type, the agency possesses other services, and the practitioner suspects or wants to know if the client can become interested in them.

The problem search procedure contains dilemmas. It is a way to try to draw out specific client target problems under an adverse condition. The client does not reveal on her own initiative that she is concerned about or will share with the agency problems other than the ones identified. It can be argued with conviction that a practitioner ought to refrain from intrusion into aspects of the client's life that the client has closed off. In fact, the value position of the task-centered model supports a nonintrusive posture.

Practitioners are faced with a sense of obligation or a responsibility when problems are mandated, despite the client's lack of acknowledgement of these problems. There are two options for a practitioner under these circumstances.

Option 1. The practitioner must insist on attention to the mandated problem. The legitimacy of such insistence is the authority vested in the practitioner as an agent of the authority that produced the mandate. Following are typical examples of option 1 when the client has no self-formulated problem:

Child referred for misconduct or underachievement in school

Mother referred for correction of child management practices as a condition of having her children returned from foster care

Parents referred for correction of child abuse

Under normal conditions, clients authoritatively referred because of serious, incapacitating, threatening problems do state problems of their own, related logically to the mandate. If nothing else, the pressure placed on them by authorities is aversive. They want to be rid of an implied or overt threat, such as not graduating, going to jail, having children placed. Sometimes their problem comes down to "getting that agency, teacher, judge, doctor off my back." It is often sufficient to deal with a mandated problem in terms of what the client has to do to reduce the pressure of authorities.

Option 2. The client can be offered an *extra two-session problem search.* I suggest from experience that if the client does not come up with a personally perceived target problem in two interviews, further attempts will be useless. Some clients do not produce a target problem under these conditions anyway, so that option 1 becomes the operating procedure.

The rationale for option 2, the problem search, rests on professional judgment. Having received the referral information, a practitioner may believe that the mandated problem is embedded in a host of other problems. The practitioner has a right and an obligation to explain this reasoning to a client. The obligation is especially pertinent if resources exist and are accessible for reducing these other suspected problems. In order to attempt to persuade the client to open up other problem areas, the practitioner can propose a set of two interviews for a problem search. Clients under authoritative pressure usually agree to the procedure.

There may be no mandated problem. There may be a professional judgment that the client ought to consider other problems, that resources exist for their solution. The practitioner believes there should be an attempt to broaden the problem scope from a specific concrete request to other areas. Here are typical examples: a discharged mental patient, receiving posthospitalization follow-up, finds that the boarding house landlord is failing to provide services for which payment has been made; a mother trying to live up to child and home management standards required by the court is in jeopardy because the public aid department has inexplicably cut off her grant for homemaker service; a married couple, both employed, are threatened with loss of income due to garnishment of wages, or wage assignments, from bill collectors. Assume that in all three of these cases the client targets the problem as lack of legal counsel. The clients come to a legal aid service for a legal remedy. Given these circumstances, it is easy to consider a variety of problems in living in which the perceived lack of a legal remedy is encased. Most human service practitioners would feel obligated to suggest exploration beyond the legal remedy, on the assumption that social remedies are available and will help the client more fully.

In order to proceed with a problem search to broaden the client's target problem, the following steps could be taken:

1. Provide an explanation of the rationale for a broader examination of the problem. ("I suggest that you and I discuss the suitability of this boardinghouse for you. I can probably help you improve your housing and help you handle your landlord's behavior to you better, so you won't have to worry about it so much.")

2. Inquire about how the client perceives the relevance of an extension of exploration to these other areas. ("What would you think about discussing your housing and its effect on you? Why would you prefer not to do this?")

3. With the client's agreement to proceed, or if a judgment that the client is being endangered is made, the recommendation is to do a problem search—two interviews, maximum. ("Since you think that maybe you could benefit from more discussions, let us set up one or two interviews to do that." Or "I strongly urge that you come to see me once or twice more before you decide against doing anything about the hospital's child abuse report. You are in danger of the authorities taking drastic action if you do not do anything. I could help you.")

4. The problem search should begin with no more than three problems recommended by the practitioner. The client should be informed as fully as possible why these three are chosen for examination. ("I suggest we review your medication to see if it is giving you trouble. You might be lethargic due to your medication and that could give your landlord ideas about taking advantage of you.")

5. The regular procedures for exploring and specifying target problems can then be followed. The difference is that the focus is initiated and largely determined by the practitioner who must be highly active and talkative, ask questions, reflect verbally on responses, make explorations and suggestions. In the discussion the client should be provided with ample opportunity to consider the relevance of the practitioner's questions, whether to become interested in them, or the rationale for leaving them alone. The client can be expected to spin off on his own into a problem formulation more fitting to him or his situation. If this does not happen, then the practitioner's obligation is fulfilled and the problem search is ended.

These problem search procedures have been devised from practice experience. They are plausible procedures if the agency has the responsibility to try to influence and convince a client and if services and staff are available. The problem search is a task-centered adaptation of *outreach*, which is common in many sections of practice. Outreach is based on assumption of responsibility to extend maximum services, with the hope that services can be supportive to problem solving and to clients' well-being. There has never been any firm evaluation of the benefits of outreach. Credible evidence from a number of respectable research studies casts strong doubt on the effectiveness of outreach processes (Mullen et al., 1972; Fischer, 1976). The inclusion of a problem search process in the task-centered model recognizes the sense of obligation felt by service workers and their agencies and required by some public social welfare regulations and legislation.

Probably the important point about the problem search process is that many clients will view it as intrusion and be reluctant to participate. Its effectiveness is questionable. However, since outreach will be done, it is advisable that the intrusiveness by limited, constrained to problems clearly and explicitly stated by practitioners, and offered in a climate respecting the client's right to refuse. Lack of success in a problem search does not have any negative moral connotations.

Drawing boundaries around problems

Boundaries need to be drawn around problems. *These boundaries and how they are defined are the crux of the task-centered model. First,* boundaries to problems create the structure of intervention. *Second,* the boundaries tell the locus of the problem, the area it covers, its substance or content, its scope and range—in other words, *focus*—so that effort can be concentrated on specified sectors of a problem situation. Delivering services in a clearly bounded problem area starts the process of structuring, which is essential to efficiency and good outcomes (Chapter 6). The idea of *target problem* can organize efforts to provide services humanely and efficiently. The task-centered model starts with finding out from the client what is the target problem in her considered opinion: *the client's problem*, not the court's, the mental health clinic's, or mother-in-law's.

THE ESSENCE OF TARGETING PROBLEMS

Task-centered practice provides a way of making a decision about problems, despite the welter of confusion that exists about problem definition. (See also Chapter 10.) The principles follow:

1. It is obligatory to define and identify problems. The whole sense of the human service enterprise is to solve or abate problems.

2. The best known way to reach a practical focus is to start with and stay with the particular client's definition.

It is immensely practical to state a problem definition that is congruent with the client's sense of a situation. Staying with the client's definition clarifies the issue of motivation—a besetting dilemma for decades. In the past it was assumed that an important cause of client dropouts and failure to change was *low motivation*. But motivation for what? Too often it was believed that the client ought to be motivated to make changes in his personality, attitude, and beliefs because these conditions were assumed to be responsible for his poor state of affairs. Many therapy approaches were developed to change clients' ideas about themselves, others, and the world. Many clients are aware, to greater or lesser degrees, that they have faulty cognitions that cause them to misinterpret events and to act wrongly, hurt others, get hurt themselves, fail to influence people satisfactorily. Clients who have such awareness often welcome intelligent help to change their ideas. But many do not.

Task-centered practice respects the client's own motivation because he must give *informed consent* to interventions. There is no way in the world to stretch a client's motivation, to maneuver him into a commitment for a personal change he does not want, does not seek, does not accept. It is true that some clients, for many reasons that could be speculated about, will submit or pretend to go along. Reluctantly, some clients will adopt a recommended viewpoint. Some will even embrace a recommended viewpoint. *Clients, however, eagerly seek help and value help that makes sense to them, is useful in their daily lives, gets or keeps them out of trouble.* The whole purpose of the task-centered model's emphasis on target problems identified by clients is to *take maximum advantage of the existing client motivation.*

The client's statement of the target problem puts necessary boundaries around the exploration and intervention. However, sometimes if done literally, the boundaries can be drawn in a trivial manner. A wide-ranging problem of death of a close relative was bounded in one case as "lack of information about where to get Medicaid forms." In another a conflict between a mother and son was bounded as "She does not make peanut butter sandwiches."

The opposite is also possible. The client's target problem may be stated as "depression," a word covering a multitude of affects and conditions. More often than not, a client who feels depressed is reacting to some loss or the absence of some essential life condition. The client is lonely, has no friends, has nothing to do and no place to go, is consumed with repetitive thoughts about fearful possibilities. The client, for example, can feel depressed because of owing too many bills or being misunderstood by important other people. Defining the target problem in words that state the action(s) which seem to produce the problem *(behavioral* terms) immediately suggests both boundaries and possible intervention strategies.

It is sometimes necessary to move the assessment procedures (Chapter 10, Step 3) up to Step 1, at least to begin some assessment procedures early. Starting assessment early is called for if the client target problem is too vague, too uncertain, and too different from the referral source's opinion or mandate. The assessment procedures help to clarify an obscure or uncertain target problem. Assessment should be started in Step 1 only to resolve strong obscurities. The reason, as will be discussed in Chapter 10, is that assessment is a process which structures the practitioner's thinking about how to implement intervention. Assessment, in the task-centered model, does not determine the focus. The client's target problem determines the focus.

TASK-CENTERED PROBLEM TYPOLOGY

The task-centered model suggests a rough typology (Reid, 1978) useful for putting some systematic boundaries around target problems. It helps to keep the classification in mind as a fence, to contain the content of the discussions, suggestions, tasks.

Problem classifications, task-centered approach

1. *Interpersonal conflict:* Overt conflict between two or more persons who agree that the problem exists, such as marital conflict, parent-child conflict

2. *Dissatisfaction in social relations:* Deficiencies or excesses that the client perceives as problems in interactions with others, such as dissatisfaction in a marriage, with a child or parent, with peers

3. *Problems with formal organizations:* Problems occurring between the client and an organization, such as a school, court, welfare department

4. *Difficulties in role performance:* Problems in carrying out a particular social role, such as that of spouse, parent, student, employee, patient

5. *Decision problems:* Problems of uncertainty, such as what to do in a particular situation

6. *Reactive emotional distress:* Conditions in which the client's major con-

cern is with feelings, such as anxiety and depression, rather than with the situation that may have given rise to them

7. *Inadequate resources:* Lack of tangible resources, such as money, housing, food, transportation, child care, a job
8. *Other:* Any problem not classifiable as nos. 1 to 7 after careful analysis

Basic actions

Problem specification. The practitioner plays an important part in specifying a target problem. Normally, clients will have indicated the location of the problems as they define them. This means the client will have *established and acknowledged the actual presence of a problem* and stated what that problem is. The practitioner must phrase the problem in a way that is concrete so that it can be developed into a statement of what is to be changed.

There are right and wrong ways to phrase target problems. The right way gives information that leads to plans for change *(tasks)*. The wrong way contains insufficient information to lead to ideas about what can be changed.

Examples of target problem specifications

RIGHT: Arthur fights too much with his foster father.
WRONG: Conflict in the foster home
RIGHT: Ben hits his mother every day. He broke windows in the apartment three times in a fit of rage. Mrs. C believes her son is too interested in sex.
WRONG: Mrs. C cannot control Ben.
RIGHT: Mr. and Mrs. D quarrel too much.
WRONG: Marital conflict.
RIGHT: They leave the children alone.
WRONG: Inadequate parenting

The phrases in the "wrong" column may be accurate, and they may be useful shorthand statements. They are wrong as target problem statements because they convey both too much and too little information. They are abstractions. *A target problem statement must be a concrete, individualized description of the condition to be changed.* "Arthur fights too much with his foster father" means that the goal will probably be a reduction in the frequency of these particular fights. "Conflict in the foster home" has no boundaries and no specificity. This wording can go all the way from leaving the cap off the toothpaste to a vague, general climate of unease and resentment among the family members in general.

Specification of conditions or behaviors to be changed. What is to change is implicit in the target problem. "Arthur fights too much with his foster father" implies that the change desired is reducing the frequency of those fights. Being particular and explicit about the conditions to be changed is to be sure that the problem is consistent with the goal.

If the conditions to be changed are not specified, it is easy to disconnect the problem from the goal. This disconnection can be illustrated with the case of Ben. Take the target problem "Ben hits his mother every day." This problem implies that the goal will probably be to eliminate Ben's hitting his mother altogether. Supposing, however, we were to avoid clarifying that the condition to be changed is exactly stopping that behavior. We could easily jump from Ben's hitting his mother to a goal of improving the mother-son interactions. Making that jump would lose the mother's attention, would open up too wide an area for Ben to handle, would stretch the boundaries of the target problem immensely. In other words, the structure would weaken.

Goal statements. These statements confirm what the end product of the sequence is supposed to be. If a goal statement lacks concreteness, there is no way to find out if it was attained or how much was attained. A diffuse goal statement prevents achievement or lack of achievement from being recognized. It can act like a carrot dangled before a horse's nose. Now it's here, now it's further away, and maybe it can't even be seen if it gets too far outside the horse's line of vision. Goals are not limited, nor are they ultimate or stretchable. Either they represent a reduction in the target problem, or they represent nothing. For Mr. and Mrs. D who "quarrel too much" and "leave the children alone," problems they acknowledge and want to do something about, the only logical goal for the first target problem is cutting down the quarreling. For the second, there are two alternatives: making safe child care arrangements when they are gone, or staying home.

Explorations in the course of specifying target problems. Defining target problems involves a large amount of discussion. In many instances specifying the problems, conditions to be changed, and goals is not easy (Reid, 1978). Sometimes the problem seems to change in the different phases of an interview or a whole sequence of interviews. Although every effort should be made to get hold of firm statements, if the target problem is not certain or is starting to appear uncertain after being stated, there should be exploration.

Exploration, as a technical term in the helping disciplines, has been variously interpreted. Exploration means to make a systematic search and to examine minutely. What is to be examined in the task-centered model is the problem. Social context and client characteristics are examined in order to shed an immediate light on the problem. In Chapter 10 the use of information obtained from exploration to make an *assessment* will be discussed. Exploration and assessment tend to occur simultaneously. However, in Step 1, making the target problem identification, the purpose of exploration is to specify target problems so that intervention can start as soon as possible.

There are a number of processes to be used to explore a target problem. Some are essential if there is to be a reasonable amount of certainty about the problem. Some are optional.

Social context. Obtaining information about the social context is obligatory. It is a primary source of information on which to base assessment of the meaning of the problem. A good deal of information about the social context normally evolves spontaneously and with a little guidance during the process of problem specification. Missing parts can then be found.

No client problems exist in a vacuum. All problems have a *social context.* This context consists of housing and neighborhood conditions, work and school conditions, socioeconomic status and financial constraints, health condition and health-care provisions, family and peer relationships, cultural and ethnic background.

It is necessary to make observations and inquiries to get *gross* information about each of these context areas. A gross exploration of the social context is *not* a license to hunt in clients' lives or to collect massive and comprehensive detail about them. It is doubtful what use this would be to a practitioner in ordinary circumstances. Total life situation explorations have a place in anthropological and sociological studies that have the objective of learning everything which can be gleaned about a person's life. In intervention practice this cannot be done. If such information were obtained, its volume would overwhelm the objective of practice—to act. A gross assessment means securing plain, obvious information that is evident (not obscure) and narrow in scope. This type of exploration means *outlining the circumstances* in which the problem exists. The reason is simple. Problems mean different things under different circumstances. Some problems are closely associated with socioeconomic conditions. The social circumstances also give a rough gauge of what opportunities exist for problem solving.

A gross exploration of the social context requires relatively little time. Information normally obtained in the course of targeting the problem usually contains what is needed. Noting this information and expanding it with a few questions provides the essential facts. These are the facts, however, that provide an impression of who clients are in their particular circumstances.

A gross exploration of this type is likely to identify important deficits or exploitive and oppressive conditions that may be present. Enough information about these special circumstances should be secured to show how much they are responsible for the problem. Observations and inquiry should attempt to identify the source of stresses that are precipitating and maintaining the client's problem. Attention should be held to present environmental stress. A long history of environmental stress often has a cumulative effect and may give a strong coloration to the client's physical and psychological situation. However, some of the undesirable effects of long stress are reversible if the stress is lifted. There are various theories and some research findings that can be of use in pointing up particular stresses commonly understood to initiate or exacerbate problems (Knox, 1977; Golan, 1978). Common sense and experience are probably the best guides to pinpointing grave stress. Among those conditions likely to produce excessive stress are separation from and loss of close relatives and friends; status changes; unemployment; tedious, demeaning, and poorly paid work; hostile authorities, unsanitary, ugly, and unsafe housing; poor health; discrimination; unattractive and offensive client personality traits and habits; low intelligence.

Client characteristics and mode of functioning. The kinds of information needed to fill out a gross picture of the client is what will give an image of the person (Chapter 4). Most of the necessary information about a person is immediately available when simply observing the individual in the interview. A practitioner can size up whether a client is timid or aggressive, suspicious or trusting, angry or calm, reasonable or unreasonable, perceives cause and effect logically or illogically, is lethargic or active. Sometimes, if a client is very upset or cognitively confused, it is necessary to confer with other people who know the person. Information about intellectual and psychiatric status sometimes is important, particularly if the client is hard to understand. Information obtained from others, however, can be misleading. A judgment always has to be made about how much credence should be given to secondhand information. Having a firm hold on a client's target problem will restrain unnecessary explorations and help make a decision on the appropriateness of the views of other informants.

Previous problem-solving efforts. Finding out about previous problem-solving efforts, particularly *recent past efforts around the same target problem,* can be enlightening. These past experiences offer analogies that can be drawn on for good ideas about actions to repeat, change, or never do again.

PRIORITIES

Every human condition is characterized by multiple aspects. There is no simple human condition. Human problems, of the types handled in human service programs, are identifiable as lacks of resources and lacks of social skills. The resource deficit may be extreme or minor, obvious or inferred. People perceive resource deficits as serious restrictions on their freedom and well-being. Deficits in social skills may vary from being simply awkward to being life threatening.

Resource deficits are both tangible and intangible. The basic tangible resources are those which sustain and maintain body and basic social subsistence. Food, clothing, and shelter are the essential minimums. When a person lacks income from employment, it is the role of the social welfare system to supply food, clothing, shelter. Beyond the basic minimums are other tangible resources considered in modern societies to be necessities of life: furniture, utilities, laundry equipment, pots and pans, heat and cooling equipment, telephones, medical care, educational opportunities.

Social skills deficits are always intangible. Social skills are a developed and acquired power to perform physical and cognitive acts, to use knowledge effectively and proficiently in the performance of particular and necessary acts. Deficits in social skills vary from inability to talk to abrasive garrulousness; from inability to concentrate to rigid obsessive fixation on a single idea; from inability to learn to inability to play; from obsessive concentration on one's own internal state to total ignorance of one's own feelings, attitudes, beliefs; from absolute insensitivity to others to offensive attention to others; from inability to be alone to complete withdrawal into one's private self. Most social skills deficits include a basic lack of problem-solving skills.

Persons referred to social agencies as well as those who seek help voluntarily often come with a long "laundry list" of problems. Being deluged with quantities of problems is one sure way to produce a crisis, to become overwhelmed and immobilized or frantic. To restrain this tendency to immobilization ("I don't know what to do: I can't do anything.") or frenzy ("These things have to be all done at once or else!"), priorities must be established.

Priorities can be established according to several criteria, including the characteristics of the method being used, mandates from authorities, and viewpoints of the client. All three of these factors are present in all decisions on priorities. However, which viewpoint is the most powerful determinant of priorities makes a sizable difference in how the priorities are structured in an intervention strategy. These priorities can be set by a professional, acting on sets of practice habits or styles, having more or less reliability.

Methods priorities

Methods priorities come about from a style of thinking that follows certain consensual conventions. These conventions have evolved in all the helping occupations and are similar, regardless of the source of the method, its name, or its attachment to a particular "school" of intervention. Methods priorities result from an attempt to explain a problem according to the practice theory espoused. There may be a partial explanation of problem causation attached to a method. Ordinarily, the beliefs about causation are incomplete and variable.

What seems to be most powerful about setting priorities based on method of intervention is style. Practitioners learn and, often, agencies support and may require certain actions that are interpreted to be consistent with a method. The consensual style is played out with innumerable variations. It consists of (1) a broad exploration of person, problem, social content; (2) exploration of one or more narrowed areas; (3) a tentative judgment about causation of the problem; and (4) a more or less formal agreement with the client on focus. The focus chosen is a judgment based on worker and agency opinion about optimum change goals, feasible change goals, and change goals that are acceptable to the client, practitioner, agency, and reference groups such as referral sources.

The key factor in allowing the method to determine the priorities is a judgment about the capability of the method to influence the client and the problem situation. The key action in carrying out a methods priority is the practitioner's judgment about priorities. Emphasizing methods priorities results in such strategies as putting priority on a client's attending sessions regularly, gaining *insight* or *facing problems, forming a good relationship,* and so on. These are all expressions that describe the client's attitude toward the method.

Mandated priorities

Mandated priorities can be set according to an authoritative direction determined by a powerful institution, usually the referral source.

Mandated target problems are those which originate with a legal or social authority, whether or not the client is in agreement. Such target problems can be ranked according to the power of their source. Mandates to act in a certain manner imply that there is an obligation placed on the client and the agency to change a situation, sometimes in a predetermined way, by restraining or curbing identified actions.

Sources of mandated problems. There are several broad categories of sources of mandated problems. These vary according to their degree of influence and jurisdiction.

Legislation. Some legislation requires that agencies or clients act according to the provisions of specific statutes. Problems of the client are governed by rights and restraints set forth in the applicable statutes, for example, legal prohibitions of assault and theft.

Police and court orders. Problems of the client are public. It is demanded that the client act differently, for example, in the case of (1) a police arrest and a legal charge and (2) a court order.

Impending police and court order. Problems of the client are public. There is a real threat of police or court order, for example, in case of a complaint of child abuse by a legally designated authority.

Professional opinion. Problems of the client are identified because of professional opinion, for example, an opinion registered by a school official or mental health professional recommending foster care for a child.

Public opinion. Problems of the client are identified because of a complaint about the client's behavior from a person in the community: a relative, neighbor, acquaintance, newspaper reporter, government official.

• • •

Only legislation and police and court orders have real power to create consequences of the highest seriousness for the client: deprivation of liberty, coercive removal of children, coercive commitment to correctional institutions. Threats of police or court orders, *if real,* have almost the same power.

Professional and community opinion are ambiguous. Professional opinion is likely to be more powerful to other professionals than to clients who dislike or reject the opinion. Community opinion, since it may express the wishes of prestigious or significant persons on whose goodwill the agency depends, may, like professional opinion, exert much pressure on an agency. Staff may easily feel compelled to maneuver the client, if possible, into submitting to the wishes and expectations of other professionals and influential community people. Professional and public opinion is, at times, capable of becoming escalated to a point where new laws evolve that become high-order mandates on agency clients.

How powerful are mandates? Only legislation and police and court orders, actual or impending, have the power to influence clients directly. Practitioners in agencies have authority, as legally sanctioned agents, to inform the client and explain exactly what consequences are to be expected if mandated problems are ignored. A list of specified actions the client will have to take to avoid negative consequences should be drawn up. The client should be helped to avoid those consequences by making the change specified.

When it comes to clients who ignore professional and public opinion, that is another matter. Clients have the right morally to make a voluntary choice about the propriety of opinions held about them by others. Professional helping people sometimes have an inclination to speak out with more authority than is warranted by the state of their knowledge. The ability of professional opinion to predict harmful acts is low. This is not meant to suggest that professional opinion can be ignored at will. But experts frequently disagree about "psychosocial diagnosis," treatment of choice, and predicted consequences. Also, there are degrees of expertness. In the helping disciplines it is sometimes hard to know who is and who is not really an expert. Public opinion about a client is capable of being genuinely altruistic but may also be spiteful, prejudiced, and exploitative.

There is little payoff in efforts to motivate, influence, and induce unwilling clients to agree to recommendations and commands of referring professionals and community people. However, it is common that clients referred, if given the opportunity, will target a problem differently from the referral source. They may include a factor from the referral source's list of problems and they may not. Where the involuntarily referred client is under a low-level mandate, the client's target problem choice should be accepted and work begun on it.

However, if the mandated problem is identified by a source with real and legal power, with actual negative sanctions for disobedience, two parallel sets of target problems can be established: one mandated and the other identified by the client. It is likely that these two sets will be related and may merge.

Legislative mandates do not ordinarily identify, specify, or command the focus of cases in the social welfare system directly. Legislative mandates are the most direct for persons charged with crimes: homicide, theft, sale of prohibited drugs, and so forth. Even for persons who are so charged, the court and welfare systems mediate and interpret the application of the law to individuals. Legislation establishes rules for conducting the affairs of a society. These are enforced by punishment or threat of punishment if they are violated. Legislation reflects history, social conflict, and social change. There are always ambiguities in what the law is and how it should be applied in individual instances.

To give an example of how legislation affects one type of case problem frequently encountered, take the question of determining child custody. Four issues dominate the present legal situation (Mnookin, 1975):

1. How much weight should be given to the rights of natural parents in a custody dispute with a child welfare agency?
2. How much discretion should be allowed in defining what decision is least detrimental to a child?
3. What legal doctrines should prevail in custody disputes? Divorce law? Guardianship laws?
4. Who should decide custody disputes and how should they do that? Adversary proceedings? Evaluations by social workers? Psychologists? Psychiatrists?

Related issues are: Can available human behavior knowledge be depended on for a clear-cut prediction of what is in a child's *best interests?* Should the courts focus on settling disputes or protecting children?

Court orders are one of the ways laws are transformed from general rules to specific rules to govern the management of a particular case. Because violation of a court order can have disastrous consequences, when a problem to be alleviated is identified in a court order, it is a high-power mandate, commanding the most attention and highest concentration. Police powers result in high-power mandates because they contain the possibility, sometimes the probability, that ignoring the police will result in being arrested. When the police refer a case to a welfare agency, their problem identification cannot be ignored.

Administrative regulations are a source of many mandated problems. Agencies are established, sanctioned, and funded to effect types of outcome or results with certain classes of persons who are identified as deviants. Partly to carry out their mission as they perceive it and partly to continue to receive public sanction and funds, agencies develop complex regulations. Some regulations are highly specific; for instance, a person is ineligible if income exceeds a stated ceiling. Most eligibility regulations are based on an applicant's income: a means test. Another variant of the means test is fixing a sliding-fee scale for applicants above a stated income ceiling. Beyond the means test, agencies develop regulations about various circumstances in which they will or will not provide goods and services. Most of these regulations contain large amounts of discretionary power and are interpreted variously case by case. Usually supervisors and higher-echelon staff exercise the formal power in specific cases. But in the daily routine of practice, the regular practitioner is exceedingly powerful.

Mandated problems with involuntary clients or semivoluntary clients are a major source of difficulty in practice. The prevailing intervention custom holds that direct service provision (resources) and social treatment (skill training or therapy) are one inseparable package. On the one hand, the ethic of social treatment cares for client voluntarism. On the other hand, the expectation of social control is authoritative. The dissonance between voluntarism and social control is immense. The probability is that these two aspects of social welfare should be separated. The reality of much practice makes that separation impossible, at least at present.

It is often simply not possible to fuse treatment and social control. It is therefore advisable to deal with them separately, even though both aspects are present in a case. This means, as has been said earlier, (1) confronting ourselves and our clients with the opportunities and requirements of *both* social treatment and social control and (2) using the authority we have been given by legislation and collaboration (as with courts and police). Since clients understand the source of authority very well, open admission of it is no surprise to them. Covert disguise of authority as "treatment" gets the distrust it deserves.

Problems "mandated" by professional opinion probably cause practitioners more distress than clearly powerful mandates. There is a problem of power involved here also, but quite a different type. Inside our heads, most practitioners in human service occupations are possessed by utopian dreams. Like Thomas More, we are beheaded (figuratively) and, like Thomas More, we are canonized (figuratively). Much as we may be "turned off" by the disagreeableness and suffering of our clients, we are also altruistically eager to rescue, save, and reform them. This kind of mission is embedded in the culture, particularly of intellectuals, both in our own time and as far back as the emergence of the Judeo-Christian prevailing set of moral values and ethics. Our assumed mission is a powerful influence, which, however, we have no right to impose on vulnerable clients who see their world differently.

Practitioners are also subject to the expectations of other professionals, especially high-status ones. Practitioners often sense that colleagues and superiors are expecting miracles of them. Mostly, this is not the case. But when others use esoteric language in their expectations, especially when they use jargon to describe a situation and a client and follow the custom of stating or inferring large, abstract goals, a sense of great powerlessness is set up in a direct service practitioner. Jargon is a secret, technical language that, at best, identifies the user as an accredited member of a profession. Translated into English, the ideas are less impressive but more informative. Jargon is also unintelligible gibberish when it has no robust technical sense. There really is no point in being either afraid of jargon or impressed by it.

Client priorities

Client priorities (Chapter 3) can be selected from client statements of how the problem is perceived, individually, in the particular circumstances. Client statements are put in order according to a leading question: Which three, if fixed, would make the most difference to you in solving your problem?

The most effective way to set priorities follows:

1. Establish what are the client's priorities or the target problems. The three most important to the client make up the priority list.
2. Include the mandated priority (if any) as one of the three.
3. Recommend to the client, if necessary, a preferable priority list. It is unlikely that the client will work on any but his own priorities. However, many clients are receptive to professional advice about a preferable priority list when it can be shown that another order will achieve more.

How to set client priorities

1. Start with the client's list, the array of problems.
2. Introduce the worker's recommendations, if any; include here any mandated problems, stating the degree of authority they carry.
3. Classify the problems according to logical combinations. The task-centered problem classification can assist in making such combinations. However, ordinarily problems are organized by their consequences.
4. Name, state, and review each problem as specified.
5. The practitioner makes an independent judgment about which elements in a multiple-problem list are most important. Judging importance means considering together those problems which (a) weigh most heavily on the client's situation, (b) have the most negative consequences, (c) would have the most positive consequences if corrected, (d) interest the client most, and (e) for which a moderate degree of ability and opportunity is available to make at least minimal changes.
6. The client makes a judgment about importance or reviews and agrees with the practitioner's judgment.
7. Listed problems that exceed the *rule of three* are put aside. They will be activated later if there is time and if they are necessary. The rule of 3 refers to using a single set of interventions, or a task-centered sequence, for up to three problems.

Illustration: specifying client target problems

Ron (Chapter 7), in interviews 1 and 2, acknowledged two target problems, specified the behavior to be changed, and stated his target problem and goals, as follows:

1. *He is too fat.*

   He has been fat for the past four years. His peers humiliate him because he is fat; they call him insulting names. His mother and sister are overweight. In addition to three full meals, Ron eats snacks four times each day—leftovers, pie, potato chips. He would like to lose weight. He would like to be normal size. This means losing forty pounds.

2. *He soils his pants.*

   At home, after he wakes up and before he leaves for school, Ron has one to three loose bowel movements. In the past seven days, he had such bowel movements on six days: every day of the week except Sunday. After he gets to school, he has loose bowels again; he is embarrassed about leaving the room to go to the toilet so often, and so he soils his pants. Ron thinks his soiling is caused by the loose bowels, which are, in turn, caused by his eating so much food and so much junk. The teacher says he soils on four out of five school days. Ron says he has had this problem since he started school, and that he used to soil at home before he started school. Ron's goal is to stop soiling.

Working explanation of the problem, review of past problem-solving efforts, and social context of the problem

This information was obtained from the first two interviews with Ron; two interviews with the mother separately; and the referral source, the teacher.

Ron has an unkempt appearance. He is worried about his problems. Peers avoid him. He is interested in a girl who is friendly to him but he fears he will lose her. He is inactive. Mostly he watches TV and eats. He plays basketball occasionally. He would like to bike but his bike is always broken. He thinks of food all the time. His three basic meals are heavy on fats and carbohydrates. His demeanor is friendly. He acts as if he would like to be close to people and less lonely. His attention span is short. He does not sit or stand still, jiggling around most of the time.

Ron lives with his mother and 9-year-old sister. His parents were divorced seven years ago. His father died less than a year ago. Ron did not want to discuss his family. He was pushed to give basic information. He said that the family is supported by social security benefits. The mother is generous with food and toys. She prefers the children to stay in the house or close by. The mother is overweight.

Ron's mother said that he was a colicky infant, who did not sleep soundly. He was given enemas. He had surgery at 4 years for undescended testicles. The surgery scared him. That was when he started soiling. He refused to use the potty. The mother is intelligent and conscientious. She pays lots of attention to Ron, but she is characteristically critical of him.

The medical information contains no known physical basis for Ron's incontinence. A report from the physician and a psychiatrist concluded that Ron has "a moderately severe behavior problem." As a result of getting that report, the mother enrolled Ron first as a patient in a child guidance clinic. He did not change, and so he was sent to a residential treatment center, and then to a special education school, where he is at present. He takes three prescribed medicines: for diarrhea, for hyperactivity, and for depression. The several therapeutic agencies that Ron has attended have been in agreement about the presumed cause of his problems: (1) strong fear reaction to his surgery years ago and (2) anxiety about his mother's serious consideration of remarriage.

Agency priorities and mandates

The referral source, the teacher and the school social worker, thought Ron's target problems (being fat and soiling) were perfectly reasonable priorities. The teacher was willing to aid in scheduling trips to the bathroom as an aid in forestalling soiling. There were no powerful mandates with drastic consequences. No destructive acts were either being committed or needed to be controlled.

REFERENCES

Brown, Lester B., 1977. Treating problems of psychiatric outpatients. In W. J. Reid & L. Epstein (Eds.), *Task-centered practice.* New York: Columbia University Press.

Epstein, Laura, 1977. A project in school social work. In W. J. Reid & L. Epstein (Eds.), *Task-centered practice.* New York: Columbia University Press.

Fischer, Joel, 1976. *The effectiveness of social casework.* Springfield, Ill.: Charles C Thomas, Publisher.

Golan, Naomi, 1978. *Treatment in crisis situations.* New York: The Free Press.

Hardwick, Elizabeth, 1978. Domestic manners. Proceedings of the American Academy of Arts and Sciences, *Daedalus 107*(1), 1-12.

Knox, Alan B., 1977. *Adult development and learning.* San Francisco: Jossey-Bass, Inc., Publishers.

Mnookin, Robert H., Summer 1975. Child-custody adjudication: judicial functions in the face of indeterminacy. *Law and contemporary problems,* Duke University School of Law 39(3), 226-293.

Mullen, Edward J., et al., 1972. *Evaluation of social intervention.* San Francisco: Jossey-Bass, Inc., Publishers.

Reid, William J., 1978. *The task-centered system.* New York: Columbia University Press.

CHAPTER 9

Second step: contracts

goals, tasks, time limits, other agreements

Step 2	Contract
	COVER Priority target problems (three maximum) Client specific goals (accepted by practitioner) Client general tasks Practitioner general tasks Duration of intervention sequence Schedule for interviews Schedule for interventions Parties: who are to be included

A contract is a contemporary form of the conventional practice wisdom that recommends a client-worker agreement as an essential ingredient of intervention. The assumption underlying the idea of agreement is *self-determination*. The assumption underlying a contract, a formal agreement, is commitment to work. A contract in direct service work is an agreement to do something.

WRITTEN AND ORAL CONTRACTS

Written and oral contracts are presently in use. The written contract has an advantage in circumstances where a high degree of explicitness is deemed necessary to control the parties, meaning staff, clients, and collaterals. Written contracts are becoming common in public social welfare where the majority of clients are involuntary, often reluctant participants.

High staff turnover, uncovered case loads, and absence of strong case monitoring are all factors that detract from an agency's ability to produce its services. Clients may be misled about what they can expect, becoming confused, untrusting, and irate and suffering lack of available and appropriate services. Clients who have gone through careful discussion and planning should be more clear about what they have to do to reduce their problem effectively. Making a contract is a significant action to achieve clarity. Both client and worker will think twice about committing themselves to something that is not reasonable, not specific, and not feasible. Oral contracts should be and can be as specific as written contracts.

Advantages and disadvantages

Written contracts have a clear advantage in accountability (Maluccio and Marlow, 1974). Anyone can check out whether or not given actions were agreed to and what those actions were to be. Finding out whether the actions did or did not occur is relatively straightforward. A written document, with signatures of the participants, is an easy way to keep track of what is supposed to be done and who is responsible. Clients, staff, supervisors, administrators, and consultants can use the written contract to make judgments about performance. In situations of high staff turnover, the written contract is a device for giving important information quickly to staff new to a case.

Written contracts have only begun to be used within the last decade. Only a small amount of information has been gathered about the extent of this practice and its effectiveness. Nevertheless, the idea of written contracts has caught hold in the field. What little evidence exists is positive. Clients have reported liking the specificity (Salmon, 1977). One study found that clients' willingness to develop and sign a contract was a good indicator of effective action to return children home from foster care (Stein, 1977). In juvenile delinquency cases and in foster care custody adjudications, judges have used written contracts as criteria for decisions (Hofstad, 1977; Rooney, 1978).

Written contracts present a number of practice problems. For one thing, there has been as yet no test of their legal status. We do not know if a client could sue a practitioner or an agency for failure to perform on a contract. We do not know if a contract is legally binding on a client and what, if any, sanctions can be applied if the client fails to perform. Furthermore, there may develop a trend toward evaluating staff performance, deciding to promote or not, deciding to raise salaries or not according to the results of a goal attainment scale that might be the same or similar to a contract (McCarty, 1978).

The problem with basing personnel decisions on client performance of a contract is uncertainty about the cause-effect relationships. Clients' failure to perform as well as clients' success can be related to personal and situational conditions that are largely uncontrollable. Nevertheless, the basic idea of connecting client and worker performance is logical, but the manner of making those connections are uncertain and not reliable.

As computerized management information systems develop, contract items will probably be tracked. Potentially these data, now largely unavailable, are exceedingly interesting and could be obtained from such systems. However, the accuracy and meaning of such data depends on its quality: how good the information is in terms of appropriateness, relevancy, and accuracy. For instance, if the staff members believe that they will be judged by the quantity of performance on certain contract items, they will become skillful at contracting for easy, simple actions. This is not necessarily bad. It is conceivable that if an agency performed maximally on all the easy, simple actions, it might provide quantities of badly needed services. On the other hand, overemphasis on easy actions could lead to a concentration on trivia and avoidance of serious problems that require risk taking. Since the reasons for poor performance on a contract are hard to discern and difficult to identify, contracts are not the only, or necessarily the best, data from which to judge performance. They are one source of usable data.

Involuntary clients are the chief cause of concern about misuse of contracts. Involuntary clients tend to be vulnerable and powerless. They may agree to a contract that is not realistic for them and find themselves punished for failure: not getting their children returned to their custody, for example, where the resources for putting their situation in order were not available or not provided. Staff workers may find themselves given poor performance ratings for failing to act because they did not know how and did not get all the supervision and consultation they could have used.

Clients who are highly vulnerable—extremely ill, confused, very young, imprisoned, and others—may lack the ability and the resources for making contracts on their own. If contracts can be made for them by caretakers, that would be a solution. On the other hand, caretakers may be unwilling or may enter into contracts with reservations.

For the most part, in the bulk of ordinary practice, contracts can and should be used. Despite the problems of administering written contracts, the practice has some obvious merits. Written contracts can certainly be used but should not be viewed as a panacea or as a rigid piece of machinery for driving a case toward some hard and fast end.

Contract revision

There is also a problem about contract revision. The written contract tends to be solidified, and amending it gets to be difficult. Written contracts should be amended when the original one becomes more or less irrelevant. That occurs either when a good deal of change takes place or understanding of the situation changes in some major way. Amendments can be made rationally if the contract sticks to major items rather than great amounts of detail. For example, the contract should state that "Lester is to look for housing," rather than "Lester is to read the housing advertisements in the *Daily Express* on Monday, Wednesday, and Friday, at 8 o'clock after breakfast."

Oral contracts

Oral contracts are much more flexible, adaptable, and easier to handle than written contracts. Oral contracts are really semiwritten. In normal agency practice their substance should be written into the agency record, shown to the client, and at least initialed. The record of an oral contract can also serve for administrative control purposes, that is, for case accountability and client and staff performance measurement. Oral contracts, when written into the record, are about the same as written contracts, with the same advantages and disadvantages. What they lack is the appearance of firmness that is present in a written contract document. This appearance may or may not be important, depending on how much the staff is trusted, responsible, and professionalized and on how many agencies are involved in carrying a particular case.

Practitioner contracts

One of the advantages of a contract is that the practitioner states what she or he will do to ameliorate the target problems. There are distinct advantages to practitioner statements of that type, particularly if written. It is a fair procedure. It can greatly increase the clarity of a client's understanding about what will be done by the agency. In terms of staff performance evaluation, it is possible to find out that a practitioner did or did not do what was promised.

HOW TO MAKE A CONTRACT

There are eight basic elements that should be included in a contract. These are itemized in the following list, with illustrations provided.

Contract processes	**Illustration**
	Rick, a 15-year-old black youth, who is in foster care, and his *mother*
1. Specify the *priority target problems* (three maximum).	*Rick* Too many people are trying to raise me. My mother pays too much attention to my aunt's advice. *Mother* Rick does not go to school. He stays out too late at night. He keeps bad company. *Mandated* BY COURT: Minor in need of supervision BY AGENCY OPINION: Mother too strict
2. State the specific goals: client goals accepted by the practitioner.	*Rick* to be discharged from foster care: to return home and to enroll in school *Rick and Mother* to agree to a set curfew time *Aunt's interference* to stop
3. State the client's general tasks.	*Rick* to decide what vocational training he wants and to start enrollment procedures *Mother* to decide on latest possible curfew time; in exchange, *Rick* to advise Mother of a plan for reporting lateness to her *Mother* to put limits on aunt's interference
4. State the practitioner's general tasks.	To arrange vocational testing for Rick To get and deliver to Rick and Mother all available information about work training programs To confer with aunt about her role in mother-son conflict To prepare recommendation for court about Rick's discharge from foster care To negotiate Rick's reenrollment with school officials
5. State the duration of the intervention sequence: the calendar time to be used, or the time limits.	Two months
6. State the schedule for interviews: dates planned and the location of the interviews.	*Rick:* Eight interviews, once weekly on specified dates; four in office, four in home *Mother:* Four interviews in home with Rick

Contract processes	Illustration
7. State the expected schedule for interventions: their order, sequence, and timing.	Weeks 1 and 2: curfew planning Weeks 2 and 3: vocational training arrangements planned Weeks 3 and 4: Aunt's involvement decided Weeks 5 to 8: All the above, concentrating on those showing least progress
8. State the parties who are to participate in the intervention: names and relationship to primary client.	Rick, Mother, Aunt, foster parents

How to state priority target problems in a contract

The contract should state at least one and no more than three target problems. This can be done properly only after the array of problems has already been elicited. They should be put in priority order, determined by the client. If there is a mandated problem from a powerful source, this problem should be among those given priority. See Chapter 8 for process of establishing priorities.

Following are the guidelines for stating a problem in a contract:

Client name → is → deficit, excess, conflict, or dissonance
(subject)   (verb)   (object)

EXAMPLE: Mrs. A → is → lacking in adequate child care.
John → is → fighting too much with his mother.

These can be shortened:

Mrs. A lacks adequate child care.
John fights too much with his mother.

Avoid long phrases that purport to explain the problem. Explanations are not necessary in the contract.

Stating target problems in a multiple-person case. Where a case has more than one participant, as in the example of Rick, it is possible to state three problems from the viewpoint of each participant. Normally there will be considerable interrelatedness between the viewpoints of the different participants. When several people participate, the firmer the target problems of each, the better.

In multiple-person cases, for example, a whole family or a part of a family, it is preferable to interview each person alone to elicit her or his views about target problems. Then, when the group meets together, the separate statements are made to the group. Differences of opinion can be aired and negotiated to the extent possible before the contract is set.

Because of lack of time or because of other logistics such as distance to be traveled to come together, it is not always feasible to conduct separate interviews with each participant. In that case, time needs to be spent in the group, arranging to give each individual as much leeway as possible to give his or her viewpoint.

It is to be expected that when the target problems of the individuals become public in the group, there will be differences. These differences are to be negotiated in the group session. Some differences seem so extreme at times that they become, for all practical purposes, nonnegotiable. Also, some members may state problems that seem not to be connected to what others have brought up. Some differences that seem disconnected are not. They are mirror images; that is, between two persons in a conflict, the problem statements are opposites of one another, but the connection is that they are about the same condition. The disconnection is that different solutions are being implied.

To reduce the problems stated by a number of persons to three, workers have three options.

Option 1. Settle on the three problems about which there is the most agree-

Options in multiple-person cases

Problems	Persons			Target problem			
	A	B	C	Group	A	B	C
	a	a	a	a	a	a	a
	b		b	b	b		b
	c	c		c	c	c	
	d						
		e				Hold e	
			f				Hold f
	g				g	Hold g-j	
	h				h	or indi-	
	i				i	vidual	
	j				j	inter-	
						views	

ment. These are three problems for all participants. Hold the remainder for later consideration, after work has begun on the three agreed-on problems.

Option 2. Settle on up to three problems, with or without agreement among the participants. All participants will have separate lists (as in the illustration of Rick and his mother). These separate lists will be interrelated but not identical. This option makes for a complex situation because time has to be allotted to give proper consideration to each participant's work, often by interspersing individual sessions between group sessions. Option 2 is the most common process in multiple-person client sequences.

Option 3. Settle on up to three problems to be dealt with in group sessions, *but* provide additional individual or subgroup sessions for those problems on which there is extreme disagreement or lack of group interest. Option 3 can be used alone or together with the other options.

The chart on p. 199 illustrates how these options work.

In the chart, problems *a*, *b*, and *c* would appear in the contract for the group. Problems *e* and *f* could probably be held, since they may be unique to each of the persons and not as vital as those on which there is more agreement. Person A, however, has many more problems. These could also be held, but their number suggests importance. This person (A) could secure additional help in an individual contract. The chart is suggestive. It can be used as a guide and be flexibly changed to fit individual circumstances.

How to state goals

The contract should state the goals (Chapter 6) of the intervention *from the client's standpoint, not the agency's.*

The number of goal statements should be low and address the priority target problems. It should be possible to show a direct connection between the problem and the goal.

If the agency has use for recording its own goals, distinct from those of the client, these should be properly labeled as agency goals or agency service objectives and recorded separately. Caution is called for to avoid imposing agency goals on clients. Agencies will often want to keep tab of their own organizational goals in a given case to evaluate themselves and to conform to requirements of legislative and funding bodies. Agency goals are necessary and legitimate. What is worked on with clients are client goals.

Examples of right and wrong goal statements

RIGHT: Temporary foster care home is to be available on 24-hour notice in case Mrs. A needs to enter the hospital

WRONG: The family needs assessment.

RIGHT: Information about work at home and application procedures for public financial assistance are to be available to Mrs. A at once.

WRONG: Mrs. A is to keep the agency informed of developments.

RIGHT: The frequency of John's fights with his foster father is to be cut 50%.

WRONG: John is to report for counseling.

HOW TO HELP CLIENTS PLAN TASKS

Client tasks are actions they plan to take. Client tasks are expected to reduce the target problem. Practitioner tasks are actions to be taken on the client's behalf to reduce the same problem. Tasks are a particular kind of problem-solving action, planned and agreed on between practitioner and client, and capable of being worked on by the client and the practitioner outside, as well as inside, the interview.

Tasks fit into the problem-solving paradigm (Chapter 8).

Problem-solving paradigm		Task-centered model
General orientation	→	Problem exploration
Generation of alternatives	→	Task possibilities developed
Testing/implementation	→	Tasks tried out
Verification (evaluation)	→	Results tallied

TYPES OF TASKS

There are two broad types of tasks: general and operational (Reid and Epstein, 1972; Reid, 1978).

General tasks. General tasks state the direction of an action but do not spell out exactly what is to be done. They are similar to what many agencies call "service objectives." General tasks always suggest the client goals. Often a general client task and a client goal are the same. They refer to two aspects of the same phenomenon. The general task says what is to be done, and the goal says what the condition will be when the task is done. It is not necessary to obey the purest logic in separating general tasks from goals. They may converge. It is necessary to get both stated and understood.

Examples of general tasks

RIGHT: Ray is to enroll in the Adjustment Training Center.

WRONG: Job training

RIGHT: Ray is to find and maintain living arrangements near the Center

WRONG: Independent living

A general task is what the client will do as a whole: "To obtain medical care." The general task is not limited to a single definite action. *It consists of many definite actions.* The definite tasks are *subtasks* of the general task: "Mrs. A will phone the doctor tomorrow; she will get an early appointment; she will explain her health problem to her children before her next medical appointment." *Subtasks come and go as they develop to implement the general tasks. The contract should not be encumbered with subtasks.*

Operational tasks. Operational tasks state the specific actions the client is to undertake. They are subtasks of a general task because they contain information about definite actions. However, operational tasks are themselves often broken down further into subtasks.

Examples of operational tasks

RIGHT: Fill out and submit an application to the Center.
Visit the Center.
Keep an appointment for psychological tests.
Have an interview with a public information officer to get an advertisement placed in the newspaper, seeking a boarding home.
Visit boarding homes.
WRONG: Come for regular counseling.
Obtain psychological and social assessment.

Other types of tasks. General tasks and operational tasks have particular characteristics related to how frequently they are to be done, how large or small is their scope, and with whom they are to be done.

The various subtypes of general tasks can be defined as follows:

1. *Unique tasks:* Planned for a one-time effort ("Mrs. A is to see the foster home finder Tuesday.")
2. *Recurrent tasks:* Planned for repetitive action ("Mrs. A is to talk to her children each day to explain how she feels and what she is doing to regain her health.")
3. *Unitary tasks:* A single action requiring a number of steps ("Mrs. A is to arrange for her hospitalization.")
4. *Complex tasks:* Two or more discrete actions that are closely related ("To discuss with her physician the several possible types and effects of surgery and consider what each would do to her ability to work, to care for her home and her children.")
5. *Individual tasks:* To be carried out by one person
6. *Reciprocal tasks:* Separate but interrelated tasks to be worked on by two or more persons; usually *exchanges* ("Mrs. B will refrain from yelling at Arthur, and Arthur will tell his mother what worries him instead of running out of the house.")

7. *Shared tasks:* Two or more persons doing the same thing ("Mrs. B and Arthur will talk to the psychiatrist together.")

Tasks may be cognitive (mental) as well as involve physical behavior, for example: "Mrs. E is to think about what exactly she likes, dislikes, and is uncertain about in her marriage." Care must be used that cognitive tasks do not degenerate into pure and unproductive ruminations that have no references to present problems. At the same time, it seems reasonable that being aware of and understanding what one wants, needs, and deserves can clarify one's priorities and help in making choices and decisions (Ewalt, 1977).

Interrelations between task types. Ordinarily, operational tasks flow from the general tasks throughout the whole sequence. They are a prominent part of Step 3, task achievement. They may be started, and often are, as a result of making the contract. However, they do not need to be written in a formal written contract because operational tasks change frequently. Operational tasks begin usually as an immediate result of the contract. They continue as a heavy activity into the problem solving, task-achievement stage to be discussed in the next chapter.

How to plan tasks

Task planning starts after target problem specification (Chapters 3 and 8). Task planning consists of generating alternative tasks in discussion and crystallizing a plan of action (strategy). Tasks are agreed on, and task implementation is planned. The whole strategy is summarized. Task planning *starts* with the contract and *continues* into the next steps as often as necessary. It is necessary any time there is uncertainty or lack of information about what to do next. However, to keep up momentum, tasks should be planned *to take care of major actions.* Minor or peripheral uncertainty or lack of information can be put aside in the interest of making progress with major work.

"Piecemeal" planning. It is possible for a task plan to be made in one session, following the problem specification. It is more usual for tasks to emerge piecemeal, during several phases of a single interview and over two or more interviews. Whereas target problems tend to remain stable over the life of the case, tasks change often. Tasks change because they are done, are not done, or cannot be done. Completed tasks are dropped. Tasks not done are analyzed to obtain information about the barriers to task achievement. They are then revised.

Sources of information for task planning. The sources of information about reasonable tasks to reduce a problem follow:

1. Clients' own experience (the basic source)
2. Expert knowledge about reliable or reasonable problem-solving actions
3. Practitioner's own experience

Client experience. The first step in planning a task is to find out from clients what they think they could do to cut down their target problems. Most clients have sound ideas on this subject once they are convinced that it is safe to state their own ideas and that their ideas will be respected. The practitioner is responsible for clarifying and molding clients' suggestions and introducing tasks for consideration to clients who do not readily generate their own ideas.

Expert knowledge. The role of expert knowledge needs explanation. Knowledge in the social sciences and in the human service professions is broad in scope. The disciplines that generate social science knowledge are many: sociology, psychology, medicine (particularly psychiatry), social work, law, anthropology, history, economics, political science, philosophy, and theology. Readily available knowledge from these sources is often of poor quality and outdated. New information is produced at an enormous rate. It is impossible for any single practitioner to sift all this knowledge and keep abreast of revisions and innovations.

It has been common for service workers to depend on familiarity with a treatment method for knowledge to use in their cases. Selective information from general reading, conferences, and advice from supervisors and consultants is used as well. It is preferable for a practitioner to have access to knowledge that is directly related to the problems in his cases. This access is obtainable. A lawyer has to look up the latest court decisions. A physician has to look up the latest drug information. A social worker, nurse, or counselor has to have access to libraries and consultants to locate relevant knowledge. Since practitioners do not have time to run down this knowledge for themselves, the information has to be secured for them by resource people on the staff, by cooperating specialized agencies, and by consultants.

Practitioner experience. Practitioners should not hesitate to draw on their own practice and personal experience to suggest client tasks. If we have had a similar experience ourselves, we have ideas about actions that failed or succeeded. Especially pertinent is a collection of previous practice experiences with similar situations.

Formalizing tasks. After task alternatives have been generated with a client, the next step is to reach an explicit agreement about which ones will be undertaken. Then details of implementation should be discussed. This means agreeing on what is to be done, when, with whom, where, under what specific conditions (if any), and how. The client should emerge with a clear idea: *a blueprint to aid in doing the tasks.*

Each task agreed to must have discussion of how the task is to be started up and followed through. Tasks that involve actions familiar to the client need only to have a brief review of the expected actions. Tasks involving novel actions require detailed stepwise discussion, including alternative actions in case of expected and unexpected developments. All task agreements should be briefly summarized at the end of a session.

Summary: how to plan client tasks

A. Purpose: to devise and organize actions to reduce the problem
B. Basic actions
   1. Generating alternatives
   2. Agreeing with client on tasks
   3. Planning details of implementation
   4. Summarize

PRACTITIONER TASKS

Practitioner tasks are actions that the practitioner commits herself to do between sessions. Formal practitioner tasks and formal client tasks compose the structure of getting the intervention done. *All practitioner tasks are supplements to client actions for the purpose of facilitating the client's work.* They consist of negotiating and conferring. *Negotiating* actions are transactions *with agency and community officials.* Negotiations are conducted for a number of purposes. These are to *transfer* resources, services, and good will from the organization to the client; to *package*, or design, those resources, services, and good will in a way to reduce clients' target problems; and to satisfy the official terms and conditions, as well as powerful mandates held by the organization. *Conferring* resembles negotiating, since conferring also is for the purpose of transferring reinforcements from those who have them to the clients who do not have them. The difference between negotiating and conferring is sometimes minor. Conferring is used to describe negotiations with nonofficials. It implies influencing people, such as a parent or spouse, to help the client in particular ways.

Negotiating with agency and community officials

The types of negotiations are varied. A list of the most common follows:

1. Identify the terms and conditions the agency requires the client to meet.
2. Specify what persons must or should participate.
3. Specify what documents must be produced, by whom, and where they are to be delivered.
4. Specify the authority for the requirements or expectation, that is, what legal, judicial, professional, or customary authority exists to justify the expectations.
5. Elicit a clear and concrete understanding of an agency's or official's intentions and plans.
6. Secure information possessed by the agency or official about the problem.
7. Secure information about the agency's special knowledge concerning a client and a problem area.
8. Secure information about the agency's resources that are available for use by the client.
9. Reach agreement on resources and services to be supplied by the agency or official.
10. Influence the agency to take a positive attitude, to ease the client's entry into its system and to encourage participation.
11. Request that the agency or official report back, confirming or revising agreements.

Conferring with collaterals

Conferences can be held with the client's family, friends, teachers, physicians, a state's attorney, and so forth. The major purpose is to win them over to take one or more actions to reward, legitimize, respect, teach, or help the client. These actions are intended to fit the plan for task achievement and should be specific.

DURATION OF SEQUENCE, OR TIME LIMITS
General rules

Normally, task-centered intervention should be planned to take place in no more than eight to twelve in-person interviews with the clients, spaced out by a regular schedule over a two- to three-month period. Negotiating and collateral conferences of any number are included. The number may be reduced if the problem has its own time limits; for example, if Mrs. A is to be incapacitated only four weeks, the time limit could be one month.

It is not known what the "rules" are for time limits. There has been no research that we know of to study what time limits are "best" for any particular problem, age group, personality type. Agencies develop practice styles about how they apportion time. Agencies using time limits make judgments based on various criteria. Some use number of interviews—from about three to twelve. Available staff time is another way time limits are set. Still another is experience. Where third-party payments are made, it is customary to set the limit to equal the amount of service that will be paid or reimbursed by another agency or an insurance company. In some agencies the number of interviews is combined with a loose rule about the total amount of calendar time to be allotted to a case.

The experience of the research projects on which the task-centered model is based suggests a "rule of thumb"—eight client interviews, plus any number of agency negotiations and collateral contacts, over a two- to three-month span. The contract for an eight-interview sequence can be shortened or extended.

The reasons for setting time limits are several. They appear to produce a mobilization effect. Like any deadline, they set an objective around which energy and expectations are organized. Time limits seem to cause a push effect that gets things done. Rarely do clients object to time limits. Those who do often have been habituated to an open-ended style as a result of previous treatment experience. No deleterious effects from using time limits have been reported. There appears to be a significant decrease in dropouts when explicit time limits are compared to planned open-ended sequences. Time limits also put the client-practitioner relationship on a work basis, cutting down on the development of unnecessary client personal dependence on the practitioner.

Special conditions for time limits

There are a number of conditions where special time limit conditions pertain.

Child in foster care; adult in chronic care facility. In foster care or chronic care, living arrangements are being provided. These arrangements can be separated from counseling service, as they often are. The counseling should follow the usual rules for task-centered intervention addressed to specific target problems, including time limits. The contract for living arrangements is distinct. The living arrangement contract can be open ended if it is planned to endure permanently or indefinitely. If this is not intended, the living arrangement plan should specify what the expected duration, discharge plan, and alternative plan are to be. While the particular living arrangement exists, there may be a series of separate task-centered sequences. Critical points in such settings that would normally call for such sequences are admission, personal crisis, changes in living plan, and discharge.

Child or adult in legal custody with court-ordered requirements. The typical incidences of legal custody with court-ordered requirements are the child wards of the court ordered to be in foster care and the child or adult on probation or parole. The terms of the court order may exceed the task-centered model's normal time limits. The contract for intervention should follow the normal task-centered time limits. Thereafter, additional sequences can be contracted for, if advisable, or the situation can be placed in a minimal monitoring status.

Child or adult receiving medical or mental health treatment. Clinics vary a great deal in their expectation that medically supervised or medically oriented treatment will be openended or time limited. The provision of medication almost always requires continuous medical supervision. Medical and psychiatric care may involve some regular checkup or monitoring to survey the development of a chronic health condition. In case the medical or mental health agency opts for extended time and the social welfare agency agrees to this stipulation, the intervention plan proceeds according to the medical recommendations. Interventions concerning the problems in living, however, should be restricted to one or more task-centered sequences. Minimal monitoring by a social agency cooperating with a medical or psychiatric agency is usually necessary (Chapter 11).

Child being counseled directly; adult who is ill, aged, or mentally handicapped. Young children have relatively short attention spans that are considered when planning the eight-session interviewing schedule. Young children may be interviewed in short segments of time, with two short segments counted as one for purposes of the interview scheduling. Ill, aged, or mentally handicapped adults may be scheduled the same way.

Reeducating parents in child care and training. There is evidence that parent education is an effective activity to reduce parent-child conflict problems and modify child-rearing practices (Hawkins et al., 1966; Levenstein, et al., 1973; Pinkston, 1979). There is also some evidence that frequent contact and service beyond the usual two to three months characteristic of task-centered intervention—up to one year—enhances effectiveness in dealing with these types of problems (Sherman et al., 1973). In view of this evidence, it would be appropriate to contract for extended duration. The extremely important proviso is that *cases be kept open only when definite plans and implementation are actually desired by clients and provided by practitioners.*

Other

Where convincing empirical evidence exists, there should be no artificial barrier to extending time limits. In the face of lack of evidence, extending a contract has no known value. It would be better to conclude with the completion of the planned brief intervention sequence. There should be no bar to reopen cases if requested to do so or in case an involuntary client is referred again.

The reasons why some cases continue for long or very long periods of time are varied. Some types of medically supervised interventions are established to be continuing over long periods of time, partly out of habits and style, partly because of beliefs held or facts known about stages of development in diseases. Types of interventions that involve large investments in reeducation of children and adults may justify long-term intervention. The fact is that the state of knowledge does not justify any hard and fast conclusions about the conditions under which long-term intervention is justified.

The present tendency is to curtail the length of time used in interventions. Especially where cost is important and where effectiveness is doubtful, planned long-term interventions are not justifiable. The numbers of people who benefit from brief, focused interventions are large and potentially larger. It is to this population that the task-centered model is addressed.

SCHEDULE FOR INTERVIEWS

The most preferable way to schedule interviews is to establish how often they will occur, the place they will be held, the specific dates they will be held, and the amount of time to be used per interview. These time and place specifics can be changed later if they prove to be inconvenient. However, to start off without a systematic schedule is to invite uncertainty, inattention, and misunderstanding. In managing a case load, a fluid and diffuse mode of scheduling time invites drift.

SCHEDULE FOR INTERVENTIONS

Taking the target problem priorities as a guide, the schedule of interventions should start with itemizing what is to be done first, second, and third.

Interventions have a way of losing specificity and order. The chain of events they often start is not capable of being anticipated. Many actors and actions get involved that influence the sense and form of interventions.

The best practice is to start off with a specific intervention schedule and revise it on the basis of concrete experience. The revisions should be explicit, even when they call for trying out one or several things to see what happens. Intervention schedules should be definite. However, they should be changed readily in the face of obvious need. Their purpose is to push and to make clear what the intervention program is to consist of. The intervention schedule is not a test of performance, but a framework to organize performance.

PARTIES: WHO ARE TO BE INCLUDED

The universe of persons who can be involved in an intervention sequence is closed. There are only certain categories of includable parties:

- A specific person
- Family members
- Peers
- Nonfamily persons in the household (girlfriends, boyfriends)
- A relevant group: interest group, age group, neighborhood or civic group, for example
- Immediately influential authorities: teachers, doctors, caregivers, for example

If possible and if feasible, those who are an immediate part of the problem and its solution should be included in the contract. They should be included only if they have expressed a willingness and ability to participate. Some people can be included because their social role commands their involvement, such as parents of minor children.

Persons can be deemed an immediate part of the problem and its solution if they are in a continuing current relationship with the central client and if they occupy a position that seems to precipitate, exacerbate, maintain, or restrain the problem. Persons whose social role commands their involvement are those who exercise direct care of and give financial support to the central client.

In deciding which parties are to be included in the contract, the crucial factor is their willingness. Rarely do persons of potential value to the success of an intervention agree to total involvement. They have their own agendas, which come first. It is not uncommon, however, for a married couple or parents and children to agree to joint interviews. It is occasionally the case that whole families will come together for interviews or that girlfriends and boyfriends will attend together. Mostly, however, persons other than the central client will take a lesser degree of responsibility. They can contract for moderate or minimal inclusion. They may be prepared to attend only once, only occasionally, or they may take on only telephone contact. The degree of involvement of persons close to the client is not crucial. What is crucial is that there be discussion with them to find out what they are ready to do and to commit them to it.

A good example of the probable criticalness of including an extended family is the Corey case (Chapter 3). In that case the maternal aunt and grandmother demonstrated openly and clearly their wish and willingness to involve themselves in planning for the children. They were a potential resource. They should have been encouraged to participate. The forever unanswerable question about the Corey children's fate would have been less obscure if that step had been taken. To have known the relatives could not take care of the children is a different thing than to have inferred that they would not take care of them. Inferences based on weak predictive theories carry no weight.

REFERENCES

Ewalt, Patricia L., 1977. A psychoanalytically oriented child guidance clinic. In W. J. Reid & L. Epstein (Eds.). *Task-centered practice.* New York: Columbia University Press.

Hawkins, Robert P., et al., 1966. Behavior therapy in the home: amelioration of problem parent-child relations with the parent in a therapeutic role. *Journal of Experimental Child Psychology 4,* 99-107.

Hofstad, Milton O., 1977. Treatment in a juvenile court setting. In W. J. Reid & L. Epstein (Eds.). *Task-centered practice.* New York: Columbia University Press.

Levenstein, P., Kochman, P., & Roth, H., 1973. From laboratory to real world: service delivery of the Mother-Child Home Program. *American Journal of Orthopsychiatry 43,* 72-78.

Maluccio, Anthony D., & Marlow, Wilma D., 1974. The case for the contract. *Social Work 19,* 28-36.

McCarty, Loretta M., 1978. A protective service caseworker performance scale. *Child Welfare 52*(3), 149-155.

Pinkston, Elsie M., 1979. Educating parents as behavior change agents for their children. In S. P. Shinke (Ed.), *Community Application of Behavioral Methods.* Chicago: Aldine Publishing Co.

Reid, William J., 1978. *The task-centered system.* New York: Columbia University Press.

Reid, William J., & Epstein, Laura, 1972. *Task-centered casework.* New York: Columbia University Press.

Rooney, Ronald H., 1978. Prolonged foster care: toward a problem-oriented task-centered practice model. Doctoral dissertation, School of Social Service Administration, The University of Chicago.

Salmon, Wilma, 1977. A service program in a state public welfare agency. In W. J. Reid & L. Epstein (Eds.), *Task-centered practice.* New York: Columbia University Press.

Sherman, Edward A., Neuman, Renee, & Shyne, Ann W., 1973, *Children adrift in foster care: a study of alternative approaches.* New York: Child Welfare League of America.

Stein, Theodore, Gambrill, Eileen, & Wiltse, Kermit T., 1977. Contracts and outcome in foster care. *Social Work 22*(2), 148-149.

CHAPTER 10

Third step: task achievement, problem reduction, problem solving

Step 3	**Task achievement, problem reduction, problem solving** **(use all or select)**

	DEFINE AND SPECIFY CLIENT TARGET PROBLEM (three maximum)
	State and name what the problem is: the particular conditions and behaviors to be changed
	Assess
	   Problem
	      How often the problem occurs (frequency)
	      Where it occurs (site)
	      With whom (participants)
	      What immediate antecedents
	      What consequences
	      What meaning
	   Social context: What social conditions precipitate and maintain the problem
	      Work-school circumstances
	      Health care circumstances
	      Economic status
	      Personality-intelligence traits
	      Family organization
	      Peer group organization
	      Housing state
	      Cultural background
	      Other
	
	Continued.

Step 3	**Task achievement, problem reduction, problem solving (use all or select)**

GENERATE ALTERNATIVES

Find out and identify a feasible range of possible problem-solving actions

Negotiate supportive and collaborative actions of other persons and agencies

DECISION MAKING

Design intervention strategy

  The basic interventions

  Timing and sequence

  Participants

Get client agreement and understanding

Get agreement and understanding of necessary others

IMPLEMENT (carry out strategy)

Develop tasks

  Get client understanding and agreement to tasks

  Get client understanding of rationale and incentives for tasks

  Devise plans for client task performance

  Summarize tasks

  Summarize plans for task performance

  Review task performance

Support task performance

  Review number of sessions outstanding

  Obtain and use resources

  Find out obstacles to resource provision

  Show client how to perform tasks

    Give instruction

    Give guidance

    Do simulations

    Accompany client for modeling and advocacy

    Discuss cognitive barriers

      Fears

      Suspicions

      Lack of knowledge

      Lack of cooperation from others

      Lack of resources

 Find out obstacles to task performance

 Plan and state practitioner tasks

  Inform client of practitioner tasks

  Review implementation of practitioner tasks

 Review problem state

Step 3	**Task achievement, problem reduction, problem solving** **(use all or select)**

	VERIFY (check, test, confirm, substantiate probable effects of intervention)
	Monitor and record problem status regularly
	Revise contract, or some parts of it, if
	    Progress unsatisfactory
	    Progress exceeds expectations
	    New problems emerge
	    Problem takes on different characteristics
	Revise tasks not performed or poorly performed
	Revise supports and resources if ineffective
	Revise practitioner tasks if not feasible or ineffective

PROBLEM SOLVING: WHAT IS IT?

For practitioners the gist of their work is problem solving. In the short run, many problems can be alleviated. The short run, the present, the current circumstances are the arena for effective intervention.

Social science studies of problem solving have been mostly confined to psychological processes. A modest amount of research has been done concerning how children and adults think about problem solving and how they act, presumably as a result of their thinking. There is a whole world of material and social resources that we assume has a great deal to do with problem solving. Exactly what material resources, in what quantity, of what quality are effective for problem solving has not been specifically studied. What knowledge we possess about material resources is found in macrosystems studies. These studies indicate clearly that there is a close association between low socioeconomic status, poverty, and deviant behavior. In our world there is a strong philosophical, moral, and political consensus that all citizens need and should have a basic quantity of material resources to provide proper conditions for managing their lives. There are also strong beliefs in modern society that certain modes of child-rearing, peer relations, marital relations, and work experience are conducive to practicing good problem solving.

Nearly all experts have expressed a firm belief that corrective experiences during treatment develop problem-solving skills (Brown, 1977). The basic ideas about problem-solving processes in their modern form seem to have originated with the philosopher-educator John Dewey (1933). He adapted the framework of scientific investigation to teaching and learning in schools. Subsequently, formulations defining and explaining problem solving were augmented by other areas of knowledge: information theory, computer science, administrative science, and linguistics, for example (Newell and Simon, 1973).

Spivak et al. (1976) in their review of the literature suggest that Jahoda (1953) made the earliest statement about the probable relationship between problem-solving thinking and personal adjustment. Until recently, the development of this credible idea has been pursued in two directions. One direction has been the widespread dissemination of speculative thinking about *coping*. The concept of coping seems to add to problem solving some unspecified and wide-ranging abilities, probably more extensive than particularized problem solving. Another direction followed by researchers has been studies of discrete *intellectual problems* such as puzzles and anagrams.

It is widely assumed that intervention in human problems is problem solving. Nevertheless, emphasis on defining, describing, and tracing problem-solving processes and its substance is a recent development. The character of available research and theory about problem solving is as yet too abstract for immediate use in practice, or it is too narrow for application in a natural life environment. Despite the weaknesses in the knowledge, the idea of problem solving as the theme of intervention is useful and promising. The task-centered practice model can be interpreted as a set of problem-solving techniques. The term *problem solving* is a neat way of capturing the theme of intervention. This term, however, as used here, means a process leading to problem reduction, or decreasing the frequency and quantity of problems. It also means problem alleviation, referring to a decrease in the intensity of problems.

Problem-solving processes should *always* take into account that increasing the material or social resources activates and perpetuates problem solving. A single-minded concentration on psychological conditions in isolation should *never* be adopted. *All* problem solving includes *programs* that represent and depict the substance and transactions of the processes. It is *wrong* to focus on what a client *feels* about a problem unless *at the same time* we find out and say with some finality *what this problem is in the real world*. It is *wrong* to lead a client into talking without that talk rapidly resulting in action that lifts burdens, straightens out lifelines, provides concrete benefits.

PROBLEM-SOLVING PROCESSES IN COMPLEX, NATURAL CIRCUMSTANCES*

A basic framework for problem solving can be visualized in five parts. These parts do not represent stages; that is, the parts overlap continuously. However, they have a logic that is sequential. One part will tend to dominate first, followed by the second part, and so on.

General orientation. This orientation identifies the particular stresses that have extruded the problem: the social context of the problem, its environmental, interpersonal, and personal features; the beliefs, attitudes, feelings, meanings attributed to the problem; and the goals and resources available for problem reduction.

Problem definition and formulation (Chapters 3 and 8). This refers to the detail and outline of the problem circumstances and actions and the statement of the problem in clear, brief language.

Generation of alternative problem-solving strategies (Chapter 9). This means to produce ideas about lines of action. The particular ideas called for are those which will probably reduce the problem. To be a strategy rather than a wish, the ideas have to be credible, reasonable, and feasible.

Decision making: selection of intervention strategy and tasks (Chapter 9). Decisions are predictions. Making predictions in human service work is an uncertain thing. *Probability* is what we depend on. We think: if we do this, it is probable *that* will happen. Ideas about probability of the effects of intervention are constructed by four modes of reasoning: (1) that the past will repeat in the future; (2) that a present trend will continue unchanged; (3) that the problem's assumed cause determines its fate, and (4) that an analagous condition whose solution is already known applies to the present situation.

In the real world, all four of these types of reasoning are used. The one most likely to be relatively free of distorting bias is the last one, reasoning by analogy. *A strategy that has demonstrated its efficacy already with the same or a similar problem in a similar social context is the most promising one to select.*

Implementation. This means carrying out the strategy and verifying its outcome, the heart of problem solving. *This chapter concentrates on implementation.*

•   •   •

---

*I am indebted to D'Zurilla and Goldfried (1971) and Brown (1977) for the organization of this discussion. My interpretation of the components of the problem-solving process is different in some respects from those two sources.

With the best will in the world, many human problems evade reduction. We do not know the answer to many problems. At the present level of knowledge, some problems are intractable. The overall objective is to put practitioners' efforts on those problems which are likely to be influenced by presently known methods and to put effort and funds into research on the more obdurate problems.

IMPLEMENTATION OF THE TASK-CENTERED MODEL

In the practice of the task-centered model, the implementation phase, or Step 3, uses most of the time. In the usual circumstance, implementation occurs during the time when interviews 2 through 7 take place. *The major objective of implementation is to help clients achieve tasks. Problems usually are reduced and alleviated as tasks are achieved.*

Implementation starts with refining the problem definition and specification, if that is necessary. In the implementation, or middle phase, the processes of generating alternative actions and making decisions about actions to take continue and develop. Earlier decisions are reviewed. They are elaborated on and revised. Keeping the target problems firmly in the forefront gives the necessary structure.

The heaviest thrust of the implementation phase is the provision of necessary resources to assist problem solving, identification and resolution of obstacles to task performance, and instructing and guiding clients in efficient means to achieve tasks. All these efforts are subjected to periodic verification to find out what effect the interventions are having.

In Step 1, the work consists of *finding out the problems,* the client's problems and the referral sources' mandates. In Step 2, the work consists of making a contract in which the *priority target problems are set* as specifically as possible.

In real life practice, target problems often have a tendency to become "slippery." What seems to occur is that the client and the practitioner have "second thoughts" about the problem characteristics. This may happen to the practitioner due to greater familiarity with the case. Both client and practitioner have probably given more thought and made more observations about the problem. At any rate, it is not uncommon at the point of commencing intervention to reconfirm the contract target problems and to refine and elaborate them. This reconfirmation and elaboration rarely require change in the target problem, although that is possible.

Throughout Step 3, task achievement and problem solving, the target problem is reviewed. If movement is occurring, the review may be cursory. If movement is not occurring, one source of the impasse may be that the target problem has been lost sight of or has changed.

Assessment

To assess a problem means to explain that problem by formulating what it consists of, its size, importance, and meaning. An assessment is never complete and never fully objective. It should be as factual as possible and contain as few as possible unverifiable inferences. One should not guess, conjecture, or surmise from scanty information what the problem and its characteristics are. Nevertheless, considering the complexity of the human problems confronting a human service agency and the pressure to act quickly, it is always necessary to act with limited information and in a situation where there is uncertainty. Assessment partakes of opinion, habits, and style of the practitioner; it also reflects agency style and professional norms as understood in the particular setting (Chapter 3). Theory often guides assessments. However, theory in the social sciences is weak, and its explanations often lack empirical verification and the ability to be verified. Nevertheless, it is virtually impossible to proceed without some plausible explanation of the problem, or assessment.

When the client's problems were found out (Step 1) and then arranged according to priorities and goals (Step 2), they were *explored*, not *assessed*. The problems were searched out, discovered, examined, which is needed to make a contract and get on with problem reduction.

Assessment is a judgment of use to practitioners. It seems to be of little direct use to clients. Assessment affects clients, nevertheless. It may result in a more knowledgeable and expert professional understanding. Presumably, this degree of understanding will help a practitioner design the most productive interventions. Assessment for its own sake makes little sense. Assessment that considers only one factor of a situation will inevitably be distorted. At best, it will not benefit a client; at worst, a distorted assessment might do injury.

The kind of assessment that has been useful for understanding the client's problem in task-centered practice answers the following questions:

- *What* is the target problem, stated behaviorally and descriptively?
- *How often* does the target problem occur?
- *When* does it occur?

- *With whom?*
- *Where?*
- With what *consequences?*
- With what *antecedents?*
- In what *context?*

Examples of problem assessment: Mrs. F

RIGHT: Mrs. F found a lump in her breast four weeks ago. She became afraid she might have cancer of the breast, followed by mutilating surgery and serious illness in the future. She worried all day and could not rest or sleep well, regardless of who she was with or where she was. She became fatigued, overwhelmed, confused, and anxious. She procrastinated for two weeks, trying unsuccessfully to ignore the matter. She finally saw a doctor who confirmed her worst fears. While not definitely making the diagnosis of cancer, the doctor recommended that Mrs. F enter the hospital for a biopsy.

WRONG: Mrs. F is supposed to go into the hospital for a biopsy.

WRONG: Mrs. F is feeling threatened by the prospect of surgery.

Mrs. G

RIGHT: Mrs. G is greatly worried and resentful that her only son Arthur, 12, hits her in the stomach and on the face. In the past year he has done this about six times. The last time was a week ago. Arthur hit his mother last week right after she yelled at him to stop being so curious about a girl. Mrs. G and Arthur were alone when he hit her. She recalls they have been alone each time and in their own apartment. The last time she ran into her bedroom and slammed the door after the incident, and Arthur ran out of the house.

WRONG: Mrs. G cannot control Arthur. He acts out in a violent manner.

WRONG: Teenaged "acting out" related to mother's conflict about Arthur's developing sexuality.

Assessment and diagnosis compared. Assessment is a judgment, an opinion, or appraisal of the problem for the purpose of understanding and interpreting it. Assessment is not the same as *diagnosis,* which means the act of recognizing disease from its symptoms. In many practice settings we are not dealing with disease but with routine to extreme problems in living. It has become popular to believe that problems in living are symptoms of disease: mental illness, developmental arrests, deficits, disorganization, or emotional turbulence or disorder. Even personal conflicts of a universal type are sometimes labeled "sick." It may be that some problems can be best understood from a practical standpoint as mental disease or an emotional disorder, but such an assessment should be made *last* and only after failing to acquire a reasonable understanding based on a factual appraisal of the problem.

Ordinarily, neither an assessment nor a clinical diagnosis will indicate what the treatment or intervention should be. Clinical diagnosis of so-called psychopathology does not ordinarily include prescribing treatment. There are exceptions, however. Contemporary scientific investigations have developed some treatments that are relatively specific to certain diagnoses. Depression, for example, is a problem for which a specific treatment regimen has been developed (Beck, 1973). It is advisable to have ready access to resource staff who can look up the current literature or who are experts in a particular problem area. They can advise practitioners what is known about how to intervene successfully.

Baselining. Baselining helps one understand the problem in detail in order to design the interventions as relevantly as possible. Getting a baseline means simply getting an accurate account of the frequency, intensity, and characteristics of the problem. A baseline can answer the assessment questions stated earlier in this chapter. A baseline is a necessity if there is to be an evaluation of progress or change.

Ordinarily, the baseline information is obtained after the problems have been decided on and the contract made. The baseline is the first implementation act. However, a baseline can be taken earlier if it will help to make the target problem more specific. Baselines are of two types: current and retrospective.

Current baseline. To be most concrete and most useful, the baseline should give accurate information about how things are. The most common ways of getting current baselines are *direct observation* and *logging* Direct observation means that the practitioner is present when and where the problem occurs and keeps a record of observations in a systematic way. If it is possible for someone else who is reliable to make the observations, the objectivity of the information may increase. Logging refers to the client's keeping a record. Logging one's own situation has a way of shedding large amounts of light on a problem. It often leads a client to generate a change strategy quickly.

Retrospective baseline. The practitioner can lead a client to think back in time. The practitioner can get examples from the client's memory about frequency, site, antecedents, consequences, and meaning of the problem. A retrospective baseline puts some form into the assessment and at times could be the only information available. Clients are not necessarily accurate informants about details of problems. Their information is influenced by their memory lapses and distortions, their mood, and their beliefs about the kind of information a practitioner and agency think is acceptable. Retrospective baselines may be improved by collateral information from other sources. Other sources may be biased and inaccurate. However, a retrospective baseline is better than none.

Example of a baseline in a natural setting: Tina

Tina, a 22-year-old woman, has two children, 4 and 6. She has no husband and is on welfare. The agency provided her with training as a typist. For two months she has had employment in a large firm as a clerk-typist, her first job. The agency secured day care for the 4-year-old. Tina's mother provides after-school baby-sitting in her own home for both children.

Tina gets up at 5 AM to do housework, prepare meals, take one child to the day-care center and the other to her mother's. Then she travels 45 minutes to work. She is already frazzled when she gets there. After work she picks up the children, eats, puts on the TV, and collapses.

Tina's supervisor has reported to the job program office that Tina is in danger of being fired. The work she does is satisfactory, but she is not energetic and she causes trouble. Called in by the counselor, Tina disposes of the lack of energy problem. There is nothing she can do about it because she is legitimately exhausted by her schedule. Tina does not want to be fired. She admits that she cannot restrain herself from insulting her supervisor and fellow employees. This is the trouble she causes. She says she is "too mouthy" and she would like to cut that out. The goal of the contract is to reduce the frequency of her insults to her supervisor and the others.

Initial exploration and retrospective baseline information result in complications. Tina says that her boss and the others treat her as if she were "invisible," meaning unworthy. Meanwhile she observes other employees making mistakes and goofing off. That gets her goat because she tries so hard. Her boss does not like her because she fails to "con" the supervisor with compliments and gratitude the way the others do. She does not think her supervisor has very good judgment. She suspects the supervisor holds her job because of friendship with "bigwigs" in the company. Tina is always so tired and so offended that she blurts out insults to all of them, all the time. She rages inside about their disrespect toward her.

At the start of Step 3, Tina agreed to keep a log, daily, for 10-minute intervals at critical times in the day's work flow: from 8:30 to 8:40; from 10:15 to 10:25; from 1:30 to 1:40; from 4:00 to 4:10. The log appears on p. 223.

What this log showed was that Tina insulted two people and did not insult

Log (simplified)

Time slot	What I said	To whom	Where	What happened
8:30-8:40	Your papers are illegible.	Corinne	Corinne's desk	She cried and complained to other workers.
10:15-10:25	Talked about TV show	Betty	Coffee room	She was nice.
1:30-1:40	Bad food at lunch	Betty	My desk	She sympathized.
4:00-4:10	Corinne and Helen don't fill out forms right.	Supervisor	Supervisor's desk	She glared; said I should mind my own business.

two persons. Each insulting statement was preceded by a need to work on someone else's papers. With this assessment, the problem was cut down to size. Being "too mouthy" became "mouthing off at certain named people who usually give me bad work to follow up."

Usefulness of baseline information
1. A baseline gives an estimate of the frequency, magnitude, duration, antecedents, and consequences of specified events and behaviors.
2. It reveals whether or not a problem is sufficiently important to warrant intervention, and what is important about it.
3. It provides data from which to measure change or nonchange.

Baselining in problem conditions. A baseline is possible to obtain when the target problem is a behavior of a person; for example, insulting the boss, fighting with other children or a spouse. There are, however, no techniques for baselining a problem situation. Many target problems are bad social conditions; for example, a mother does not have custody of her children; an elderly person does not have an adequate home; someone has been refused care at a mental health clinic; or a parent has been refused privileges to visit the children. These conditions call for accurate identification of the problem condition, that is, a combination of circumstances or a state of affairs. Some conditions of a complex type, containing many parts and many persons acting in relation to one another, can be baselined by selection. If some behavior can be isolated that is crucial and if change in this behavior can alter the situation, then a baseline can be taken. If the condition is too complex for taking a baseline of behavior, exact information should be obtained about the important facets of the condition.

Assessment of social context. Starting from the gross exploration of the social context, the assessment attempts to judge what factors in the environment and in the problem situation are precipitating and maintaining the problem.

The social context is a source of strength and help. The positive elements should be identified as carefully as the negative. A comfortable apartment or house, moderately understanding relatives and friends, interested teachers and authorities, moderately good health, basically adequate income with health insurance and access to credit, individual talents and interests—all add up to opportunities, latent or overt, that can be called on to aid problem solving.

Proceeding from the earlier exploration of the gross features of the social context, assessment helps make a critical judgment. The practitioner may conclude that some feature of the social context is precipitating or perpetuating the problem. This assessment leads to the development of an intervention strategy that will concentrate on work to influence and change the conditions of the social context. Having such an assessment gives the practitioner the ability to give advice and make recommendations about actions to the client, referral sources, family members, and other agencies. On the other hand, the social context assessment can lead to the conclusion that the social context factors cannot be changed. That judgment is again the basis for advising the client and attempting an alternative strategy.

Assessment of client characteristics and mode of functioning. An assessment can be organized by using the observations made about the client during the exploration (Step 1, Chapter 8) and adding other related information. When summarizing an assessment, we make a conclusion, a judgment, about what talents and capabilities the client has personally, what are the personal inadequacies, and what is the style or pattern of conduct. This assessment gives a practitioner some criteria to use to understand what the client may do to precipitate or exacerbate the problem, what potentials and limits there are to personal change.

It is especially around this assessment that the tendency arises to overuse psychiatric examinations and to arrange for psychological tests. It is true that making such examinations and giving such tests is required in many settings. They are sometimes informative, valuable, and useful. They are often excess baggage.

The decision of interest here is in those circumstances where a practitioner can exercise choice in arranging for psychiatric and psychological assessment. The criterion for referral for specialized diagnosis is that the client's actions are extremely odd: they are not understandable, or they show sensational contrasts or striking incongruities. Such clients may be helped, or protected if need be, by being directed into the psychiatric treatment stream of intervention. Certainly if there is a real possibility they will be helped or adequately protected, such resources should be used. A clinical diagnosis may aid in designing the intervention strategy. For the most part, unless a clinical assessment results in hospitalization, clients' negative traits and patterns of conduct are an obstacle to intervention. With this understanding, it is usually possible to help them to learn ways to minimize their undesirable behavior and make it less visible where it brings on undesirable consequences.

Other possible assessments. There are certain additional areas that, in individual instances, may be helpful in rounding out an assessment. The assessment, however, should be brief. Information should not be gathered, and time should not be spent to gather information, that is not of immediate use in the present problem-solving effort.

Working explanation. Some clients appear to need to know reasons why they are in the problem situation. In our society we are oriented to seeking causal explanations for events. Real knowledge, however, about causation in social and behavioral events is weak. Various theories exist that try to identify causation, but these theories ordinarily have little meaning for directing problem solving. Perhaps a reason for the popularity of the medical model in social welfare practice is the power of the medical view that knowledge of causation directs the practitioner to proper intervention. This ideal, however, often cannot be achieved in medical practice and rarely in social intervention practice. Furthermore, styles of assessing causation come and go and change a great deal over time.

Nevertheless, some people want explanations in order to obtain a cognitive map, to provide boundaries, to simplify a condition and reduce it to manageable proportions. A working explanation can be obtained from the client's reflections and from the practitioner's and agency's knowledge and experience. A working explanation should be as simple and realistic as possible. Complex explanations, not subject to verification, should be avoided.

Elaborate explanations purporting to give a developed and detailed analysis of a problem should be avoided. These are likely to be unduly time consuming, esoteric, and lacking in credibility. Interpretive explanations, purporting to go beneath the surface, are likely to be fictitious.

The human services have been taken in by a belief in "the underlying problem." In actuality, there is one developed theory, psychoanalysis, which suggests that human problems are caused by unconscious conflicts among contending sectors of personality. In this approach, unconscious conflicts are uncovered in order to reroute or dissolve them. In addition to psychoanalysis, it is a common belief among many "schools" of treatment that there is always, or usually, something behind the facade of beliefs asserted by a client. These theories and observations are not whimsical and often seem to have some truth. They are, however, no more than hypotheses and hunches.

It is not at all clear or certain that there are underlying problems or that the concept is necessary. It is highly unlikely that their existence can be verified in ordinary human service practice. A commonsense explanation of problems or one based on experience is a perfectly good explanation. A rough working explanation is all that is needed. People who deeply want self-understanding—and they exist—should seek out practitioners rigorously trained in the art of developing self-understanding: psychoanalysts, advanced social work or other therapists, philosophers, and wise religious people. Solving problems in living does not ordinarily require so much rigorous self-understanding.

Past problem solving. A moderate amount of information about what the client has recently done to try to solve the problem can be helpful, providing history taking of broad scope is avoided. Recent past problem solving provides information about possible tasks to take and to avoid. Delving into an adult's past is ordinarily unlikely to exhume much that can be used to guide present problem solving. If a target problem is chronic, the past three to six months should provide adequate information on which to make an assessment.

Past history. History of development of the problem should be restricted to a *gross estimate* about prior occurrences, duration, and fluctuations in its course. Ordinarily the history of a problem is only slightly important for organizing tasks. The mere fact that the problem is old does not by itself predict the difficulty of present problem solving. However, an old and obdurate problem will have set up habits in the client, in his social network, and among social agencies. Knowing this, one can help a client and his significant others choose tasks to overcome habits. The area not likely to be changeable can also be left alone.

Generating alternatives

The basic alternatives for work on the problem will have been laid out in the contract. These are the general tasks. As implementation proceeds, new tasks appear. Especially, many subtasks need to be formulated to keep the work related to the events that start to unroll. Generating alternative tasks is needed frequently to answer the question: What do I do now?

The source of alternative actions (tasks) are (1) the client's own experience, (2) the practitioner's personal and professional experience, (3) literature and expert information. The generation of alternatives consists of a discussion, open ended at first and narrowed thereafter, to get one or more answers to two questions. This first question is addressed to the client: What kinds of things could you do to "lick" this problem? The second question is addressed to the practitioner: What can I do to help the client lick this problem? The practitioner has to clarify and shape these alternatives into understandable form.

Important persons and officials in the client's social network should also be asked what actions they can, will, should take. As far as possible, what these other persons and agencies suggest should be pinned down and discussed with the client.

Decision making

Out of the alternatives generated, choices should be made. They are the result of considering what is known to be an effective or reasonable program to reduce the target problem; what is within the resources of the client and agency; and what is perceived by the client to be most suitable to her.

The product of these choices is the *intervention strategy*. It consists of a *list* of actions to be taken *in general*, when they should be taken, in what order, and who will do these actions. It is of the highest importance that the client know and understand the strategy. It is equally significant that important others are well informed so that their reluctance be neutralized and their support obtained.

Implementing the intervention strategy

Developing tasks. The basic rules for planning tasks were explained in Chapter 9, dealing with the initial statement of general tasks for the contract. During the middle phase, implementation, new tasks can be expected to be established as movement (or its absence) occurs. In establishing new tasks, the basic rules in Chapter 9 also apply. In addition, the implementation of task-centered practice requires additional work on developing the tasks so that the client gets all the help possible in carrying them out.

The following basic guidelines are suggested to develop tasks. These guidelines are expected to enhance the ability of clients to achieve tasks. What is wanted are tasks that have a reasonable possibility of being performed.

Client understanding. Enough discussion time needs to be allowed to be sure the client understands and agrees to the tasks. Tasks should *never* be assigned. It is common for the practitioner to suggest tasks. However, client performance can be expected only if the client is committed to the actions. The *only* time clients should be *directed* is when they have asked what to do. Clients ask this question often. If the practitioner knows what the clients should do, they should be told by such statements as: "What I suggest is this: _____ ." Clients are likely to change these suggestions or contradict them. That is fine. This process adds up to realism in the intervention.

Incentives. Establish incentives for task completion. The client needs the belief that the effort is worthwhile, that it will alleviate the problem. (For example: "Talking to the children about my health problem will be stressful but it will calm the children's imaginary fears.")

Rationale. Establish the rationale for the task work. There must be an understanding of a compelling reason why the difficulties of task work should even be attempted ("I have to do these things in order to live through the distress of my illness and be in a position to resume some kind of normal life later, even if I am left handicapped.")

Expectable difficulties. Anticipate expectable difficulties. Raise, discuss, and elicit the client's fears about obstacles that will be encountered working on tasks. Sift out what is probably real and not real. Reassure the client maximally but do not mislead him.

Supporting task performance

What to do in an unexpected difficulty. The practitioner should *always* state that unexpected difficulties can arise. Strongly advise the client how to slow down, stay cool, temporize, procrastinate, evade, and avoid unexpected difficulties. Advise her to take time to think, consult the practitioner or others. Affirm that if she feels relatively sure of herself, she can and should act on her own.

Teaching through instruction, simulation, and guided practice. The practitioner should inform the client about conditions he does not know or understand, about the people he will interact with, the expectations of others he will confront, the location and structure of places he will be going to, the normative behaviors that will be expected by other people.

1. *Instruction* of various types is the main technique for showing clients how to perform tasks. This means imparting information, giving training in skills, and furnishing direction.

2. *Didactic instruction* is systematic imparting of information a client needs in order to act in the most effective manner. Following is an example: "I can see from what has already happened that you need a lot of information about how to deal with your husband's anger. We have decided already that you will start a conversation with him as soon as he comes home in the evening. The conversation will be about what was good and bad in his day at the shop. Let me go over the kinds of things you could say and what would be important to him. You already know that there is a lot of talk about the plant's closing down or moving South. That worry is on his mind all the time. You could start out with: I'm glad you're home. What's the news today about what they are going to do with the plant? Any new gossip? Since it will be a novelty for your husband to hear that from you, you could expect a grumpy response." This kind of instruction will be interspersed with the client's reaction and further instructions to handle those reactions. This is just one kind of instruction, given to depict what is meant.

3. Another type of instruction is *role playing.* The practitioner can set up a stage where the client rehearses the actions to carry out the tasks. The practitioner, for example, can act the husband while the wife tries out the tasks. Role playing provides a vivid means to learn skills and also to find out obstacles to task performance. Role playing is easy with children. With adults it is possible but should be avoided if either the client or practitioner is embarrassed.

4. *Guided practice* can occur in an interview where the problem is played out in the session. Practitioners can guide the client by modeling, for example, behaving toward a child, spouse, relative in the preferred manner. Family quarrels often occur in an interview. The practitioner can intervene with suggestions and create discussion intended to clear up misunderstanding and wrongdoing. Practitioners can *accompany* clients to see landlords, lawyers, judges, and relatives to show and teach clients how to handle troublesome affairs. Guidance of this kind should be partial; that is, it should con-

centrate on a few key actions. Clients should not be hindered from following their own bent and style, nor should their confidence be undermined. They should not ever be denied advice available.

5. Work toward task achievement in *increments*. Break tasks down into parts, attending to the easiest first and adding on. Care should be taken not to underestimate the client. However, it is easier to raise the demand from simple to more complex so as to generate success than to go backward after a failure.

6. Devise any necessary *plans* to help clients perform tasks.

7. *Summarize* the plans for task performance often, especially whenever there is a new phase.

8. *Review* task performance regularly in a systematic way. Keep understandable and simple notes on task performance. Agency resources can be developed to keep uniform records (measurements) of task performance. An example of one form for this purpose is the task-centered project's Task Review form (Reid and Epstein, 1977).

Task review is begun by an inquiry about what the client has been able or unable to do since the last session. Complete, substantial, or satisfactory performance should be credited and put aside. The inquiry then proceeds to what were the circumstances that stood in the way of performance, or the identification and analysis of barriers.

9. *Review* time limits and number of sessions remaining. This is a simple and straightforward matter that causes difficulties only if not done.

10. Obtain and use *resources*. Organize and procure the needed resources to support the client's task work. Unless the client can quickly obtain resources on her own, the practitioner should make the arrangements. The idea is to get the resources, not to engage the client in a process. One exception is if the client is being instructed in how to obtain resources. Such training could stand in good stead for the future, but it is usually not in the forefront. Usually what is wanted from task performance is to get the resource.

11. Find out *obstacles* to resource provision. Some resources obviously are in short supply and are not easily obtained. Slowness of resource procurement and meagerness of resources can be expected to be substantial obstacles to task performance. The best substitute available will have to be used. Clients sometimes need advice, instruction, and guidance in how best to use resources, once obtained.

Techniques for providing resources. Weissman's (1976) research on linkage technology offers a promising methodology for linking clients with resources. This methodology can be outlined as follows.

Locating and selecting the appropriate community resources. To accomplish this activity, an agency must have extensive lists of available resources that are up to date. Knowledge of the caliber of the services is also needed. The role of the practitioner is to describe and explain to the client the character of the resources and how the particular agencies operate. The practitioner should also provide the client with an evaluation of the quality of the resources' services. The client is then in a position to make an informed choice among the possible resources and to have some idea of what can reasonably be expected of them. The client can also opt for not using the resources, weighing the advantages and disadvantages of either course. Most often, the client will seek and should be given the practitioner's opinion of the usefulness and drawback to using the resource.

Connecting. Obtaining a good connection between client and resource is where many such efforts fail (Kirk and Greenley, 1974). It is often assumed that there is or should be a fit between what the client needs and what the resource can do. This assumption, however, is often illusory.

Various connection techniques have been described in Weissman's work:

1. *Simple direction:* This means writing out the name and address of the resource, how to get an appointment, transportation directions, and basic expectations (what the resource can be expected to provide). Simple direction appears to effect the connection when clients already know what they need but have not known how to locate the resource.

2. *Directions plus a name:* This technique adds to the directions the name of a person to contact.

3. *Providing a letter of introduction:* This step adds a brief written statement, read and approved by the client, describing the problem and what the client would like done.

4. *Facilitating phone calls:* In addition to or as a substitute for the foregoing, the client makes the phone call to contact the resource from the referring practitioner's office. The practitioner assists, if necessary, by making the call and turning it over to the client.

5. *Facilitating in-person contacts:* The practitioner may accompany the client to the other agency or may request a relative or friend to go with the client.

6. *Cementing:* These are techniques for assuming that the connection will get results.

   a. *Check-back:* The client reports back to the practitioner on the effects of contact with the resource immediately after the initial connection.

b. *Persisting:* The practitioner contacts the client at frequent intervals to find out what is taking place.

c. *Interspersing:* The referring practitioner has an in-person contact with the client both before and after interviews with the resource.

d. *Monitoring:* The referring practitioner monitors the resource provision at scheduled interviews for that purpose or during regularly scheduled interviews.

•   •   •

Weissman's preliminary findings in his study of the effectiveness of these techniques suggests that the majority of referrals in the setting studied (industrial social work) were successful. The simpler techniques were effective when the target problems involved obtaining legal, financial, and health resources. Complex social-environmental and mental health problems required the most elaborate of the techniques.

What to do if tasks do not get done

Types of obstacles to task achievement. There is no way to ensure that all clients will work on all tasks and be successful. It is, however, a reasonable expectation that most clients will work and that most, but not all, will be successful. There is enough evidence in the numerous trials of the task-centered model to be optimistic about outcomes. Generally satisfactory performance on tasks is correlated with satisfactory problem alleviation, although this relationship is not perfect.

The following reasons seem to explain low task performance:

1. *The client lacks concrete resources* to facilitate task work. Examples of necessary sustaining resources are money, medical and psychiatric care, adequate housing, adequate work and school, adequate child care such as available relatives, homemakers, day care.

2. *The client lacks reinforcements* necessary from other persons such as family, peers, authorities. They may be estranged, not caring, unable because of their own problems, hostile, oppressive, or exploitative.

3. *The client lacks skills,* not knowing how to do the task work. The client may be painfully awkward or may have only enough skill to perform incompletely or erratically.

4. *The client has adverse beliefs.* These may lead to thinking that the tasks have little value or may have negative consequences. There may be fear of taking the task actions.

5. *The client lacks capacity* for task performance. There may be some incapacity to make attempts. There may be misunderstanding of the task.

6. *The practitioner may be biased and unskilled.* Negative attitudes toward the client, such as anger, contempt, resentfulness, will adversely affect work. Also, a client who is fearful, forgetful, anxious, discouraged may react negatively to a practitioner.

Guidelines for overcoming obstacles

LACK OF CONCRETE RESOURCES. The practitioner procures the resources at once by ordering them, if that is possible, or by using the referral techniques discussed earlier.

If necessary resources are not available and accessible, the client should be instructed and sustained to withstand delay. Alternatives should be developed. At worst, the client should be helped, as best one can, to tolerate and relinquish expectation of the resource. However, if a genuinely necessary resource is totally unavailable and if no satisfactory substitute can be made, then task performance is not within the control of the client and probably will not occur.

LACK OF REINFORCEMENTS. The practitioner discusses and guides the client, showing him how to communicate and behave toward important other people, show others how to respond, communicate what actions others should take, and let others know that what they do will be reciprocated.

The practitioner can undertake *facilitating tasks* to approach the important other people (teacher, spouse, parent, child, relative, etc.). The practitioner should interpret the client's actions; learn what the other persons could do to help the client; discuss what the others might gain; and plan a program with them. The practitioner can confer, refer, request, instruct, negotiate, and accompany the client and, if necessary, advocate on the client's behalf.

LACK OF SKILL. In the sessions the practitioner carries out work with the client to help the acquisition of skills. The techniques of instruction have already been described. The practitioner can refer the client to available experts to augment this learning of social skills.

ADVERSE BELIEFS. The client's own experience may have induced beliefs, convictions, or opinions that hamper or inhibit task performance. Examples are low self-esteem; awareness of cultural and economic oppression and discrimination; firm thoughts that others view him as lowly; and a genuine disregard and disapproval of dominant customs, folkways, ethics, social conventions.

Unrealistically low self-evaluations are learned attitudes. They decrease with factual, realistic discussion of their inappropriateness. This is particularly so if these discussions are supported by real experience with some others who like, respect, appreciate the client. Few people cling to low self-esteem if it can be transformed into a more satisfying self-appraisal. Some people might not be able to make this switch, but they are few indeed.

However, beliefs based on a negative attitude toward dominant customs may be intransigent. Possibly an appeal to basic self-interest and time taken to freely air the pros and cons of a particular view may succeed. The person's opinion may not change. At least the client can understand how to be protected from clashes with convention.

LACK OF CAPACITY. First, caution is called for to avoid underestimating clients, be they young, antagonistic, old, or mentally handicapped. Obviously, children too young to have developed verbal and thought skills and persons seriously deteriorated and ill represent a floor of incapacity for many acts. Such people should be cared for and protected.

However, the actions usually called for are to scale down the tasks to be within the person's capacity and to involve others in doing the tasks for and with the client.

PRACTITIONER BIAS AND LACK OF SKILLS. Practitioners should exercise discipline in restraining their biases. Lack of skills should ideally be filled by in-service training and professional education. However, experience is a masterful teacher. Experience and access to a library or a good resource person are excellent ways to improve skill.

SUMMARY OF OBSTACLES AND INTERVENTIONS. If tasks do not get done, here is a checklist of what to look at:

1. Are you working on a problem of high interest to the client?
2. If working on a mandated problem, does the client understand the consequences of ignoring, avoiding, or failing to change?
3. Does the client understand the tasks? Has he been shown how to do them and given help in getting them done?
4. Is the goal specific?
5. Have you reviewed the target problems and tasks sufficiently, adjusted the tasks often enough to fit the client and the situation?
6. Have all the available resources been fully provided?

Practitioner tasks. Practitioner tasks are actions to be taken by the practitioner on behalf of the client and between the in-person sessions. These are actions intended to support the client's task performance.

Practitioner tasks are of three types. One is *getting information* the client needs in order to perform. Another is conferring with other agencies to interpret the client, develop a positive attitude toward her, and arrange for commitments to deliver services. Another type of practitioner task is conferring with relatives, friends, and officials such as teachers to negotiate actions they will take on the client's behalf.

Practitioners are obligated to report to clients what they did, what they found, and in case of nonperformance, what the reason was.

VERIFICATION

In order to verify the effectiveness of an intervention in a simple manner, the interventions and their results are *monitored* (checked) periodically. The purpose is to test, confirm, substantiate the effects of the intervention. Such periodic monitoring is not the same as scientific research into effectiveness (Chapter 6). On a case-by-case basis, however, periodic verification as part of practice is both common sense and makes for accountable practice.

Monitoring the intervention process

At each interview, check the following:
1. Task performance
2. Problem status and change
3. New or revised problems

CAUTION: *Do not expect spectacular improvements. Do not be surprised by no movement. Do not be surprised by real or supposed new or revised problems. These are all ordinary happenings in the intervals between contacts.*

There are many ways to track cases. Some methods need sophisticated research techniques (Chapter 6). These are not practical unless an agency provides staff with the necessary training, time, and consultation. Simple monitoring devices (p. 236) can be used. Although these simple methods will not satisfy the demands of research, they will satisfy minimum accountability demands. They will provide concrete information to guide practice in particular cases toward productive efforts.

What to do with the verification checks

When monitoring task performance, complete or substantial achievement is an excellent result. Partial or minimal achievement is a signal to study what obstacles there are. Obstacles can often be resolved by following the guidelines already given. Another way is to revise the tasks. Study of task-centered practice suggests that if a task is not done after three attempts, that task should be changed. Observing that the client had no opportunity to carry out the tasks provides information to interpret failure objectively.

Example of a simple case monitoring chart*

INSTRUCTION: Put check mark indicating the rating.†

1. Task performance

	Complete	Substantial	Partial	Minimal	No opportunity
T_1	☐	☐	☐	☐	☐
T_2	☐	☐	☐	☐	☐
T_3	☐	☐	☐	☐	☐

2. Problem status

	No longer present	Considerably alleviated	Slightly alleviated	No change	Worse
P_1	☐	☐	☐	☐	☐
P_2	☐	☐	☐	☐	☐
P_3	☐	☐	☐	☐	☐

3. Problem altered   **Explain**

P_1

P_2

P_3

---

*Modified from Reid, William J., and Epstein, Laura (Eds.), 1977. *Task-centered practice.* New York: Columbia University Press.

†Definitions for this scale are given in detail in Reid and Epstein (1972 and 1977). However, the terms are self-explanatory. If such a scale is used by a single practitioner or a group of them, they should think over and write down how they interpret the terms in order to get some uniformity from case to case and from practitioner to practitioner.

KEY: *T*, task; *P*, problem.

When monitoring problem status, a rating of *considerably alleviated* is a success. Under adverse conditions, *slightly alleviated* is not a failure. However, when ratings are in this or the *no change* categories, the intervention strategy perhaps needs revision. If ratings are *worse*, that might or might not mean that the interventions are responsible. Such ratings might be the result of stresses in the environment. *Worse* ratings signal a need for thorough reevaluation, starting with the client's health; deterioration in the environment; hostile actions from relatives, friends, and authorities; and adverse effects of an agency program. At least, any conditions identified as jeopardizing the client could be attended to. The possibility always is that we cannot find out or understand what is the cause of deterioration. It stands to reason, however, that if a client's problem becomes worse, more of the same interventions are not called for. At present, not much is known about the cause of deterioration in the course of intervention. Closer attention to this issue may, in time, develop leads about strategies to follow.

Monitoring problem status leads to clear pictures of *alterations in problems*. During intervention a problem can change its appearance enough to warrant redefinition and a revised contract.

Contract revision should follow the checkup if progress is unsatisfactory, or exceeds what was expected, if new problems emerge, and if old problems take on different characteristics. Contract revisions can be made at any time during the established time limits. They do not necessarily call for extension of the time limits. The new contract can facilitate the achievement of goals already set. However, anytime an extension is justified, it should be provided (Chapter 11).

Without necessitating formal contract revision, anytime that task performance is poor, it should be revised. If the support services already in place do not work or if the resources supplied are ineffective, *remedial planning* should take place. This means that the negotiations with other agencies should be reviewed and changes made. Understandings arrived at earlier with relatives and officials should be revised. When it turns out that the practitioner-supported tasks are not feasible or are ineffective, they should be revised.

The whole purpose of verifying the effects of the intervention is to make midcourse corrections while the case is active. These corrections will temporarily destabilize the structure of the task-centered model. However, as soon as a revised intervention strategy is decided on, the regular procedures can be put back into place.

Case examples of task-centered intervention: Eleanor
PRIOR TO TASK-CENTERED INTERVENTION

Eleanor, a 15-year-old black girl, was referred by the Juvenile Court for foster home placement. She had been living since early childhood with her widowed grandmother, a recipient of social security. Her grandmother had complained to the police that Eleanor was out of control. She was pregnant, refused to attend school, was argumentative and disobedient. The grandmother feared that Eleanor's future was in jeopardy and wanted her to be "straightened out." The police took Eleanor to the detention home, with her grandmother's consent.

Eleanor was in good health with no evidence of mental handicap or disturbance. Her grandmother was elderly, infirm, poor—a decent, caring person, worried and concerned about Eleanor's bad conduct. The grandmother's home was plain and comfortable, located in an insecure public housing high-rise.

Eleanor's father left when the child was an infant. She was an only child. Her mother was an excitable woman, given to bouts of public drunkenness, lonely, often receiving public aid, and sometimes working as a day housecleaner. Eleanor was given over to the maternal grandmother to be reared. For short periods she lived with her mother to give her grandmother a respite. Eleanor and her mother fought because the mother was excessively demanding that Eleanor be perfect.

The grandmother cooperated fully in placement planning for Eleanor. The court's reason for placement was to see Eleanor through her pregnancy, arrange for child care for the baby, arrange continued schooling for Eleanor, and provide supervision to control her sexual behavior and argumentativeness.

Eleanor stayed in the foster home two years with her baby girl. She attended school erratically and eventually dropped out altogether. Infant care was left to the foster mother. The infant was healthy and normal. Eleanor fought with the foster mother. She continued to be argumentative, disobedient, and undisciplined. Then she ran away and left her baby in the foster home.

Months later, Eleanor reappeared and went to live with her grandmother again. She came back with a second baby girl. The father was a 22-year-old unemployed youth, also the father of the first child. Their relationship was a continuing one. He was the only boy Eleanor dated. Both her grandmother and her foster mother disapproved of him because they thought he was a "layabout" without prospects. When Eleanor became pregnant for the second time, her boyfriend took her to his relatives in the South until after the baby was born. The grandmother was stretching her social security to provide for herself, Eleanor, and the second baby.

TASK-CENTERED INTERVENTION
Application

Eleanor applied to the agency for return of her first child.

Client target problems

1. Eleanor does not have custody of her child.
2. Eleanor is herself still a ward of the court.
3. Eleanor does not know what the agency requires of her in order to be freed of their control.

Mandated problems

COURT: Minor in need of supervision, referring to both Eleanor and her first child (legal mandate)

AGENCY: Eleanor lacks adequate parenting skills, education for becoming self-supporting, income for self-care; probably emotionally disturbed (professional opinion)

Client priorities

1. Get custody of her first child.
2. Find out the law and agency requirements preventing her from getting her child back.

Negotiating strategy

1. Intra-agency conferences to support work on the client's priorities.
2. Conferences with the court to provide evidence of Eleanor's ability to care for her child.

Assessment

Eleanor became a ward of the court because of having become pregnant out of wedlock and her own family's lack of resources and skills to cope with this problem. She did not behave maternally toward her first child because of youth and inexperience. Her anger was due to being kept away from her stable relationship with her boyfriend and her feeling of being denied satisfactory work and life opportunities. Now only a few months away from being 18 years old and automatically freed of court supervision, Eleanor wants to be independent and get what belongs to her—the child in foster care. Eleanor is capable even though she lacks social skills. She has a basically good relationship with her mother, grandmother, and boyfriend. She lacks confidence in herself and is fearful of the power of the court and agency.

Contract

TARGET PROBLEMS

1. Lack of child custody
2. Lack of skills and resources for independent living

GOALS AND GENERAL TASKS

1. Obtain child custody
2. Enroll in continuation school
3. Obtain public assistance grant

TIME LIMIT: Eight weeks

Major interventions

1. Eleanor was fully informed about legal and administrative requirements to explain her status as ward of the court and her child's status.
2. Specific tasks were planned to help her acquire basic child care information, to follow procedures for reenrolling in school and obtaining public assistance, to share household duties with her grandmother.

Client's response

Eleanor became extremely agitated when she found that she could not be freed of court supervision unless she changed her child care behavior. Once this was clear, Eleanor was committed to doing what was required in order to win her independence.

Practitioner tasks

1. Teaching basic child care in interviews
2. Mediating with grandmother about housework planning and implementation
3. Instructing Eleanor in legal and agency administrative requirements
4. Negotiating on Eleanor's behalf with the agency, court, public assistance, and school

Obstacles to task achievement and interventions

1. *Eleanor's rage at authorities.* The rules of the agency were explained. Their rationale was discussed. What seemed unfair was openly confronted.
2. *Eleanor's inconsiderateness of her grandmother.* Joint sessions with the grandmother were held. Reciprocal tasks were developed so that the grandmother could get some benefit from keeping Eleanor.
3. *Foster mother's resentment of plan to return child to Eleanor.* The practitioner taught Eleanor how to refrain from provoking the foster mother on visits to her

child. She was not to visit in the home but to take the child out and return her clean, cared for, and comfortable. The foster mother was offered an opportunity to express her opinion through agency channels and in court. She did not do so.

4. *Eleanor's delayed contact with school for reenrollment.* The practitioner gave repeated drill in how to talk to school officials so as to diminish Eleanor's fear of them. It was that fear that made her delay contacts.

Outcome

Eleanor became adept at feeding and clothing both children, keeping them clean, and responding to them. The grandmother helped generously. Eleanor completed all steps to obtain public assistance for herself. Last, she finally completed reenrollment procedures for school. The court was pleased but cautious. Hence, although they ordered the child in placement to be returned, they set up a six-month continuance for the agency to monitor and help maintain Eleanor's gains.

Elaine
Referral

Elaine, a 5-year-old white child, was referred by a public assistance worker because of "bizarre" behavior.

Social context

Elaine lived with her widowed maternal grandmother (age 73) and her maternal unmarried uncle (age 45). She could not be cared for by her parents. Her mother most of the time was either in the state hospital or under its supervision in semi-independent living. Her father lived alone in bachelor housing. He was a seasonal farm laborer with meager earnings. The grandmother reported to the public assistance worker that Elaine stayed in bed under the covers in cold weather. She had tantrums, could not talk in sentences, could not be toilet trained. The grandmother feared Elaine will be "mad" like her mother. The grandmother and uncle were both illiterate. Both were responsible and concerned persons, kept a clean home, were decent and considerate to neighbors and authorities. They were supported by public assistance.

Target problems

GRANDMOTHER: (1) She was unable to provide proper developmental conditions for Elaine. (2) She was afraid Elaine is crazy.

Mandated problems

MENTAL HEALTH AGENCY, PUBLIC HEALTH AGENCY, COMMUNITY SERVICES AGENCY: All agree Elaine is "developmentally disturbed." The mental health agency diagnosis is mental retardation; their recommendation is special education.

Client priorities

GRANDMOTHER: Proper training resources for Elaine

Negotiating strategy

Questions were raised in the interagency conferences about the propriety of this grandmother, at 73, being the chief person responsible for Elaine's rearing. Since she might be short-lived and become infirm, some agency officials thought that Elaine should be placed in an institution. Consensus was achieved that the agencies would respect the caring qualities in the grandmother's home and her cooperativeness. This meant that for the time being no plans for placement away from the grandmother would be made.

Assessment

Elaine is a mentally retarded child being reared by relatives of limited intellectual capacity. Elaine's eccentric behavior is due to lack of training in speech and social skills. The home climate is excellent.

Contract

TARGET PROBLEM: Lack of child training resources
GOAL AND GENERAL TASK: Secure child training
TIME LIMIT: Eight weeks

Major interventions

1. Psychological and psychiatric evaluation was secured.
2. The results of these evaluations were explained to the grandmother and uncle.
3. The grandmother agreed to apply for Elaine's admittance to a local day-care facility. Transportation was arranged for the grandmother to attend parent education sessions.
4. Resources were obtained as follows:
   a. The day-care center officials were influenced to admit Elaine alternate half-days despite her developmental deficits. The primary agency assured the

day-care center that services would be provided to augment the regular day-care program.

b. Individual speech therapy was obtained in a clinic located in another city. Transportation for several times each week was arranged.

c. Elaine's admittance to a local special education class in the public school was secured for alternate half-days. She was to learn motor coordination. Transportation was arranged.

d. A schedule for Elaine's attendance at all these resources was made up. The schedule was distributed to all agencies and explained fully to the grandmother and uncle.

e. Regular reporting and coordinating conferences were set up between all the involved agencies.

f. It was arranged for the grandmother to join and participate in a parent group at the day-care center.

Client response

Positive

Practitioner tasks

1. Arranging for evaluations
2. Locating and developing child training resource in a sparsely populated rural area

Obstacles to task achievement and intervention

1. *Some of the local agencies opposed Elaine's remaining with her aged and limited grandmother.* This was resolved through numerous conference discussions.
2. *There was a lack of readily available resources for child training in the locality.* The practitioner organized and packaged the resource by combining various existing services.
3. *The grandmother was sometimes late to pick up Elaine from the various places she was attending.* This was overcome by planned, regular reminders.

Outcome

The "crazy" behaviors stopped. Elaine began learning to talk and play with others. She liked music and water play. She started to use scissors, modeling clay and cookie cutters. She was clearly a happier child.

John
PRIOR TO TASK-CENTERED INTERVENTION

John, 15, a black teenager, lived with his grandparents who were his legal guardians. At age 13, he began running away. He was finally made a ward of the court and referred to the agency for supervision. After two more runaways, John was placed in detention and thereafter in a foster home.

TASK-CENTERED INTERVENTION
Client target problems

GRANDPARENTS: (1) John does not want to go to school. (2) He stays out too late at night.

JOHN: (1) Too many people are trying to raise me. (2) My grandmother pays too much attention to my aunts' advice.

Mandated problems

COURT: Minor is in need of supervision (legal mandate).

AGENCY: Grandparents are too strict (professional opinion).

FOSTER MOTHER: Too many people are involved in supervising John (individual opinion).

Client priorities

GRANDPARENTS AND JOHN: John to return home

Negotiating strategy

Intra-agency conferences reached agreement on goals; conferences with the court provided information about what evidence was needed to order John returned to his grandparents' home.

Social context

John was friendly and willing to talk. He had a realistic appraisal of the bad consequences of not attending school. He stated that his truancy, staying out late, and running away were a "disease." The grandmother was cooperative but anxious. The grandfather left all decisions up to his wife. The housing is a single dewlling in an old and rundown public housing project. There was no evidence of health or psychiatric problems. The natural parents were not in the picture. The father had been absent for years. The mother was in a state hospital. The grandparents were on social security.

According to John, the grandmother discussed every bit of his behavior with his aunts. The aunts were "all over him" and his grandmother, telling him and his grandmother what he must do. John stayed away from home frequently overnight. This is the runaway behavior. He went to a friend's house. He did not call home because he was afraid his grandmother would holler. He did not have any safe way to get home late at night. So he stayed overnight with whatever friend he was visiting. John ditched school because that was more "fun" than staying at school. John and his friends were not into drugs or any other antisocial behavior. They "play around" with girls. This worries the grandparents.

Assessment

This problem is one of unskillful handling by anxious grandparents and an expectable rebellious attitude in a normal teenager.

Contract

TARGET PROBLEMS
1. Separation of family
2. John's staying out late
3. John's not attending school

GOALS AND GENERAL TASKS
1. Reunite the family.
2. Arrange for safe transportation and phone calls home to cut down staying out late.
3. Cut down truancy from school.
4. Stop the aunts' interference.

TIME LIMIT: Eight weeks

Major interventions

1. Negotiations with the school resulted in their agreement to readmit John.
2. Negotiated agreements between John and his grandmother set rules for his staying out and getting transportation home.
3. Negotiated rules with the aunts regulated their contacts. They are to talk directly to John, rather than go through the grandmother.
4. John went home on a trial basis.

Client response

Moderately positive, with reservations

Practitioner tasks

1. Explored possibilities of school's accepting John and of alternative schools
2. Interpreted situation to court

Obstacles to task achievement and interventions

1. *The Grandmother was afraid to tackle the aunts about their interference.* Rehearsal and guided practice were repeated several times. The practitioner conferred with the aunts.
2. *John could not tolerate going back to school.* The problem was *retargeted* to *lack of job training.* Referrals were made to explore job training opportunities for teenagers.
3. *John was erratic in following the rules of staying out late.* There was review and repetition of the contract, explaining the effect of nonperformance on the court: the court would be reluctant to let John go home.

Outcome

John agreed to the necessity for seeking job training instead of reenrolling in school. The plan to stop the aunts' interference was fully performed. Staying out late was cut down 80%. The court released John to his grandparents.

INVOLVING FAMILIES IN INTERVENTIONS

It is commonly believed that family welfare leads to individual welfare and social welfare. The minute interactions among family members are sometimes cited as the source of grave social problems. Fascination with "family treatment" among the helping disciplines is a reflection of the belief in the importance of family life to individual well-being. There has been an explosion of literature on "family pathology" and family treatment, divided into many particular viewpoints or "schools" (Bell, 1971; Stein, 1973; Haley, 1976). The family treatment field, however, has not produced studies of practice that establish the superiority of any one viewpoint over any other, nor is the superiority of family treatment to individual treatment established (Briar and Miller, 1971).

Is family life a social problem?

We are not so sure as we used to be about what constitutes good family life because social conditions today are changing family characteristics. The number of marriages is decreasing; divorce is increasing. The percentage of mothers in the work force doubled between 1948 and 1974. The majority of female-headed families are below the poverty level.

There is a large risk of oversimplification if we judge a family deviant because it departs from mythical standards of family life. Modern demands on family life are impossible to meet (Aries, 1978). We are only in the beginning stage of evolving basic understandings of family life in the present day. The families of the nineteenth and early twentieth centuries have been idealized. Those families were based on the husband's being employed and supporting financially dependent women and children. The unmarried single adult was aberrant: an "old maid" or a "bachelor." The unmarried woman with children wore a scarlet letter. Today, the Western world is moving toward less specialized family roles. More egalitarian marriages are evolving where husbands and wives share in the economic and child care supports of their children. Single adults, with or without children, are struggling for new role definitions.

A recent study spells out many enlightening details, culled from analysis of available data from many sources (Ross and Sawhill, 1975). Although many questions remain unanswerable, close analysis of what is known is enlightening. *It does not appear that the family is an endangered institution. It is a changing one.* The majority of adults and children live in traditional families. The parents do not separate or get divorces.

The number of families headed by women is up, from 9% of all families in 1960 to 15%. This growth occurred among all segments of the population, but particularly among young women and black women. However, for most of such women, their state is temporary, typically lasting no more than five or six years. They then marry or remarry, establishing a traditional home life.

The major cause of the family headed by a single female is not illegitimacy, although that too is rising. The cause is divorce and separation. Although there are many explanations of the rising divorce rates, one explanation seems to fit best. A study of 2500 families indicated that marital instability is associated with a husband's having employment problems and a wife's having her own earnings from employment. Black families are as stable as white families with the same economic and demographic characteristics. The continued growth of female family heads in the black population is probably due to the continued urbanization of blacks and high unemployment and underemployment of young and least educated black men. It is probably the unemployment and underemployment of black men that inhibits marriage and remarriage of black women.

One further observation about the modern family concerns the children in the so-called "broken homes." First of all, these children are likely to be poor. It is an error to attribute problems associated with poverty to the absence of a father. These are distinct and separable conditions. The evidence of childhood "pathology" in families headed by women is weak and poorly understood. The way a family functions cannot be determined by any one characteristic such as personality of a mother or the "pattern" of family interaction. Family functioning is heavily influenced by the family's social circumstances and its environment (Herzog and Sudia, 1973).

Task-centered interventions

There is little doubt that changes in family life and uncertainty in public policy toward economic and social support systems are associated with family disasters. Based on practical experience, we cannot doubt that involving total families in problem solving is a good thing to do. However, it is not necessary to assume that total family involvement is essential in dealing with individual case problems and with the so-called multiproblem or special hardship families. Both good and poor outcomes result from using either the family or the individual mode.

It is possible to consider several levels of family involvement in individual cases, all of them satisfactory.

No involvement. A single individual, an adult or older adolescent, is involved alone. Young minor children should not be seen in intervention sessions without parental permission. They are minors who have legally responsible parents (or parent substitutes). Adolescents, although legally minors, are in an ambiguous social position because of their approaching adulthood.

Minimal or episodic involvement. Because of the interrelatedness of family members, it seems worthwhile to include family members who are part of the client's target problem or part of its solution. Occasional and collateral involvement of family members, with the client present, or separately if more feasible, is possible and probably desirable. There should be no prejudice or penality to a client if relatives participate minimally or episodically. The process of treatment is not the objective; problem reduction is the objective. Working people ordinarily cannot take time from income-producing employment to attend treatment sessions. Fatigue and urgent interests may consume their off-work hours. It is false to interpret the minimal involvement of relatives as "resistance" unless all other explanations have been explored.

Substantial involvement. A few families may want and agree to regular attendance at sessions. If dealing with several family members at the same time seems a good idea, it should be done.

Guidelines for making contracts in a multiple-person case were discussed in Chapter 9. Briefly reviewed, those guidelines call for the following:

1. Obtaining target problem specifications from each individual, possibly changed in the course of family interaction during sessions
2. Organizing the individual family member's target problems into clusters of shared problems, despite opposing views of their nature
3. Reducing the array of problems to no more than three, chosen according to the family members' priorities
4. Putting aside excess problems or providing additional individual sessions on high priority problems excluded from the family contract

The basic rules for task-centered intervention can be followed in work with families. However, the changeable, fickle, and conflictive atmosphere of the group process adds stress to the processes. This book is not the place for a necessarily extensive review of family group processes. There are numerous writings on this subject that can be used for reference, but no recommendation is made.

The special features of task-centered intervention in family work are in the assessment and in the types of tasks. The basic rules for social context assessment fit family work. However, what seems to be more important than assessment of client individual characteristics is how the family is organized. This means observing and drawing some conclusions about the *objectives* of the family group. For example, is the family geared mainly for survival, for status, for interpersonal satisfaction, for security? Also, what kind of *hierarchy* exists to fulfill the objectives. For example, who is the boss? What are the arrangements for giving orders? What are the means for controlling and disciplining children? What are the avenues for redress of grievances? What is the division of labor?

Tasks in family work are typically shared and reciprocal. Shared tasks are those to be worked on together by two or more persons. Reciprocal tasks are those where one person takes an action that benefits another, *and in return* the other takes a different action to benefit the first person. Experience with interventions in families suggests that reciprocal exchanges of tasks are the most common. It is also common that sharing and reciprocation occur among dyads: husband-wife and parent-child. Examples of these types of family tasks are found throughout this book, but especially see Eleanor and John in this chapter. (For more information see Bass, 1977; Ewalt, 1977; Tolson, 1977; Wexler, 1977; Wise, 1977.)

TASK-CENTERED INTERVENTION IN FOSTER HOME CARE

It would sometimes seem from the amount of newspaper and television coverage and professional writing that children are an endangered species. Again, the facts do not support such a conclusion. There are 80 million children in the United States under 13 years of age and 16 million teenagers. Only 325,000 are placed in foster homes and institutions. However, that small proportion is a source of high concern and the center of attention for large numbers of agencies and practitioners.

The majority of the children in placement in the United States, living away from their families, are the responsibility of social welfare agencies. Foster care programs are complex and expensive, and their outcomes are in doubt (Rooney, 1978). Institutions for children usually do not live up to expectations (Pappenfort and Kilpatrick, 1969; Pappenfort et al., 1973).

Children in a family headed by a woman have a high probability of living in poverty. Being poor, belonging to an underprivileged minority, living in a female-headed family—this combination is prominently associated with children who became separated from parents, siblings, and neighborhoods and are placed in foster care. After placement, some children return home quickly. Many children, however, are in foster care for a long time, five to ten years (Fanshel, 1978).

The association of foster care with poverty is well understood. Nevertheless, in daily practice, children are in foster care because of adverse judgments of their parents, particularly mothers (Shapiro, 1976). Parental fault accounts for 65% of the reasons given for placement. When children are older, the reason (or blame) for placement shifts to adverse behaviors on the part of the child (Lash and Sigal, 1976). Studies of pilot projects providing resources to the natural parent, instead of placement, suggest that provision of homemaker help and day care, in combination with counseling, are promising interventions to avoid placement (Jones et al., 1975). Yet these resources are commonly of meager quantity in American communities.

The task-centered approach to service delivery in foster care cannot solve basic policy issues. As stated repeatedly in this book, intervention techniques are constrained to operating within some existing institutional frame-works. The kind and quality of services depend on the nature of current child and family law and its administration by juvenile and other courts, on the manner of allocating funds to develop services, on local agency service juris-dictions, on maintaining established and often inefficient and ineffective ser-vice procedures (Chapter 5). Task-centered interventions—together with im-proved staff training, supervision, and monitoring—could be of assistance in solving certain technical issues such as lack of discharge planning, early de-cisions about termination of parental rights, maintaining contact with nat-ural parents, concentrating with the children on alleviating current unhappi-ness and making future plans. Task-centered interventions, if adequately de-veloped, may have the potential for reducing the number of children in foster care who should be in their own homes (Rooney, 1978).

The most sensible strategy to rationalize foster care is to provide family supports, particularly homemaker help and day care, to those impoverished families overwhelmed by stress. These supports are available in varying de-grees, with variable quality, in some localities. They are provided by social welfare agencies because the families are too poor to purchase them in the commercial market. Medical, psychiatric, housing, employment, and in-come-maintenance services for the families, certainly to the maximum of availability, as early as possible and in sufficient quantity, could restore basic family functioning in some instances. Adoption or quasiadoption plans can be implemented. Older children already in placement after two years can be offered an opportunity to explore whether or not their own family can be reconstituted, whether or not they can be adopted. If these options are clearly unavailable, there should be an open and explicit plan to rear the child in the foster home indefinitely.

A number of public child welfare agencies are interested in the potential for adapting task-centered guidelines in handling foster care case loads. To date, however, only one well-designed and carefully executed study has been made, in the South Area Office of the Illinois Department of Children and Family Services, Chicago (Rooney, 1978). Certain special adaptations have been worked out as follows.

Target problems. Identify *client target problems for each person involved.* This means a thorough exploration with the natural mother and father, with the child, and with other family and extended family members living in or close to the household (see examples of Eleanor and John in this chapter). Be-cause of the multiplicity of persons in a foster family care case, there will be *multiple sets of target problems* for each participant. Therefore *the aggregate number of target problems may exceed the ordinary limits of three per case.* Obviously, the fewer the number the better. But the *rule of three,* which ordinarily is adequate in task-centered practice, may not be adequate in some highly complicated foster care cases. Each set for each participant should be limited to three target problems. These may be shared or not shared. To the extent target problems are shared among two or more participants, sessions may be scheduled with two or more participants or in any practical combination. The crucial factor is that it is perilous to avoid, ignore, or deprecate any participant in a foster care case. Parents of placed children are often viewed as unpleasant at best and destructive at worst. But children are always deeply connected to their parents, who are also victims (Jenkins and Norman, 1975).

Social context. Thorough evaluation of the *social context* of client-identified target problems is called for, primarily to define *resource deficits* in the environment such as ill health, bad housing, lack of available public benefits. Equally thorough definition of supporting or potentially supporting resources such as relatives, schools, agencies is also called for. *The evaluation of social context should be more thorough in a foster care case than in a regular task-centered case.* The reason for added thoroughness is that the most direct route to avoiding placement and unifying separated families is to provide the resources fundamental to the child care in the home: food, shelter, and supervision if the parent is absent due to employment or illness or if the parents' child-caring skills are deficient. Parent training is an additional resource needed, as is treatment or reeducation of the child sometimes.

Involvement of agencies, relatives, community. *Consultation and negotiation* is necessary with professional, kinship, neighborhood, and legal system participants who have routed the family into the placement system. The intent is to influence and convince these important participants in the client's social network to understand, tolerate, aid, and support avoidance of placement or reunification. A program to prevent or reverse placement affects a large number of influential people in a way unheard of in an ordinary case. Foster care cases are public matters, not private troubles. The contending interests of all influential persons or organizations must be dealt with to overcome the weight of organizational pressures that could maintain the child in placement. The practitioner attempting to prevent or reverse placement is a community organizer, for all practical purposes.

Informed consent. *Clear and accurate information* must be provided to all the participants, but especially to the family in jeopardy, about the terms, conditions, legal restrictions and requirements, and agency restrictions and requirements (see example of Eleanor in this chapter). Informed consent to what parents and children will confront if the child is placed or discharged is necessary. The participants must understand accurately what is expected of them and what they can expect from the agency, the court, the foster parents, and each other. In other words, all the rules should be open, stated, and communicated clearly. The participants must also know the basis of the rules: the particular laws governing them and the agency, as well as the administrative regulations. The prevailing practices of the agency related to living conditions must also be explicit: rules for parental visiting, obedience to foster family living practices, contacts with social workers and medical personnel, school attendance, and so forth.

Regular task-centered guidelines. *Regular guidelines of task-centered practice can be followed, with adjustments.* Regular application, however, may be overwhelmed at times by the large number of participants, each with a different agenda. This means that a practitioner will be managing *several sets of task-centered sequences, running concurrently, and related to one another. Management problems can be handled by keeping straight and distinct the terms of the contract with each participant.*

Regular application may become overwhelmed by the extrusion of *crises, emergencies,* and *ultimatums.* When these occur, task planning and implementation should be put aside temporarily and for as limited a time as possible. All effort is expended to abate the crisis, emergency, or ultimatum. Regular work should be resumed as soon as practical. The contract may be extended, if need be, to take into account lost time.

Time limits. In foster care, when a contract is ended, the child may still be in the custody of the agency. If the case offers no immediate opportunities for avoiding placement or reuniting the family, the case should be put on monitoring status. Activity may be initiated later by the practitioner or by one of the participants. Every separate instance of activity should be structured by regular task-centered methods. The time limits in foster care exceed the usual task-centered guidelines. No rules to apply have been developed. The best rule of thumb for the present is to proceed by making a series of contracts. In that way, each intervention phase can be controlled for focus, goals, and verification of results. It is surprising how often cases can be managed within the time limits of two to three months. This limit should be tried out first.

Resource provisions. There are many agency functions involved in providing foster care that have nothing to do with social treatment but everything to do with the quality of the child's life: clothing, medical care, special lessons, recreational events, gifts, and so forth. Such activities should normally be provided on a straightforward basis by a proper administrative plan.

Discharge plan. There should be, in foster family care cases, a dominating goal: a *discharge plan*. Every case should have a discharge plan no later than one month after a child enters the system. The discharge plan can be changed, but it should exist. It may be short term or long term, provided it exists.

REFERENCES

Aries, Philippe, 1978. The family in the city. In A. S. Rossi, J. Kagan, & T. K. Harenen (Eds.). *The family.* New York: W. W. Norton & Co., Inc.

Bass, Michael, 1977. Toward a model of treatment for runaway girls in detention. In W. J. Reid & L. Epstein (Eds.). *Task-centered practice.* New York: Columbia University Press.

Beck, Aaron, T., 1973. *The diagnosis and management of depression.* Philadelphia: University of Pennsylvania Press.

Bell, John E., 1971. *Family therapy.* New York: Jason Aronson, Inc.

Briar, Scott, & Miller, Henry, 1971. *Problems and issues in social casework.* New York: Columbia University Press.

Brown, Lester B., 1977. Client problem solving learning in task centered social treatment. Dissertation research in progress, School of Social Service Administration, The University of Chicago.

Dewey, John, 1933. *How we think.* Boston: D. C. Heath & Co.

D'Zurilla, Thomas J., & Goldfried, Marvin R., 1971. Problem-solving and behavior modification. *Journal of Abnormal Psychology 78* (1), 107-126.

Ewalt, Patricia L., 1977. A psychoanalytically oriented child guidance setting. In W. J. Reid & L. Epstein (Eds.). *Task-centered practice.* New York: Columbia University Press.

Fanshel, David, & Shinn, Eugene B., 1978. *Children in foster care.* New York: Columbia University Press.

Haley, Jay, 1976. *Problem-solving therapy.* New York: Harper & Row Publishers, Inc.

Herzog, Elizabeth, & Sudia, Cecilia E., 1973. Children in fatherless families. *Review of Child Development Research #3,* 141-232.

Jahoda, Marie, 1953. The meaning of psychological health. *Social Casework 34,* 349-354.

Jenkins, Shirley, & Norman, Elaine, 1975. *Beyond placement: mothers view foster care.* New York: Columbia University Press.

Jones, Mary Ann, Neuman, Renee, & Shyne, Ann W., 1975. *A second chance for families: evaluation of a program to reduce foster care.* New York: Child Welfare League of America.

Kirk, Stuart A., & Greenley, James R., 1974. Denying or delivering services? *Social Work 19*(4), 439-447.

Lash, Trude W., & Segal, Heidi, 1976. *State of the child: New York City.* New York: Foundation For Children Development.

Newell, Allen, & Simon, Herbert A., 1973. *Human problem solving.* New Jersey: Prentice Hall, Inc.

Pappenfort, Donnell & Kilpatrick, Morgan, 1969. Child caring institutions 1966: Selected findings from The First National Survey of Children's Residential Institutions. *Social Service Review 43*(4), 448-459.

Pappenfort, Donnell, Kilpatrick, Morgan D., & Roberts, Robert W., 1973. *Child caring: social policy and the institution.* Chicago: Aldine Publishing Co.

Reid, William J., & Epstein, Laura, 1972. *Task-centered casework.* New York: Columbia University Press.

Reid, William J., & Epstein, Laura (Eds.). 1977. *Task-centered practice.* New York: Columbia University Press.

Rooney, Ronald H., 1978. Prolonged foster care: toward a problem-oriented task-centered practice model. Dissertation, School of Social Service Administration, The University of Chicago.

Ross, Heather L., & Sawhill, Isabel V., 1975. *Time of transition: the growth of families headed by women.* Washington, D.C.: The Urban Institute.

Shapiro, Deborah, 1976. *Agencies and foster care.* New York: Columbia University Press.

Spivack, George, Platt, Jerome J., & Shure, Myrna B., 1976. *The problem solving approach to adjustment.* San Francisco: Jossey-Bass, Inc., Publishers.

Stein, Joan W., 1973. *The family as a unit of study and treatment.* Seattle: School of Social Work, University of Washington, Regional Rehabilitation Research Institute.

Tolson, Eleanor R., 1977. Alleviating marital communication problems. In W. J. Reid & L. Epstein, (Eds.). *Task-centered practice.* New York: Columbia University Press.

Weissman, Andrew, 1976. Industrial social services: linkage technology. *Social Casework #57*(1), 50-54.

Wexler, Phyllis, 1977. A case from a medical setting. In W. J. Reid & L. Epstein (Eds.). *Task-centered practice.* New York: Columbia University Press.

Wise, Frances, 1977. Conjoint marital treatment. In W. J. Reid & L. Epstein (Eds.). *Task-centered practice.* New York: Columbia University Press.

CHAPTER 11

Fourth step: termination, extension, monitoring

Step 4	Termination
	End Extend: Only on evidence of client commitment Monitor: Only when mandated by law, court order, or formal agency requirements

TERMINATING

Termination tends to be difficult for practitioners and, more infrequently, for clients. Conventional assumptions about termination are nebulous. The subject has not been seriously studied. Criteria for termination have been vague judgments about clients' mental states and uncertain predictions about their future actions. Some agency rules, particularly those designed to implement reimbursement from third parties (private insurance companies and public medical benefits), have established cutoff times for services.

In the task-centered model it is expected that many clients will approximate rather than completely achieve goals. Set time limits provide structure for setting an end. Time limits enable clients to exercise control over their participation. It is a rare client indeed who truly becomes unhappy or adrift when termination occurs. Practitioners tend to overestimate the value they have as persons for a client's well-being. The rewards of termination to a client are great: more money in the pocket (if the client is paying a fee), more time, more independence. A practitioner may provoke unhappiness in a client about termination if the practitioner has overvalued the relationship and if the excess valuation has been communicated to the client by word and deed.

257

Once practitioner-induced dependency has developed, harsh termination measures may be called forth and may be unfair. Analyzing and reorganizing a client's thoughts and attitudes toward a practitioner to whom the client has become emotionally attached is time consuming. That process often involves intimate discussions about feelings, which makes most clients and practitioners highly uncomfortable. Many practitioners lack the training and skill, as well as the time, to become involved in the intimacies and complexities of discussing the personal dependency of clients, if that has occurred. It is far better to use businesslike constraint on the working relationship than to be faced with the separation troubles that accompany the loss of a practitioner who has become too important to a client.

There is a normal and natural degree of dependency many clients experience. The practitioner may in reality be a vital source of resources, advice, affection. There is nothing at all wrong with clients being dependent when they lack resources in themselves or in the environment. Practitioners should make sure that clients are fully informed about alternative sources of resources and rewards and grasp the fact that they have managed and can manage on their own. Clients can also touch base with the agency and the practitioner from time to time if they really need to, including returning for full service again for the same problem or another. If the provision of service was businesslike in the first place, termination will be the same.

EXTENSIONS OF A CONTRACT

Extensions should be avoided. It is unlikely that they will be productive when the contract has failed or resulted in ambiguous effects. Some conditions are intractable because of client characteristics, excess deficits in the environment, lack of knowledge in the field, adverse agency limitations, and lack of practitioner skill. Most social and personal problems are long-lived and recur repeatedly. Expectations of "big cures" are unscientific, unrealistic, and misleading. In obdurate problem situations, reopening a case at a later time is proper. If everything possible has been done and has failed, there is no sense to extending. If the case is reopened, things may go better the next time.

Studies in the task-centered model repeatedly produce the information that the few clients who would have liked more contact think of one or two more interviews. Therefore, it is suggested that extensions of a contract be limited to two interviews, if any, except for certain specific situations:

1. *The target problem is self-limiting.* This means that the target problem

will dissipate in the near future, and the client can use additional help to complete tasks. Examples are that a marital separation is scheduled and will occur in a few days or weeks; a discharge from a hospital is scheduled; a move from one apartment to another is scheduled for a few weeks in the future.

2. *The client asks for an extension and can state what work is to be done.* An example is that after a family has moved and is settled in a new apartment, the parents want to work on a parent-child conflict.

MONITORING

The initiative of the practitioner and the agency is needed for this process. Monitoring means to watch, observe, or check for a particular purpose and to keep track, regulate, or control.

The circumstances that call for monitoring in social welfare are of two types: those required by court orders and those advocated for professional reasons. There are numerous instances when a court orders supervision: foster care, probation and parole, legal protective guardianship. This type of monitoring can be structured by informing the client of the legal requirements clearly and accurately. Then there should be established a schedule for episodic client reporting or practitioner visitation. Monitoring for professional reasons requires discussion.

Monitoring can be set up for professional reasons, mainly to enable the practitioner to check regularly on maintenance or deterioration of gains. The intention of professional monitoring is to detect early problems and provide early interventions. This type of monitoring ought to be set up only if the client is willing. There should be some reason to believe that early detection can actually be performed and that if performed, a remedy is known and available. Most professional monitoring tends to become mere surveillance, a kind of oversight whose objective is only the act of keeping watch. One reason this happens is that in some settings, oversight of clients has become habitual—as if an end in itself. Perhaps more important is the fact that the early warning signs of problems are not well understood. They have few telltale signs by which they are surely known. They are heavily weighted by idiosyncratic opinions and intuitions. Furthermore, effective preventive interventions on an individual case basis are few and far between.

It would seem more efficient to avoid cluttering up case loads with long-term inactive cases by reserving monitoring for cases where surveillance or supervision is court ordered or where eligibility has to be reviewed due to legal or administrative requirements. Short-term monitoring, professionally initiated, would be reasonable if desired by the client and if it has a clear-cut objective. Ordinarily, ongoing monitoring in the absence of a mandate should be avoided. Instead, clients should be encouraged to return in case of need of further service.

CRISES, EMERGENCIES, ULTIMATUMS

Cases on a monitoring status are often subject to crises, emergencies, and ultimatums. A crisis is not just anything that raises a person's distress. A *crisis* is a particular state of affairs that is life threatening or threatens basic habits of conducting oneself. Crises are believed to occur if there is a severe threat, loss, or challenge (Dixon, 1979; Golan, 1978). Crises are normally sudden discontinuities in the life arrangements. Examples are sudden death of someone close to the client, onset of a critical illness, extreme and mutilating surgery, having been criminally assaulted or burglarized, having been burned out, and so forth.

Emergencies are situations where prompt action will remove or retard the threatening crisis. Examples are making a phone call to stave off an eviction, influencing a school to stop or slow up a suspension, calling the police to stop an assault, finding temporary accommodations to keep a person from living on the street, getting clothing for a person who has none.

Ultimatums occur when a caretaker pressures an agency to act "or else." Examples are to get a patient out of the hospital today, to get a child out of his home today, and so forth. Ultimatums result from a variety of complex pressures on a delivery system. They are rarely true emergencies, although they may produce a crisis state for clients unless they are buffered.

Because of the introduction of crises, emergencies, and ultimatums while a case is on monitoring status, practitioner schedules have to contain some leeway for adjustment to meet urgent problems. These should be managed by rapid problem specification, high and short-term practitioner activity to arrange for stress abatement, and termination of the episode.

REFERENCES

Dixon, Samuel L., 1979. *Working with people in crisis.* St. Louis: The C. V. Mosby Co.

Golan, Naomi, 1978. *Treatment in crisis situations.* New York: The Free Press.

Index